Advances in Science, Technology & Innovation

IEREK Interdisciplinary Series for Sustainable Development

AF820159

Advances in Science, Technology & Innovation (ASTI) is a series of peer-reviewed books based on important emerging research that redefines the current disciplinary boundaries in science, technology and innovation (STI) in order to develop integrated concepts for sustainable development. It not only discusses the progress made towards securing more resources, allocating smarter solutions, and rebalancing the relationship between nature and people, but also provides in-depth insights from comprehensive research that addresses the **17 sustainable development goals (SDGs)** as set out by the UN for 2030.

The series draws on the best research papers from various IEREK and other international conferences to promote the creation and development of viable solutions for a **sustainable future and a positive societal** transformation with the help of integrated and innovative science-based approaches. Including interdisciplinary contributions, it presents innovative approaches and highlights how they can best support both economic and sustainable development, through better use of data, more effective institutions, and global, local and individual action, for the welfare of all societies.

The series particularly features conceptual and empirical contributions from various interrelated fields of science, technology and innovation, with an emphasis on digital transformation, that focus on providing practical solutions to **ensure food, water and energy security to achieve the SDGs**. It also presents new case studies offering concrete examples of how to resolve sustainable urbanization and environmental issues in different regions of the world.

The series is intended for professionals in research and teaching, consultancies and industry, and government and international organizations. Published in collaboration with IEREK, the Springer ASTI series will acquaint readers with essential new studies in STI for sustainable development.

ASTI series has now been accepted for Scopus (September 2020). All content published in this series will start appearing on the Scopus site in early 2021.

Asma Salman · Assem Tharwat
Editors

Smart Designs for Business Innovation

Proceedings of the 3rd American University in the Emirates International Research Conference, AUEIRC'20—Dubai, UAE 2020

Springer

Editors
Asma Salman
College of Business Administration
The American University in the Emirates (AUE)
Dubai, United Arab Emirates

Assem Tharwat
The American University in the Emirates (AUE)
Dubai, United Arab Emirates

ISSN 2522-8714 ISSN 2522-8722 (electronic)
Advances in Science, Technology & Innovation
ISBN 978-3-031-49315-7 ISBN 978-3-031-49313-3 (eBook)
https://doi.org/10.1007/978-3-031-49313-3

This Springer imprint is published by the registered company Springer Nature Switzerland AG
The registered company address is: Gewerbestrasse 11, 6330 Cham, Switzerland

Paper in this product is recyclable.

Preface

The 3rd American University in the Emirates International Research Conference (AUEIRC'20) under the theme "Transition to Knowledge Economy: Challenges, Smart Opportunities and Innovation" brought together academics, researchers, and practitioners under one platform with the aim of sharing ideas and expertise in the most pressing challenges that the world has witnessed. Under the Patronage of H. H. Sheikh Hamdan Bin Rashid Al Maktoum, Deputy Ruler of Dubai and Minister of Finance, United Arab Emirates (UAE), the 3rd AUEIRC 2020, was held between August 8th and 11th 2020. The proceedings will be published in the *Transition to Knowledge Economy: Challenges, Smart Opportunities, and Innovation* book series of Springer.

As the first research conference to be conducted virtually in the Middle East, covering vital sectors of the economy and the impact of COVID-19, this conference was a testimony that digital transformation indeed leads to the continuity of exchange of knowledge. It warranted a vision, where the academics, practitioners, and policymakers from the region and across the globe engaged in a dialogue to discuss some of the most pressing issues in knowledge economy and the pandemic that has gripped the world, while focusing on the application side of the research rather than just the theoretical ones.

The scope of the conference included eight main themes, namely; COVID-19 Challenges, Entrepreneurship, Computer and Advanced Technology, Education Industry, Security and Global Studies, Law, Integrated Media, and Design Industry. The 3rd AUEIRC 2020 witnessed research paper presentations from 101 presenters in 18 different sessions under these eight tracks. The conference boasted of imminent speakers from the industry and academia covering pertinent issues and offering plausible solutions. It had seven keynote sessions, six interactive workshops, talks from 20 experts from the industry and participation from over 25 Countries during the 4-day conference. Each speaker brought with them a wealth of knowledge and concluded with a range of questions and discussions from the audience and the panels. Worthy speakers included; H. E. Mr. Mirza Al Sayegh, Director, Office of H. H. Sheikh Hamden Bin Rashid Al Maktoum (United Arab Emirates), Major Gen. Dr. Ahmed Nasser Al Raisi, General Inspector of the Ministry of Interior (United Arab Emirates), Prof. Suzanne Trager Ortega, President of the Council of Graduate Schools (United States of America), H. E. Dr. Dena Assaf, United Nations Resident Coordinator for UAE and H. E. Jamal Al Jarwan, Secretary General—UAE International Investors Council (United Arab Emirates).

The International Scientific Committee comprised of over 40 international experts in various fields as per the themes of the conference. The panels were divided based on tracks and all papers were presented in 18 thematic sessions. In an aim to bridge the gap between theory and practice, each session was organized to have an academic and an industry representative as a chair and/or co-chair. This enhanced the feedback and reflected discussions from a well-rounded perspective. Sessions were designed to start with the paper presentations and then the floor was opened for a healthy exchange of feedback. A double-blind peer review process enabled 50 full papers to be accepted for publication (in five edited volumes) by Springer.

This volume focuses on integration of informatics for modern business strategy; illustrates how ICT is addressing contemporary business challenges; and incorporates a wealth of research on State-of-the-art ICT for economics, business and society.

On behalf of the AUEIRC'20 Steering Committee, we would like to thank all the referees, track chairs, and paper authors. Special thanks to Prof. Muthanna G. Abdul Razzaq, President, and CEO American University in the Emirates (AUE) and AUEIRC'20 General Chair who contributed all resources at his disposal to ensure the conference meets the standard of excellence. We would also like to thank Major Gen. Dr. Ahmed Nasser Al Raisi, General Inspector of the Ministry of Interior—United Arab Emirates and Chairman Board of Trustees (AUE) for his valuable support. Special gratitude to members of the conference steering committee for their hard work, dedication, and continuous support throughout the preparation and implementation of this virtual conference. Moreover, we are grateful to the event management, information technology department, auxiliary services, media, protocol teams as well as faculty and staff members from different committees for their support in organizing the conference and ensuring its success.

Dubai, United Arab Emirates

Prof. Asma Salman
asma.salman@aue.ae

Prof. Assem Tharwat
assem.tharwat@aue.ae

About This Book

In light of continuous and fast-paced developments in technology and advertising and a rapidly changing world, it has become easy for any longstanding business, that is not able to adapt, to fall behind. The proliferation of smart, or 'intelligent', technologies into both physical and online businesses and throughout our economies, known as 'Smart Design', has majorly affected every sector. Security cameras, smart home assistants, thermometers, QR codes, digital personal assistants and robots, smart tech, Internet of Things (IoT) sensors, and finally, smart devices have all disrupted businesses.

However, this disruption and the current challenges and opportunities posed by market globalization have given new power to the theme of "innovation" and business value generation across industries. And because this innovation cannot rely on technologies and R&D alone, it must encompass the delivery of a unique value proposition and innovative business model designs. Nevertheless, its role remains undeniable for technological development in fostering developmental growth.

That said, the literature defines the notion of "Smart Design" as one that relates to a design process or artifact, yet one for complex challenges nonetheless. It is a data-based approach that operationalizes the S.M.A.R.T.—specific, measurable, actionable, realistic and time-based—principles to bring a user's experience to its ultimate limits whether through innovative business models or through technological insights and the adaptation of intelligent systems that humanize products, services, and experiences.

In this title, a comprehensive interpretation of different aspects of business encountered in several parts of the world is presented and it includes—but is not limited to—human resources management, marketing, and finance. This volume reports the results of Globalization and Internationalization, which have been gaining momentum over the last few years leading to a number of challenges and uncertainties for enterprises on an international scale. The impacts on these multinational enterprises are considered and theories and solutions are then presented around managerial leadership skills, people management, and more. Secondly, it highlights "**Contemporary Challenges in Business**" covering leadership competencies, strategy implementation and applications of Technologies in the military, healthcare and smart environments such as IoT, Blockchain and more.

Finally, this book also includes the significance of economics and society by pinpointing the disconnection between economic growth and social welfare. It also continues to offer a comprehensive overview of social business innovation as a way to address past and existing challenges, one of which is the COVID-19 crisis which has completely disrupted socio-economic factors of the world.

Contents

Application of a Fuzzy Delphi Method in Marketing: A Review

Nikolina Ljepava and Aleksandar Aleksic

Abstract

The Delphi method has been widely utilized in a number of scientific domains to aid forecasting and decision-making. Created by Dalkey and Helmer (Manag Sci 9:458–467, 1963), the method was developed to forecast future scenarios based on the consensus of expert opinions collected through several iterations of structured questionnaires. Although the approach was adopted in various disciplines, several shortcomings of the method, such as lack of consistent standards for result interpretation, limited generalization, the long-time needed for implementation, and susceptibility to the subjective interpretation of the qualitative results, have been identified over time. The purpose of the study is to review the available scientific literature on the application of a Fuzzy Delphi method in the marketing domain, in order to measure the interest in the method, identify the studies that have utilized the fuzzy Delphi method for marketing related topics, and determine the areas of marketing where the method has been applied so far. Fuzzy Delphi method has found the most extensive application in operation management, decision sciences, and business intelligence and has not been widely adopted as a method of choice in marketing studies.

Keywords

Delphi method · Fuzzy data · Forecasting (marketing process)

1 Introduction

In the conditions of fast and continuous changes that take place in the environment, achievement of the most critical strategic and operational goals highly depend on accurate and timely decision making. This applies to all areas of business operations, including marketing operations. For marketing strategic and operational plans to be successful, enable the organization to preserve the market position and increase competitiveness, marketing managers have to make the right decision at the right time based on the reliable and valid market information. To provide input for marketing decision-making and development of strategic and operational plans, various methods and techniques in marketing research and analytics are used. These methods are typically qualitative or quantitative, and in quantitative methods, we strongly rely on statistical tools and techniques. However, although successful forecasting in the various areas should be one of the essential tasks of the marketing managers, decision-making and forecasting tools are not often applied in the marketing decision making. Moreover, even in cases where forecasting tools are used, the techniques traditionally applied in marketing typically do not account for the uncertainty in marketing decision-making.

Obtaining useful demand forecasts can help decision-makers to determine production size, production costs as well as to assess and calculate market prices. Similarly, forecasting market and consumer trends can contribute to the development of successful marketing strategies. Effective predictive analytics can help decision-makers estimate various relevant market indices based on the historical data and/or expert opinion: market demand, market potential, production size, production costs market prices. A group of managers from different departments can bring various perspectives, knowledge, judgment, and intuition to the planning process (Minkes 1987). This is especially relevant when ideas related to new products,

N. Ljepava (✉)
College of Business Administration, American University in the Emirates, Dubai International Academic City, P.O. Box: 503000, Dubai, UAE
e-mail: nikolina.ljepava@aue.ae

A. Aleksic
Faculty of Engineering, University of Kragujevac, Sestre Janjic 6, 34000 Kragujevac, Serbia
e-mail: aaleksic@kg.ac.rs

A. Salman and A. Tharwat (eds.), *Smart Designs for Business Innovation*,
Advances in Science, Technology & Innovation, https://doi.org/10.1007/978-3-031-49313-3_1

processes, services, technologies, and markets are elaborated (Selaković et al. 2018).

Based on the literature, forecasting methods can be divided into two groups: (1) qualitative forecasting methods and (2) quantitative forecasting methods. By using the qualitative forecasting methods, the projected demand values are based on decision-makers' (D.M.s) estimates. Decision-makers base their assessments mainly on their expertise–knowledge, and previous experience. Therefore, it can be said that the predicted values of demands which are provided by using qualitative methods are highly burdened by the subjective opinions and attitudes of decision-makers. This subjectivity, as in any qualitative research, can be denoted as one of the main shortcomings and limitations of the qualitative forecasting methods. However, in a case when there is a sufficient amount of accurate historical data from the records, marketing forecasting can be conducted using quantitative methods; in this way, more accurate values of forecasted consumer demand can be obtained. Increased accuracy and objectivity are some of the primary advantages of quantitative methods; however, the quality of output is highly dependent on the reliability and validity of the historical quantitative data.

At the same time, qualitative forecasting and decision-making employ a variety of methods and approaches, including direct contact with customers, analysis of potential customers, analysis of potential customers, and the Delphi method (Tadić and Nestić 2019). Delphi method is one of the most widely used qualitative forecasting techniques in decision making. The Delphi method has been widely utilized in a number of scientific domains to aid forecasting and decision-making. Created by Dalkey and Helmer (1963), the method was developed to forecast future scenarios based on the consensus of expert opinions collected through several iterations of structured questionnaires. Later, the application of this technique was represented in risk assessment of project success (Evangelidis et al. 2002), social, cultural, and ethical impacts of e-services (Asgarkhani 2005), strategic alignment of e-services with macro policies (Viscusi et al. 2008) and economic development planning (Meijering et al. 2013). The Delphi technique is an iterative method that is realized through steps. The four features of the Delphi technique are usually unchanged, including anonymity, iteration, controlled feedback, and statistical "group response" (Förster and Gracht 2014). Aggregation estimates of D.M.s can be performed in different ways. The procedure is repeated until consensus is reached, or the number of given iterations is performed in advance. Although the approach was adopted in various disciplines, several shortcomings of the method, such as lack of consistent standards for result interpretation, limited generalization, lack of theoretical framework, the long time needed for implementation, and susceptibility to the subjective interpretation of the qualitative results have been identified over time.

To overcome the challenges of the traditional qualitative Delphi method, Hsu and Yang (1999) suggested a Fuzzy Delphi method—a modified version of the Delphi method, based on the combination of fuzzy theory and traditional decision making. It is believed that D.M.s may express their estimates significantly better by using words than precise numbers. However, the developments in mathematics, such as set theory (Zadeh 1975), has enabled linguistic expression to be quantified. There is a large body of scientific literature where D.M.s estimates are further analyzed using type 1 fuzzy numbers (Zimmermann 2010; Dubois and Prade 1980). The fundamental characteristic of these fuzzy numbers is membership functions, which can be of different forms. In the literature, modeling of estimates of D.M.s was most often performed by using triangular fuzzy numbers (TFNs) (Nestić et al. 2019). The handling of these fuzzy numbers does not require complex mathematical operations, and at the same time, the accuracy of the obtained results is satisfactory. Several authors believe that the uncertainty and vagueness of words can be better represented by using:

(a) Interval type 2 fuzzy numbers (Mendel 2017) which are characterized by two membership functions, and
(b) The intuitionistic fuzzy sets introducing another degree of freedom into a set description (membership function, non-membership function, and intuitionistic index foundation) (Atanassov 1999).

The article provides an overview of the Fuzzy Delphi method application in marketing in scholarly articles published from 2000 until 2019 and indexed in EBSCO, ProQuest, DOAJ, or Emerald scientific databases. A comprehensive database search with the keyword search "fuzzy Delphi" and "Marketing" confirmed that the Fuzzy Delphi method is rarely applied in marketing studies. This paper is organized in the following way: in Sect. 2, the primary considerations and application of the DELPHI technique are presented. The fuzzy Delphi techniques are analyzed in Sect. 3. The comparative analysis of the discussion is presented in Sect. 4. The conclusion is presented in Sect. 5.

2 Basic Considerations of DELPHI Technique

The Delphi technique can be defined as a structured process for data collection during several successful rounds conducted with subject matter experts. There are no rules about the number of experts involved in the decision-making process and the sampling process. For instance,

Somerville (2008) suggest that the choice of experts included in traditional Delphi study is better based on a combination of individuals with multiple specialties than on the snowball sampling technique based on the recommendations. The proposed approach is applied by Macnee and McCabe (2008). Somerville (2008) suggests that in Delphi, the team should present a mixture of experts with different specialties, arguing that between five and ten members are sufficient. Some researchers (Malone et al. 2005) suggested that in Delphi rounds should be conducted with fewer than 10 D.M.; however, at the same time, some other studies included more than 100 participants (Meadows et al. 2005).

The obtained result from the traditional Delphi study can be presented as a group consensus. For data collection, a set of questions measured on a Likert scale is created and distributed for expert feedback. After the first round of data collection, the mean value for each variable of interest is calculated, and in a case where there is no consensus, experts are provided with another round of questionnaires until the consensus is reached. Different studies have proposed different approaches for determining consensus in the Delphi study. Based on Habibi et al. (2015), Kendall's coefficient of concordance can be used to determine the degree of consensus of expert opinions.

2.1 Combining Delphi Technique and Other Methods

Many management problems can be solved by the Delphi technique integration with other methods. Some hybrid methods proposed in the literature are further briefly analyzed. Strategic analysis, based on provided data, judgments, intuition, and personal vision of decision-makers, is analyzed by Li (2005). His study proposed that a web-based expert system performs a rule-based intelligent reasoning process for generating outputs or strategic recommendations. The proposed web-based expert system can be conducted through several stages. The Delphi technique is then used to select criteria and their sub-criteria in the second stage of the proposed model. As it is mentioned, the demand forecast problem can be solved by using a different hybrid method. Hicham et al. (2012) have suggested the method which integrates Enterprise Resource Planning, Delphi technique, fuzzy clustering, and Back-propagation Neural Networks with adaptive learning rate. The proposed model is developed for demand forecasting in the packaging industry. The Delphi technique is used to identify the factors that represent the input data in the decision-making process. Pre-defined questionnaires were submitted to the experts, and experts expressed their estimates on a measurement scale from 1 to 5. The evaluation process is then repeated until a consensus is reached.

Many companies are aware of the strategic importance of technology commercialization and have been trying to develop innovative technology products. Several research studies have focused on exploring the general market trends or business factors for successful new product development utilizing some variation of the Delphi technique. For example, Cho and Lee (2013) have considered 25 factors according to which product development is evaluated, and the choice of factors, as well as their subfactors, was based on the Delphi technique. All participants in the decision-making process have expressed their assessment on a Likert scale, and the aggregation of decision-makers' estimates was determined based on the results of statistical analysis. These researchers considered four factors: marketability, business feasibility, technological competitiveness, and research and development capabilities.

3 The Fuzzy DELPHI Technique

Unlike the traditional Delphi method, the Fuzzy Delphi method takes into account fuzziness in the selection of the relevant criteria and interpretation of the results and includes less iteration in the data collection process.

Some studies preferred the fuzzy Delphi method to the conventional Delphi method (Kumar and Dash 2017). Argued that by taking the completeness and consistency of experts' opinions and taking into account fuzziness in the iterative process, the fuzzy Delphi technique provides more objective insights. It should be noticed that all four features of the Delphi technique are preserved in the fuzzy Delphi technique. In the fuzzy Delphi technique, expert estimates are described by linguistic variables that can be quantified by fuzzy numbers. The number and type of fuzzy numbers are determined by experts depending on the size and type of problem. Fuzzy Delphi method is mostly applied in operation management, decision sciences, and business intelligence and is not widely adopted as a method of choice in marketing studies.

3.1 Fuzzy Sets Theory

A fuzzy number is a number that does not refer to a single value but to several different possible values where each possible value has its weight. This approach enables us to incorporate uncertainty into decision making and thus make the analysis more realistic. Fuzzy sets are sets with a degree of membership, and they are determined with their membership function.

To facilitate an understanding of the methods that combine fuzzy sets theory and other methods in this Section, the basics of fuzzy sets theory are presented.

Definition 1 A linguistic variable is a variable whose values are expressed in linguistic terms.

Definition 2 A fuzzy set $\widetilde{A}$ is defined as a set of organized pairs:

$$\widetilde{A} = \left\{ x,\ \mu_{\widetilde{A}}(x) \ \middle|\ x \in X,\ 0 \leq \mu_{\widetilde{A}}(x) \leq 1 \right\}$$

where:

A fuzzy set $\widetilde{A}$ is defined on the universe set $X \in R$. In general, set X can be either finite or infinite. $\mu_{\widetilde{A}}(x)$ is a membership function of fuzzy set $\widetilde{A}$. Each fuzzy set is completely and uniquely determined by its membership function.

Definition 3 A fuzzy number $\widetilde{A}$ is a convex normalized fuzzy set $\widetilde{A}$ of the real line R such that:

(a) if exist $x_0 \in R$ such that $\mu_{\widetilde{A}}(x_0) = 1$, and (b) $\mu_{\widetilde{A}}(x)$ is piecewise continuous.

Definition 4 The triangular fuzzy number can be denoted by (l, m, u). Where $l \leq m \leq u$, l and u stand for the lower and upper value of the support of X respectively, and m for the modal value. The support of X is the set of elements $\{x \in R \,|\, l < x < u\}$. When $l{=}m{=}u$, it is a non-fuzzy number by convention.

Definition 5 If X is a set of real numbers, then a type-2 fuzzy set and an interval type-2 fuzzy set in X are called a type-2 fuzzy number and an interval type-2 fuzzy number, respectively.

Definition 6 If the upper membership function and lower membership function of $\tilde{\tilde{A}}$are two triangular type-1 fuzzy numbers, than $\tilde{\tilde{A}}$ is referred to as triangular interval type-2 fuzzy number, $\tilde{\tilde{A}}= \left(\tilde{A}^{U}, \tilde{A}^{L}\right)$ so that:

$$\tilde{\tilde{A}} = \left(\tilde{A}^{U}, \tilde{A}^{L}\right) = \left(\left(a_1^U, a_2^U, a_3^U, \alpha\right), \left(a_1^L, a_2^L, a_3^L, \beta\right)\right)$$

where:

The lower and upper bound in the domain are denoted as a_1^U, a_3^U respectively, and $a_{1'}^L, a_3^L$ respectively. The modal values are a_2^U, respectively, and a_2^L, respectively. The values of the membership function are defined as:

$$(\alpha, \beta) \in [0, 1]$$

Definition 7 Let a non-empty set is given X. An IFS from the set X may be presented in the following way (Atanassov 1999):

$$\tilde{A} = \left(x, \mu_{\tilde{A}}(x), \vartheta_{\tilde{A}}(x) | x \in X\right)$$

$$\mu_A(x) \to [0, 1]\,\mathrm{I}\, \nu_A(x) \to [0, 1]$$

where:

Membership function, $\mu_{\tilde{A}}(x) \to [0,1]$ and non-membership function, $\vartheta_{\tilde{A}}(x) \to [0,1]$.

So the following condition is present:

$$0 \leq \mu_{\tilde{A}}(x) + \vartheta_{\tilde{A}}(x) \leq 1, \forall x \in X$$

For each IFS denoted as $\tilde{A}$ from the set X is valid:

$$\pi_{\tilde{A}}(x) = 1 - \mu_{\tilde{A}}(x) - \vartheta_{\tilde{A}}(x)$$
$$0 \leq \pi_{\tilde{A}}(x) \leq 1, \forall x \in X$$

where $\pi_{\tilde{A}}(x)$ indicates intuitive index. The smaller $\pi_{\tilde{A}}(x)$, the more certain $\tilde{A}$.

Definition 8 An IFS $\tilde{A} = \left(x, \mu_{\tilde{A}}(x), \vartheta_{\tilde{A}}(x) | x \in X\right)$ of the real line is called a triangular intuitionistic fuzzy number (TIFN), so that: $\tilde{A} = \left([a, b, c, d], [a_1, b, c, d_1];\ \mu_{\tilde{A}}(x), \vartheta_{\tilde{A}}(x)\right)$ and a, b, c, d, a_1, d_1 are real numbers, and $a_1 \leq a \leq b \leq c \leq d \leq d_1$.

3.2 Fuzzy Delphi Method in Marketing Studies

The majority of decisions that we make in today's complex environment are formulated under a state of uncertainty. Conditions of uncertainty exist when the decision-maker is not aware of all available alternatives, the risks associated with each, and the consequences of each alternative or their probabilities. In the current market situation globally, most decisions that businesses need to make will have some level of uncertainty. However, in the traditional approach to marketing research and analytics, the uncertainty is often not accounted for Ljepava (2018).

Majority of publications in marketing use only traditional, non-fuzzy (crisp) methods for forecasting. To explore the application of the fuzzy Delphi method in marketing, a comprehensive review of the available scientific literature has been conducted.

One of the first studies that considered the application of this technique in marketing is a study conducted by Li et al. (2002). In their study, they proposed an integrated approach utilizing group Delphi, fuzzy logic, and expert systems for marketing strategy development. The strategy development process includes a high level of uncertainty and ambiguity, so the Delphi technique can be applied to conduct the SWOT analysis with experts. After collecting the feedback from D.M.s, results can be fuzzified using the fuzzy logic and expert systems and further utilized for setting up marketing strategies.

Buyukozkan (2004) explored digital marketplaces that were extensively developing at that time, especially business-to-business commerce, one of the dominant segments in e-business. To get more benefit from this digital marketplace, he suggested applying the fuzzy set theory and AHP. The experts' opinions, in this case, are described by linguistic terms, which are expressed in triangular fuzzy numbers (TFNs). Expert group members compared and rated various e-marketplaces available at the time. The results are derived from their initial and subsequent responses and analyzed using appropriate fuzzy algebra. Expert group members were then requested to re-examine their comparisons, and the results are derived from their initial and subsequent responses until they are completely satisfied (Buyukozkan 2004).

The market segmentation problem was considered by Hanafizadeh and Mirzazadeh (2011). They have explored market segmentation of Iranian telecommunication companies by using 19 variables divided into four groups—demographics, psychological, behavioral, and geographic. Seven marketing and sales managers (D.M.s) have participated as experts in the research. Subject matter experts expressed their estimates using a five-point Likert scale. The corresponding linguistic expression accompanied each value of the Likert scale, and these linguistic variables were further modeled with TFNs. The proposed model was obtained by the aggregation of the estimates of D.M.s into a single score. The modal values of the TFNs describing the aggregated estimates of D.M.s were calculated using the fuzzy averaging operator. The lower and the upper bounds were given as minimum or maximum of the lowest or uppers bounds of used TFNs. After conducting the analysis, the results were visualized to identify the relevant market segments.

Mir and Rashidpoor (2019) explored the factors relevant to promoting the brand personality. They conducted the study with the purposive expert sample of 15 university experts who rated the most significant factors that can impact the promotion of the brand personality. Data were further analyzed using a Fuzzy Delphi technique, and six factors were identified as leading factors in promoting the brand personality: brand, language, profitability, reliability, prestige, activism, and color.

One of the critical challenges the marketing managers face is evaluating client retention. The period of client retention within the company depends on several external and internal factors, and it can be treated as uncertain data (Gil-Lafuente et al. 2013). These authors suggested that TFNs could well describe the estimation of the lifetime period of the client staying with an enterprise. Obtaining group consensus was based on the rules of the algebra phase.

Identification of the most significant attributes for the development of a tourism strategy was considered by Liu and Chou (2016). They have divided all possible attributes into three groups: marketing strategy, brand equity, and travel motivation. Under each marked group, decision-makers rated the importance of attributes by using linguistic variables. These linguistic variables were modeled by TFNs. The consensus of decision-makers was given by using the proposed model.

The problem of assessing the importance of factors influencing digitalization in the public sector was considered by Kamalian et al. (2017). These authors considered ten groups, including education, healthcare, communication, transportation, law and justice, culture and religion, agriculture and ecology, security and citizenship rights, finance, and business services. Fuzzy rating of the relative importance and values of factors is given by using the fuzzy Delphi technique. The authors emphasized that the application of the fuzzy Delphi technique has certain advantages over other methods. Those are: (a) it is more time-effective compared to other qualitative methods of data collection, (b) it reduces the possible bias arisen from individual comments, and (c) it displays the semantic presentation of expert opinions. The decision-making process involved 32 experts belonging to development, employment, national security, communication, transportation, education, agriculture, and culture workgroups (four participants per each workgroup). D.M.s used seven linguistic expressions modeled by TFNs. The aggregation is performed by the fuzzy averaging method. Ten criteria were selected, which were associated with the highest values of the respective scales of TFNs, which described the aggregate values of D.M.s.

In recent decades, many companies worldwide have implemented end-of-life strategies such as product remanufacturing. A study conducted by Vafadarnikjoo et al. (2018) explored applying the fuzzy Delphi method for understanding consumers' motivation, which leads them to purchase a remanufactured product (bike). The study explored the major motivational factors for buying a remanufactured bike based on the consumers' and experts' opinions. The survey involved 104 participants from different universities. University students were contacted by email to fill out the online questionnaire, and for some of them, the questionnaire forms were printed out to be filled in (Vafadarnikjoo et al. 2018). Each participant used seven different linguistic terms, which are modeled by single-valued trapezoidal neutrosophic numbers (Ji et al. 2016). The consensus of D.M.s opinions is given by using the trapezoidal neutrosophic weighted arithmetic averaging proposed by Ye (2017).

After reaching the consensus, results were fuzzified to account for uncertainty in subjective judgments.

Quality and warranty were identified as the main factors influencing the purchasing decision.

The prediction of factors influencing online consumers' behavior problems is widely covered in the marketing literature (Röllecke et al. 2018). The construct of the list of changing pattern factors of the consumer perspective is performed by the fuzzy Delphi technique (Kumar et al. 2018). The preference of decision-makers is described by linguistic expressions and corresponding to TFNs. The summarized estimate of expert opinions is given by using fuzzy algebra rules, which are described by TFNs. Using the defuzzification procedure (Mardani et al. 2016), the summarized assessment is presented by crisp values. The weights vector of the possible pattern factors of the consumer perspective is calculated by the fuzzy analytical hierarchy process (FAHP).

Assessment of antecedents of customer engagement problem is considered by Jani and Zakaria (2018). It is assumed that D.M.s express their estimates by linguistic themes modeled by TFNs. The group consensus is given by using the fuzzy averaging method. It should be noted that those antecedents of customer engagement are selected where the smallest difference between individual assessments and the aggregate value of D.M.s opinions. The authors used Euclidian distance to determine marked differences.

4 Comparative Analysis and Discussion

In this Section, a comparative analysis of the proposed fuzzy Delphi techniques and its applications in marketing studies, which have been identified in the previous studies, is conducted and presented in Table 1. The advantages and disadvantages of the analyzed fuzzy Delphi techniques are further discussed.

Based on the comparative analysis presented in Table 1, it can be concluded that there is no consensus in using the number of experts (decision-makers) in different studies where authors used a different number of D.M.s ranging from 7 to 32. This finding is in line with the previous literature on the Delphi method since there are no rules on how to choose D.M.s, nor is the optimal number of D.M.s recommended, so it can be concluded that the number of D.M.s depends on the nature and problem size.

In almost all analyzed papers, D.M.s use linguistic expressions that are modeled by TFNs. The number of linguistic variables ranges from 3 to 9. Similarly, as in the case of the number of expert decision-makers (D.M.s), the choice of the number of linguistic expressions depends on the problem. Vafadarnikjoo et al. (2018) believe that modeling the opinions of D.M.s can be significantly better described by using the Trapezoidal neutrosophic fuzzy numbers.

The aggregation of D.M.s opinions into a single score can be performed using different aggregation methods. The obtained unique score is modeled by TFNs, according to fuzzy algebra rules. The lowest and upper bounds of these aggregated TFNs are given as the lowest and uppers bounds of used TFNs, respectively. The modal values are calculated by using the fuzzy arithmetic operator (Hsu et al. 2010; Habibi et al. 2015; Jani et al. 2018) and the fuzzy geometric operator (Hanafizadeh and Mirzazadeh 2011; Liu and Chou 2016; Kumar et al. 2018). Some researchers suggest a fuzzy averaging operator (Kamalian et al. 2017; Vafadarnikjoo et al. 2018) for obtaining aggregated estimates of D.M.s. All researchers believe that D.M.s involved in the decision-making process are of equal importance. In practice, this assumption cannot always be introduced. In these cases, aggregation estimates of D.M.s should be performed using the Fuzzy Ordered Weighted Average Operator (Merigó and Casanovas 2008).

The choice of treated factors is based on the proposed procedure (see Table 1). Many authors have mapped aggregated fuzzy estimates of D.M.s into precise numbers by using different defuzzification procedures. It should be emphasized that there is no rule as to the limit for accepting factors. Therefore, the decision to accept factors is highly burdened by subjective assessments of D.M.s. This can be considered as one of the basic shortcomings of the proposed fuzzy Delphi techniques. However, even with this disadvantage, it can be said that the choice of factors based on the application of the fuzzy Delphi techniques gives better results than using an affinity diagram.

Table 1 The comparative analysis of existing research integrating marketing and fuzzy Delphi technique

Author and year of the publication	Number of D.M.s	The number of considered items	The domain of application/combination with some other method	The type of fuzzy numbers/the number of linguistic expressions	Aggregation method	Defuzzification procedure
Li et al. (2002)	–	–	Development of marketing strategies	–	–	–
Buyukozkan (2004)	–	–	e-marketplaces selection/FAHP	TFNs/5	–	–
Hsu et al. (2010)	–	17	Critical factors are used as criteria for the assessment of regenerative technologies/FAHP	TFNs/9	The proposed model with the fuzzy averaging operator	Center of gravity method
Hanafizadeh and Mirzazadeh (2011)	7	19	Choosing Market segmentation variables/techniques of visualization	TFNs/5	The proposed model with Fuzzy geometric operator	–
Gil-Lafuente et al. (2013)	–	–	The estimation of the lifetime period of the client within an enterprise	TrFNs	Fuzzy algebra rules based on cuts of membership functions	The maximum presumption
Mir and Rashidpoor (2019)	15	–	Factors impacting the promotion of the brand personality	–	–	–
Liu and Chou (2016)	–	11	Attributes problem of tourism strategy/DEMATEL	TrFNs/3	The proposed model with Fuzzy geometric operator	The method of maximum possibility
Kamalian et al. (2017)	32	10	Assessment of the weights of criteria/electronic government domain	TFNs/7	Fuzzy averaging method	–
Vafadarnikjoo et al. (2018)	8	47	Assessment of the weights of motivations for potential consumers to buy a remanufactured product/FAHP	Trapezoidal neutrosophic fuzzy numbers/9	Weighted arithmetic averaging	–
Kumar et al. (2018)	–	35	Choosing factors related to the changing pattern of consumer decision making in the digital market / FAHP	TFNs/9	The proposed model with Fuzzy geometric operator	Defuzzification procedure (Mardani et al. 2016)
Jan et al. (2018)	12	–	Assessment of antecedents of customer engagement	TFNs/7	Fuzzy averaging method/Euclidean distance	The simplest defuzzification method, alpha-cut

5 Conclusion

In the conditions of various changes taking place in the environment, it can be said that even though there is more than a sufficient number of data records, in many cases, the available data cannot be considered to be completely valid and reliable. Therefore, the application of quantitative methods for forecasting demand should be applied cautiously. Considering that, many researchers suggest the application of modified qualitative methods in forecasting studies. In the literature, many management problems are stated as multi-criteria optimization problems. This can be applied in all areas of management, including marketing management and marketing decision-making.

The number of factors by which possible alternatives are assessed is determined by the assessment of D.M.s and depends on their knowledge and experiences. In order to reduce the scope of calculations, the number of factors must be optimal. Determining the optimal number of factors can be based on an estimate of D.M.s. In this case, this decision would be highly burdened by subjective assessments of D.M.s. In order to reduce subjectivity in determining the number of factors, many authors suggest the application of the fuzzy Delphi technique. The rank of alternatives is based on applying different multi-criteria optimization methods, such as FAHP. Recently, TFNs have gained popularity in the evaluation and choosing problems in a wide range of applications. Based on the literature review, a summary of the typical research conducted in marketing utilizing this method has been provided, and three main areas of application identified: consumer behavior and consumer decision-making, market segmentation, and support in the development of marketing and branding strategies.

The paper contributes to the current body of literature with two main aspects as follows: (1) it identifies the various models based on the Delphi framework which have been integrated with fuzzy sets theory and utilized in marketing studies (2) identifies various potential application areas for utilization of this method in marketing.

Although the published studies indicated that the Fuzzy Delphi method is showing as very useful in various areas of marketing, the method is relatively unexploited in marketing studies. One of the reasons behind that might be the current scope of marketing research curriculum, which is traditionally based on social sciences (Babin and Zikmund 2015; McDaniel and Gates 2010), and is not focused on training prospective graduates to apply tools and techniques from decision making and business analytics in marketing research and analytics. Future research can aim to develop fuzzy Delphi models for forecasting in marketing areas of interest by employing fuzzy sets that are not yet thoroughly examined within this domain. Additionally, researchers should not rely only on the traditional methods and techniques in their respective disciplines but aim to integrate techniques and approaches from various business disciplines to utilize the opportunities that this integration can offer fully.

References

Asgarkhani M (2005) The effectiveness of e-service in local government: a case study. Case Stud eGov 3(4):157–166

Atanassov K (1999) Intuitionistic fuzzy sets: theory and applications. Physica-Verlag, Wyrzburg

Babin B, Zikmund W (2015) Essentials of marketing research, 6th edn. Cengage Learning

Buyukozkan G (2004) Multi-criteria decision making for e-marketplace selection. Internet Res 14(2):139–154. https://doi.org/10.1108/10662240410530853

Cho J, Lee J (2013) Development of a new technology product evaluation model for assessing commercialization opportunities using Delphi method and fuzzy AHP approach. Expert Syst Appl 40(13):5314–5330

Dalkey N, Helmer O (1963) An experimental application of the Delphi method to the use of experts. Manag Sci 9(3):458–467

Dubois D, Prade H (1980) Fuzzy sets and systems: theory and applications. Academic Press Inc., London

Evangelidis A, Akomode J, Taleb-Bendiab A, Taylor M (2002) Risk assessment & success factors for e-Government in a U.K. establishment. In: Traunmüller R, Lenk K (eds) Electronic government, vol 2456. Lecture notes in computer science. Springer, Berlin Heidelberg, pp 395–402

Förster B, von der Gracht H (2014) Assessing Delphi panel composition for strategic foresight—a comparison of panels based on company-internal and external participants. Technol Forecast Soc Chang 84:215–229

Gil-Lafuente, Anna M, Mauricio OH, Ma Luisa S M (2013) Customer retention in noncontractual relationships: The Fuzzy-Delphi method and the counter-expertise through uncertain values. In Decision Making Systems in Business Administration, pp. 143–161

Habibi A, Jahantigh FF, Sarafrazi A (2015) Fuzzy Delphi technique for forecasting and screening items. Asian J Res Bus Econ Manag 5(2):130–143

Hanafizadeh P, Mirzazadeh M (2011) Visualizing market segmentation using self-organizing maps and Fuzzy Delphi method–ADSL market of a telecommunication company. Expert Syst Appl 38(1):198–205

Hicham A, Mohammed B, Anas S (2012) Hybrid intelligent system for sale forecasting using Delphi and adaptive fuzzy back-propagation neural networks. Editorial preface

Hsu YL, Lee CH, Kreng VB (2010) The application of Fuzzy Delphi Method and Fuzzy AHP in lubricant regenerative technology selection. Expert Syst Appl 37(1):419–425

Hsu, Tsuen-Ho, Tzung-Hsin Y (1999) A new fuzzy synthetic decision model to assist advertisers select magazine media. In FUZZ-IEEE'99. 1999 IEEE International Fuzzy Systems. Conference Proceedings (Cat. No. 99CH36315), IEEE vol. 2, pp. 922–927

Jani NM, Zakaria MH, Maksom Z, Haniff MSM, Mustapha R (2018) Consequences of customer engagement in social networking sites: Employing fuzzy delphi technique for validation. International Journal of Advanced Computer Science and Applications 9(9)

Ji P, Wang J, Zhang H (2016) Frank prioritized Bonferroni mean operator with single-valued neutrosophic sets and its application in selecting third-party logistics providers. Neural Comput Appl. https://doi.org/10.1007/s00521-016-2660-6
Kamalian A, Shahmehr FS, Ajdari P, Khaksar SMS (2017) Empirical study on electronic government in developing countries by using fuzzy Delphi and TOPSIS techniques. Int J Electron Bus 13(4):295–322
Kumar A, Dash MK (2017) Causal modelling and analysis evaluation of online reputation management using fuzzy Delphi and DEMATEL. Int J Strat Decis Sci (IJSDS) 8(1):27–45
Kumar A, Mangla SK, Luthra S, Rana NP, Dwivedi YK (2018) Predicting changing pattern: building model for consumer decision making in digital market. J Enterp Inf Manag
Li S, Davies B, Edwards J, Kinman R, Duan Y (2002) Integrating group Delphi, fuzzy logic and expert systems for marketing strategy development: the hybridisation and its effectiveness. Mark Intell Plan
Liu CHS, Chou SF (2016) Tourism strategy development and facilitation of integrative processes among brand equity, marketing and motivation. Tour Manag 54:298–308
Ljepava N (2018) Marketing research. 2.0. Marketing research practices in digital era. Foundation Andrejevic
Macnee CL, McCabe S (2008). SRN. Understanding nursing research: using research in evidence-based practice, 2nd ed. Wolters Kluwer Health/Lippincott Williams & Wilkins, Philadelphia, PA
Malone D, Abarca J, Hansten P, Grizzle A, Armstrong E, Bergen RV, Duncan-Edgar B, Solomon S, Lipton R (2005) Identification of serious drug-drug interactions: results of the partnership to prevent drug-drug interactions. Am J Geriatr Pharmacother 3(2):65–76
Mardani A, Zavadskas EK, Streimikiene D, Jusoh A, Nor KM, Khoshnoudi M (2016) Using fuzzy multiple criteria decision making approaches for evaluating energy saving technologies and solutions in five star hotels: a new hierarchical framework. Energy 117:131–148
McDaniel C, Gates R (2010) Marketing research with SPSS. International Edition John Wiley and Sons Inc.
Meadows AB, Maine LL, Keyes EK, Pearson K, Finstuen K (2005) Pharmacy executive leadership issues and associated skills, knowledge, and abilities. J Am Pharm Assoc 45(1):55–62
Merigó JM, Casanovas M (2008) Using fuzzy numbers in heavy aggregation operators. Int J Inf Technol 4(3):177–182
Meijering JV, Kampen JK, Tobi H (2013) Quantifying the development of agreement among experts in Delphi studies. Technol Forecast Soc Chang 80(8):1607–1614
Mendel JM (2017) Type-2 fuzzy sets. Uncertain rule-based fuzzy systems. Springer, Cham, pp 259–306
Mir S, Rashidpoor A (2019) Prioritizing the describing factors in promoting brand personality using fuzzy Delphi technique. Consum Behav Stud J 6(2):134–148
Minkes AL (1987) The entrepreneurial manager, decisions goals and business ideas. Penguin Books, Harmondsworth
Nestic S, Lampón JF, Aleksic A, Cabanelas P, Tadic D (2019) Ranking manufacturing processes from the quality management perspective in the automotive industry. Expert Syst 36(6):e12451
Röllecke FJ, Huchzermeier A, Schröder D (2018) Returning customers: the hidden strategic opportunity of returns management. Calif Manage Rev 60(2):176–203
Selaković M, Ljepava N, Đeletović M (2018) Upravljanje inovacijskim promenama u savremenom okruženju. Vojno Delo 70(3):448–459
Somerville JA (2008) Effective use of the Delphi process in research: its characteristics, strengths, and limitations
Li S (2005) A Web-enabled hybrid approach to strategic marketing planning: Group Delphi+a Web-based expert system. Expert Syst Appl 29:393–400
Tadić D, Nestić S (2019) Organization work. The University of Kragujevac, Faculty of Engineering
Vafadarnikjoo A, Mishra N, Govindan K, Chalvatzis K (2018) Assessment of consumers' motivations to purchase a remanufactured product by applying Fuzzy Delphi method and single valued neutrosophic sets. J Clean Prod 196:230–244
Viscusi G, Thevenet LH, Salinesi C (2008) Strategic alignment in the context of e-services-an empirical investigation of the INSTAL approach using the Italian egovernment initiative case study. In: Bellahsène Z, Léonard M (eds) Advanced information systems engineering, vol 5074. Lecture notes in computer science. Springer, Berlin Heidelberg, pp 163–166
Ye J (2017) Some weighted aggregation operators of trapezoidal neutrosophic numbers and their multiple attribute decision making method. Informatica (in press)
Zimmermann HJ (2010) Fuzzy set theory. Wiley Interdiscip Rev Comput Stat 2(3):317–332
Zadeh LA (1975) The concept of a linguistic variable and its application to approximate reasoning—I. Inf Sci 8(3):199–249

Towards a High-Performance Global Organization; Dimensions, Challenges and Solutions of GPM Programs

Nay Haidamous

Abstract

Globalization and internationalization are two concepts that are growing spectacularly in the last decades. However, multinational enterprises are facing the challenges and uncertainties of the cross-cultural context and struggling to maintain the effectiveness of their operations and the sustainability of their competitive advantage. Based on the literature research, the following report will thoroughly discuss five broad dimensions, namely: managers' leadership skills, people management, organization's design structure, culture and change management, which directly affect the global performance management of multinational enterprises. On one hand, it will address the theories that enable companies to overcome the challenges encountered while applying these dimensions, and accordingly maximize their tangible outcomes and their performance effectiveness. On the other hand, the report will highlight on the necessity of correlating risk management programs along with the global performance management programs and to continuously monitor their application and their alignment with the companies' international business strategy.

Keywords

Globalization · Global performance management · Multinational enterprises

1 Introduction to the Global Performance Management

Performance management (PM) has always been a hot topic among HR leaders (Boselie et al. 2012) searching to improve the organizations' business processes and internal culture understanding, and to maximize employees' performance. However, it has gained recently a critical interest worldwide, since it is affecting equally the organization itself in realizing its business strategy, and the employees in determining their career development (Evans et al. 2011).

Performance management is a strategic human resource management process described as being "*an extension of performance appraisal*" (Lindholm, 2000), where competencies and behaviors are reviewed and assessed according to previously determined parameters linked to corporate strategic goals, and where compensation decisions are then applied to the rating and evaluation of each individual.

While performance management acts locally in an organization, the term Global Performance Management (GPM) reveals a wider angle of this practice, spanning different cultures and countries, and covering Multinational Enterprises (MNE) spread globally throughout an international context (Knappert, 2013).

However, according to Mercer's 2013 survey, the efficiency of the global performance management programs have not been very overwhelming recently, and only less than 3% of the companies acknowledged that these processes were truly valuable and efficient (2013 Global Performance Management Survey Report, 2013). In fact, a number of challenges are preventing their proper implementation; the Boston Consulting Group (BCG) has identified five broad dimensions, namely: leadership, design, people, change management and culture, that influence global performance management programs and enable the accomplishment of the organization's international strategy if they are continuously examined and improved.

N. Haidamous (✉)
Bernoty Architects, Beirut, Lebanon
e-mail: nay@bernotyarchitects.com

A. Salman and A. Tharwat (eds.), *Smart Designs for Business Innovation*,
Advances in Science, Technology & Innovation, https://doi.org/10.1007/978-3-031-49313-3_2

Fig. 1 Diagram of research methodology (*Source* Haidamous, 2020)

The following report will further discuss these dimensions that challenge the achievement of a successful GPM, and how global organizations may properly address them, to consequently be able to monitor their people and operations and converge them toward clearly defined goals. The below diagram (Fig. 1) shows the research methodology adopted in this report, which will be further detailed in the following paragraphs.

2 Impact of Managers' Leadership Skills

In today's fast changing environments, effective leadership skills are increasingly becoming a scarce resource that cannot be translated solely through command and control. In fact, "*developed markets are suffering from an exodus of older executives and developing markets straining to keep up with rapid growth*" (Bhalla et al. 2011).

The primary driver that boosts the companies' performance and enables them to successfully achieve expected results is the strength of their managers' leadership skills and their ability to spread the organization's culture and objectives among the entire workforce, embracing their subordinates' humanistic needs and considerations, and aiding them to maximize their innovative outcomes through individual motivation and collective interaction. Bryan Robertson, the former director of lean transformation for Direct Line Group once said: "*Our ultimate aim was to define the role of a leader as someone who coaches others to be successful and achieve their true potential*" (Robertson, 2014).

The case of the Royal Bank of Canada that experienced a dramatic drop of financial returns in 2004, shows the extent to which a proper implementation of defined operational and behavioral objectives for leaders and managers can change the fate of an organization. In fact, further to the Bank's critical situation, the senior team has set threshold expectations of behaviors and financial targets for the bank's managers and amended the PM system to reward achieved goals. Three years later, the plan worked well and the bank's stock price had doubled. All employees agreed that the visionary transformation was clearly reflected in the daily activities and that the leaders are still following the agreed-upon values (Bhalla et al. 2011).

Unfortunately, a detrimental phenomenon is affecting the organization and its employees in the contemporary working life which is the prevalence of destructive leadership in its passive and active forms, having serious implications on the overall PM programs, on the recruitment, and on the training and development of leaders. In fact, these concepts of leadership behaviors such as Machiavellian (Christie & Geis, 1970), authoritarian (Bass, 1990) and narcissistic leadership styles (Vries & Miller, 1984) demonstrate belittling, manipulating and humiliating behavior manners towards subordinates, and can also take the form of nonverbal aggression. They focus on control and obedience, and act as mental stressors for employees. They equally affect the legitimate organization's interests, hinder the accomplishment of the strategic objectives and negatively

Fig. 2 Elements that have the most impact on the overall success. 2013 (*Source* 2013 global performance management survey report, p. 6)

When it comes to manager skills, what elements have the most impact on overall success?

	Perceived impact on organization	Actual driver of organizational impact	Percentage of managers with marginal skills
Having candid dialogue	**1st** (perceived highest impact)	3rd	33%
Linking performance to development planning	2nd	**1st** (skill with highest impact)	**48%** (lowest skill level)
Setting SMART goals	3rd	2nd	29%

impact the relationship with clients and customers (Padilla et al. 2007). They do so by neglecting or actively preventing the execution of the required tasks through sabotaging subordinates' motivation and performance, stealing or misusing the corporate resources or aiming for individual interests regardless those of the organization (Conger, 1990).

Conversely, the results of a study conducted by Müller and Turner demonstrated the effectiveness of the visionary, coaching, empathic and democratic management styles in creating a leader who succeeds in being followed and in providing adequate and enhanced work environment for his subordinates (Müller & Turner, 2007). Therefore, many companies have a big gap to fill in this regards, and Mercer's recent studies revealed an urgent need to improve managers' skills observed as the best lever of change: while candid dialogue was perceived as the most important driver of the overall performance management success, participants in a statistic survey claimed that almost half of managers are marginally skilled in linking individual performance to development planning, and 29% are marginally skilled in setting specific and measurable smart goals (2013 Global Performance Management Survey Report, 2013) (Fig. 2).

On the other hand, managers need to be comfortable with change. To successfully face the uncertainties of foreign markets, they need to cooperate with their peers and have enough flexibility to deal with outsiders and adapt to new environments. Therefore, in order to collect the desired performance from managers, global organizations need to identify the potential leaders from the early stages of their career, and provide them with the necessary coaching to enhance their leadership skills and competencies (Bhalla et al. 2011).

3 Managing People to Achieve an Efficient Global Performance Management

A global organization's workforce is strongly correlated with the success of its international business strategy, and can also be a source of sustainable competitive advantage if it is successfully managed at a global context and in the light of changing dynamics (Slavić et al. 2014).

Unfortunately, the vast majority of companies view their GPM program as the procedure of employees' evaluation directly linked to compensation decisions. This pay-for-performance philosophy often lacks clear strategic assessment of the employees' potential and competences, and rather focuses on tangible outcomes regardless of their true value. For example, only less than half of the companies focus on the personal leadership qualities of their CEO-s; instead, they address their bottom-line operational impact and achieved financial goals (2013 Global Performance Management Survey Report, 2013).

In this regard, a company is likely to adopt a GPM program that identifies and attracts talented individuals willing to challenge their capabilities. Through coaching and mentoring, they will be able to maximize their productivity and "think out of the box", yet innovate in their field and guarantee the organization's advantage over its competitors (Johnson et al. 2008); in this case, employees benefit from compensations beyond the simple financial incentives. To sustain their motivation, employees must sense the evolution of their career development, job rotation and autonomy. Hence, performance management should be strongly correlated with talent management programs where global organizations identify critical roles and talented individuals and focus contingency plans around them, but also, they recognize poor performers and act responsibly in their regard (Bhalla et al. 2011).

However, macro-environmental factors have seriously challenged people's integration, and the need to adjust the GPM processes became crucial to support changing strategies that arise by entering an unknown global market, where a number of barriers are imposed, such as meeting new legal rules and regulations, new national cultures and a number of uncertainties (Slavić et al. 2014). In this context, MNEs need to avoid the risk of discrimination and inequalities against minorities through a number of guidelines that meet the diversity of today's corporate workforce. Specifically, gender discriminating practices have become a worldwide phenomenon, and the under-representation of women in top management positions is nowadays deeply embedded in the organizational life (Meyerson & Fletcher, 2000). In France, for example, women account for only 9 percent of executive committee members (Sancier-Sultan, 2013). The literature researches showed that MNEs have put in place some initiatives aiming to avoid inequality, but have not obtained good application results for the simple reason that these measures were not very well implemented. To achieve a gender-diverse organization, an important success factor is the corporate culture that enables mind-sets to engage diversification and adaptation to dialogue, experimentation and incremental changes, to raise the levels of confidence in women leaders and to encourage the diversity of corporate management styles (Devillard et al. 2014; Sancier-Sultan, 2013).

4 The Transnational Design Structure to Insure Globalization

Global performance management researches have much debated the paradigms of convergence and divergence (DeNisi et al. 2008). The convergence paradigm seeks the adaptation of the management practices across countries driven by increased global competition and the need to find the most efficient methodologies to perform at a global context. Conversely, the divergence paradigm describes country-specific practices that remain stable over time, influenced by the organization's legacy culture and processes (Pudelko & Harzing, 2007).

While the convergence concept is a purely economic ideology, and the divergence stresses on the national culture of the organization's country of origin, today's multinational enterprises need to merge these two philosophies of GPM into the idea of crossvergence; this development in performance management practices draws a more realistic picture since it allows organizations to integrate various influences, and to consider new and innovative approaches that have not been considered before (Knappert, 2013). But most importantly, this process allows for a dynamic understanding of the foreign cultures and engages continuous learning and development of the organizations' structure and performance (Ralston et al. 2008). Accordingly, this concept of GPM must be carefully diffused to the organizations' key elements, and translated through the company's strategy into a source of competitive advantage.

To ensure the proper implementation of the crossvergence concept, global organizations must adopt a lean structure that minimizes the unnecessary hierarchical layers, where communication and top-down decision-making are faster, and where senior leaders can have a better view and follow-up on the daily operations (Bhalla, et al. 2011).

The latter discussion is typically applicable for the transnational structure that stresses on innovation and learning objectives, and is described by Bartlett and Ghoshal as being like a matrix with two specific features; the first is its flexibility to adapt to the challenges of internationalization through encouraging the interconnectedness of groups and functional silos and emphasizing change on both individual and strategic levels, and the second is having more fixed responsibilities within its cross-cutting dimension (Johnson et al. 2008).

5 Change Management for a Better Performance

In today's fast-paced world, the MNEs' ability to set new priorities and to drive change in their strategic directions quicker than their rivals became crucial (Bhalla, et al. 2011). Unfortunately, 70% of the change programs fail to achieve their goals, mainly due to a lack of two fundamentals: a proper transmission of the change initiatives from the senior executives down to the business units, and employees' resistance (Ewenstein et al. 2015).

Therefore, change needs to be spread gradually throughout the different layers of the organization following the process of "cascading change"; this process allows the organization to ensure that the goals and means of change are well received and assimilated by the different hierarchical structures, where companies achieve a minimum sufficiency by investing the required energy to succeed through focusing on the most important elements of change, and avoiding unnecessary fragmentation of efforts (Bhalla, et al. 2011).

Regarding employees' resistance, it is never easy to ask people to think or act differently from the way they were used to do things for many years. Bryan Robertson, in his interview with McKinsey & Company, stated that he has faced this issue in many of his transformation programs, and clarified that employees may take the time to accept change, but when they go themselves through the "change curve" they will finally realize that there are better ways of doing things and become strong advocates of the company's new strategy (Robertson, 2014; Financial Services Practice, 2015).

Being a critical competitive advantage, change management programs are necessary for organizations' rapid results and sustainable growth to an unprecedented degree: decision-makers have to react more quickly, managers need to adapt faster to the opportunities and threats, while frontline employees have to be more collaborative and dynamic (Johnson et al. 2008). Consequently, the introduction of digital tools will allow global organizations to adapt to the continuously changing environments much faster than the traditional workshops and training courses, and are much more efficient in the light of the scale and the diversification of their employees. Powerful digital tools will equally allow just-in-time feedbacks, create direct connections among people by sidestepping hierarchy, and minimize the physical distances between employees through achieving a level of connectivity and commitment. For example, a beverage company in Africa was experiencing share losses in its highly competitive market. The challenge was to drive more than 1000 sales representatives spread widely across countries to increase their sales. An SMS message system was implemented, and each representative received a number of daily messages that included updates on consumers and market insights along with personalized performance information. Within a year, selling increased considerably, transforming a 1.5% market share loss to a 1% gain (Ewenstein et al. 2015).

6 Organizational Culture and Performance Effectiveness

While Hofstede states that culture is the *"software of the mind"* shared by a group that acts similarly upon this software (Hofstede & Hofstede, 2004), organizational culture has been defined as being the shared values and attitudes inherited over time and resulting of corporate behavioral norms and practices adopted for problem-solving and for the pursuit of the inner strategy (Johnson et al. 2008).

Corporate culture has a direct impact on the organizations' performance: a weak and ambiguous culture underperforms employees regardless the level of their capabilities whereas a strong and positive culture can increase the productivity even with average individuals. Therefore, culture and performance are interdependent and organizations cannot seek to improve their performance without considering consolidating their corporate culture (Ehtesham et al. 2011).

Denison's theory has demonstrated this fact and has identified the four deepest cultural traits affecting the company's effectiveness, namely: involvement, consistency, adaptability and mission, as a foundation for more common cultural components such as symbols, rituals and actions (Denison, 1989). The involvement trait requires that executives and employees feel that their work is contributing to the achievement of the organization's strategic goals and objectives which provides them with a sense of commitment and belongingness. And since global organizations' culture is often influenced by national factors, the necessity of determining consistency through common behaviors and mind-sets ensures the company's stability, a high degree of conformity and an internal integration. However, effective integration can sometimes hinder change and resist new initiatives. Hence, high-performance organizations are driven by customers' needs and expectations, and have the readiness and adaptability to take risks and change path-dependent capabilities, and amend their system and processes toward a greater value and a continuous costumers' satisfaction. These organizations have equally well defined directions and strategic objectives that draw their mission and express a vision of the organization's future goals and purposes (Ehtesham et al. 2011). All these cultural values that affect organizational performance have therefore a direct impact on the performance management practices and can be summarized in the below model (Fig. 3).

Examples of how organizational culture can improve MNEs' effectiveness and their performance management are numerous. Largest insurers in North America were facing many challenges that their previous investments were not able to solve. So they have integrated a new culture into their systems through a lean management process aiming mainly to improve their workforce productivity and level of engagement, to retain and develop the existing talent, to acquire new capabilities and enhanced resources and finally to rethink and update their business models. The new culture that primarily assesses clients' values and drives changes that continuously act upon that value was implemented, and these companies have witnessed 20 to 30 percent increased returns in the first two to three years (Financial Services Practice, 2015).

A regional healthcare system located in the southern U.S. needed a step change in performance in order to encounter the challenges ahead and yield lasting results. So it consulted McKinsey, who helped designing and implementing a lean transformation, aiming to reduce costs while improving quality, and put in a performance-driven culture that ensures sustainable results. Within less than two years, each hospital has improved its productivity and revenues and secured long-term cost-saving. The new performance management system ensured that the new standards

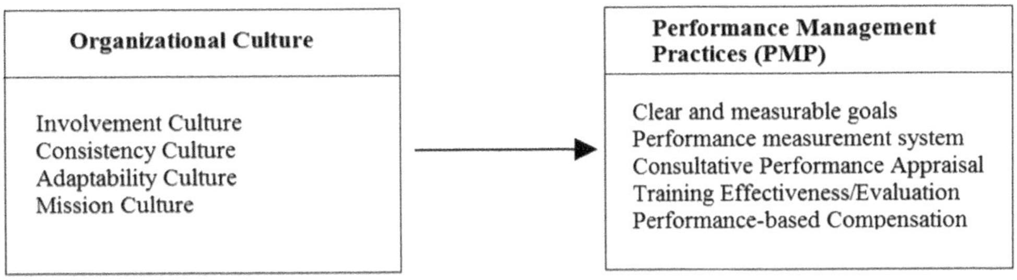

Fig. 3 A conceptual model of organization culture and performance management practices 2011 (*Source* Ehtesham et al. (2011) p. 81)

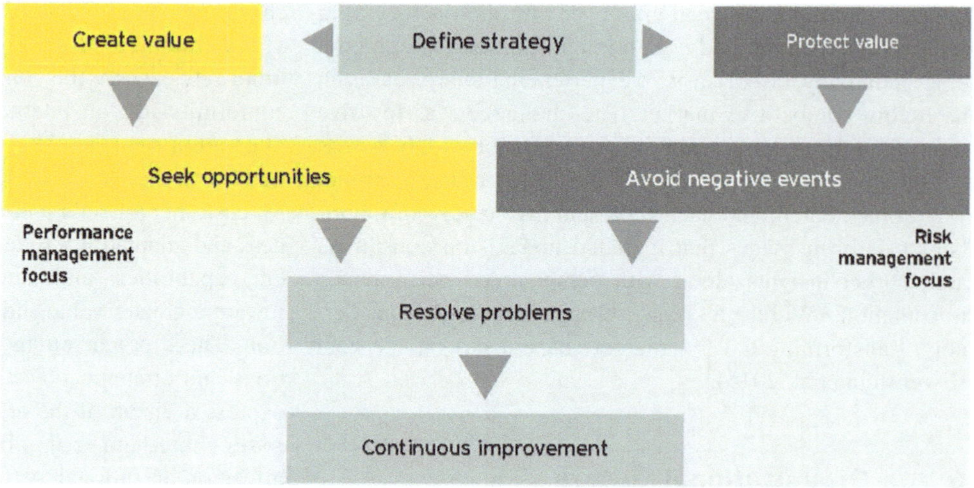

Fig. 4 Risk management aligned with performance management… two sides of the same coin (*Source* Ernst & Young, 2009, p. 2)

are shared by all employees and that real-time changes are made to continuously meet the clients' expectations (McKinsey & Company, 2016).

7 Discussion

The five dimensions previously discussed are all interrelated. They equally affect the GPM program of an organization which primary objective is to improve the company's performance, and therefore is crucial to achieving success. A fundamental principle while conducting a GPM is to continuously link it to the MNE's strategy and objectives, through a spiral process in which performance is continuously assessed and enhanced upon previously set parameters that are aligned with the MNE's international business strategy (Knappert, 2013).

Furthermore, "*risk management should not be a separate silo […]. To the contrary, risk management should be intimately linked to performance management*" (Ernst & Young, 2009). They should be perfectly aligned and treated as being two sides of the same coin. Accordingly, risk factors should be considered in every aspect of the five GPM dimensions previously discussed, to enable the MNE to face the uncertainties and challenges of the business markets, to continuously improve its resources and capabilities, and maintain its short-term and long-term competitiveness (Fig. 4).

The cyclical monitoring of the GPM will increase its effectiveness, and one of the most useful tools to do so is the Balanced Scorecard developed by Kaplan & Norton (2009). It measures the application and efficiency of corporate key performance indicators (KPIs) such as customers' satisfaction and the iron triangle (cost, time and quality), unifies culture and language, and helps in transferring the company's vision and mission into a measurable set of individual and collective objectives (Johnson et al. 2008). These objectives are either cascaded into various KPIs from a top-down perspective, or aggregated into fewer KPIs from a bottom-up perspective, and therefore, the Balanced Scorecard becomes a link between the company's different layers and integrates the financial and non-financial goals into the daily operations and into the performance review process.

8 Conclusion

The addressed challenges are all common issues encountered in today's MNEs, and consist the basis of the contemporary Human Resource activities and concern. This report has discussed the five main dimensions that align organization's needs with those of the employees, and ensure that the corporate operations and objectives converge towards an effective performance management.

As a conclusion, the major areas of GPM include the necessity of goal setting and commitment and of employees' engagement in the organization's life-cycle as drivers for successful work performance, constituting the line of sight between the assessment of goal attainment, the compensation decisions and finally the actions taken to improve the global performance of a Multinational Enterprise.

References

Bass BM (1990) Authoritarianism, power orientation, machiavellianism, and leadership. In: Bass BM, Stogdill RM (eds) Bass & Stogdill's handbook of leadership: theory, research, and managerial applications. Free Press, New York, pp 124–139

Bhalla V, Caye JM, Dyer A, Dymond L, Morieux Y, Orlander P (2011) High-performance organizations: the secrets of their success. The Boston Consulting Group (BCG)

Boselie P, Farndale E, Paauwe J (2012) Performance management. In: Brewster C, Mayrhofer W (eds) Handbook of research on comparative human resource management. Cheltenham, Edward Elgar, UK

Christie R, Geis FL (1970) Studies in machiavellianism. Academic Press, New York

Conger JA (1990) The dark side of leadership. Organ Dyn 19:44–55. 2 edn. https://doi.org/10.1016/0090-2616(90)90070-6

DeNisi A, Varma A, Budhwar PS (2008) Performance management around the globe: what have we learned? In: Performance management systems: a global perspective. Routledge, Abingdon [England], New York, NY, pp 254–262

Denison DR (1989) Organizational culture and organizational effectiveness: a theory and some preliminary empirical evidence. School of Business Administration, University of Michigan. From Denison Consulting: https://www.denisonconsulting.com/sites/default/files/documents/resources/denison-1989-preliminary-evidence_0.pdf. Accessed 11 Dec 2016

Devillard S, Sancier-Sultan S, Werner C (2014) Why gender diversity at the top remains a challenge. From McKinsey & Company: http://www.mckinsey.com/business-functions/organization/our-insights/why-gender-diversity-at-the-top-remains-a-challenge. Accessed 13 Dec 2016

Ehtesham UM, Muhammad TM, Muhammad SA (2011) Relationship between organizational culture and performance management practices: a case of university in Pakistan. J Compet (4), 78–86. http://www.cjournal.cz/files/77.pdf

Ernst & Young (2009) A new balanced scorecard: measuring performance and risk

Evans P, Pucik V, Björkman I (2011) Global performance management. Glob Chall: Int Hum Resour Manag 2:346–390. McGraw-Hill, New York, NY

Ewenstein B, Smith W, Sologar A (2015) Changing change management. McKinsey & Company. http://www.mckinsey.com/global-themes/leadership/changing-change-management. Accessed 10 December 2016

Financial Services Practice (2015) Building a culture of continuous improvement in insurance. McKinsey & Company. www.mckinsey.com/client_service/financial_services

Haidamous (2020) Towards a high-performance global organization; dimensions, challenges and solutions of GPM programs

Hofstede G, Hofstede GJ (2004) Cultures and organizations: software for the mind, 2nd edn. McGraw Hill Professional

Johnson G, Scholes K, Whittington R (2008) Exploring corporate strategy, 8th edn. Financial Times Prentice Hall, Harlow, England

Kaplan, R & Nortan, D (2009) Conceptual foundations of the balanced scorecard. Harvard Business School, pp 2–32

Knappert L (2013) Global performance management in the multinational enterprise. Berlin.

Lindholm N (2000) National culture and performance management in MNC subsidiaries. Int Stud Manag & Organ 29:45–66. Taylor & Francis, Ltd.

McKinsey & Company (2016) By creating a performance-driven culture, a health system lowered costs and raised quality of care. From McKinsey & Company: Healthcare Systems & Services: http://www.mckinsey.com/industries/healthcare-systems-and-services/how-we-help-clients/creating-performance-driven-culture. Accessed 13 Dec 2016

MERCER (2013) 2013 Global Performance Management Survey Report

Meyerson DE, Fletcher JK (2000) A modest manifesto for shattering the glass ceiling. Harvard Business Review

Müller R, Turner JR (2007) Matching the project manager's leadership style to project type. Int J Project Manage 25:21–32

Padilla A, Hogan R, Kaiser RB (2007) The toxic triangle: destructive leaders, susceptible followers, and conducive environments. Lead Q 18:176–194. 3 edn, United States

Pudelko M, Harzing A-W (2007) Country-of-origin, localization, or dominance effect? An empirical investigation of HRM practices in foreign subsidiaries. Hum Resour Manag 46. 4 edn. https://doi.org/10.1002/hrm.20181

Ralston DA, Holt DH, Terpstra RH, Kai-Cheng Y (2008) The impact of national culture and economic ideology on managerial work values: a study of the United States, Russia, Japan, and China. J Int Bus Stud 39. 1 edn

Robertson B (2014) Cultural change at direct line group. McKinsey & Company, Interviewer. Retrieved 10 Dec 2016

Sancier-Sultan S (2013) Women matter 2013–gender diversity in top management: moving corporate culture, moving boundaries. From McKinsey & Company: http://www.mckinsey.com/global-locations/europe-and-middleeast/france/en/latest-thinking/women-matter-2013. Accessed 13 Dec 2016

Slavić A, Berber N, Leković B (2014) Performance management in international human resource management: evidence from the CEE region. Serb J Manag 9(1). Accessed 04 Dec 2016

Vries FK, Miller D (1984) Narcissism and leadership: an object relations perspective. Fontainebleau, Human Relations, forthcoming, France

The Leadership Competencies During the Crisis in Aligning the TQM Success Factors in the Higher Education Sector

Ahmed Mohy El Din and Assem Tharwat

Abstract

In this new era of management all sectors are fully oriented towards producing and providing best of the products and services for the customers. This has benefitted in developing the most advanced and elaborate system of production and operations labelled as Quality management or Quality services. With the emergence of the quality concerns, the specifications for achievement of Quality also emerged. Now quality is the watchword in every sphere of activity, including academic sector. The research study is to address the leadership qualities for academic administrators including all sectors of management namely production and service sector. Total Quality Management is the matter of requirement in every production and service sector is a wide approach that recently proved its implementation importance in different sectors. Leadership plays a vital role in the success of any organization. This research aims to find out the leadership competencies for crisis management in alignment with TQM success factors. The data needed for the study included both quantitative and qualitative data, collected through discussions and interviews, analyzed based on statistical inferences to arrive at the result of the study. Senior management staff and academic leaders from the CAA accredited organizations formed the part of the population for the study. From this population, selected respondents were contacted for purpose of the study to know the approaches in which the leadership acted during the crisis situations. The factors related to the Quality management protocol with regard to the Leadership qualities namely Leadership Performance, Process Control and Improvement, Employee Involvement and stakeholder focus were discussed as part of the research study. The study in this area provided the response towards the fact that it is crucial for the top management to perform as true leaders for implementing TQM during any crisis situations. The research has administrative and theoretical implications for the design and formulation of TQM operations strategy in higher education sector during crisis situations.

1 Introduction

The COVID-19 pandemic has invaded the whole industrial scenario including the production and operation sector as well as the service sector institutions. The whole industrial scenario is on a drastic change with most of the industries and institutions fining out diversified methods to overcome the crisis situations through effective management of the resources. The Crisis pandemic affected the world of business in a diversified manner, bringing the world to a standstill. The sea of changes that happened overnight placed many organisations to bring in commendable changes to the work settings to accommodate all mandatory requirements for health and safety, while at the same time without compromising the cost, quality and value of the services. It needs to learn that as the world continues to fight with the worst ever scenario of the natural crisis due to Covid-19, the governments are battling a combined attack to protect the people, systems, and economies. It is very unclear that, even when the pandemic comes to a stop, how the events across the world are going to change in terms of quality and value in the services delivered.

The academic sector went to a drastic and commendable changes during this time period. The era of education was

A. M. E. Din (✉) · A. Tharwat
American University in the Emirates, Dubai, United Arab Emirates
e-mail: a.mohyeldeen@gmail.com

A. Tharwat
e-mail: assem.tharwat@aue.ae

A. Salman and A. Tharwat (eds.), *Smart Designs for Business Innovation*,
Advances in Science, Technology & Innovation, https://doi.org/10.1007/978-3-031-49313-3_3

going on hand in hand with the technology enabled classrooms, smart rooms, etc., to coverup the academics through traditional classroom teaching. Overnight the scenario changed. The whole education sector moved to network enabled online education system, with classrooms being replaced by laptops sitting anywhere across the globe to handle the education including the teaching learning process. Though the academic sector moved in pace with the changes in the global academic scenario, it was the need of the hour to measure the quality and value of the education that is happening and the best methods to promote value added technology enabled education with better quality and efficiency.

The present study focuses on the Quality management protocol with regard to the Leadership qualities in the academic system to manage the crisis and the crisis events. The focus of the study was mainly on the performance of the lleadership during the pandemic situation, changes in the process management protocols, and the expected outcomes in terms of the improvements. Further the study concentrated on the involvement of the employees in delivering the best of the quality with the response expectations from the stakeholders.

It is the time for the academic institutions to move towards a much-organised quality-controlled technology enabled era of education. Now it is the time to address the situation of changes in the sector. The study better focuses on the Quality side of the academics and the influence and interference of Leadership to manage the crisis. This made the researcher to think the process to analyze the basic enquiry related to the methods to handle the crisis that can happen to academic systems.

Thus the objective of the study is to understand the methods of Leadership and decision making skills which can better address the crisis management situation and at the same time to take care of Quality standards to be implemented with compromise that emerged now and can happen in future and how best similar situations were addressed during the past, which can be copied for the future, as well to emerge with new skills in leadership and decision making which can benefit the new era of technology enabled advanced era of higher education.

At present the study is planned to explore the leadership competencies for crisis management in alignment with TQM success factors among the institutions in the higher education sector in UAE. The proposed study was conducted in selected Universities under Ministry of Higher Education and Research as well as accredited by CAA. The outcome of the study is explained to address the kinds of quality maintenance requirements for better Leadership and Decision-Making in the event of a similar or any other events.

Literature references:

1.1 Leadership and Crisis Management

Leadership literature is long, complex, and emerges from a rich history. Fully exploring that literature is beyond the current scope. As Fiedler (1971). describes "there are almost as many definitions of leadership as there are leadership theories" (Antonakis et al. 2012). Leadership at its core can be viewed as "an influencing process [occurring] between a leader and followers ...explained by the leader's dispositional characteristics, competencies and behaviors, follower perceptions and attributions of the leader and the context in which the influencing process occurs" (Antonakis et al. 2012, p. 4).

Considering that crises are a time of extreme ambiguity and uncertainty across the organization's various stakeholders, leadership's role becomes more complex particularly in terms of decision-making in what is essentially a time-pressed change management process. The consequences of this on the leader–follower dynamic, and by extension the rest of the organization, emerge from the way in which information is acquired, processed, and disseminated such that it impacts decision-making (via such things as decision-making errors and biases) as well as "collective sense making and role structure and followers' belief in cultural norms" (Ibid, p. 77). Interestingly employee-centered crises are a unique case in point in that they not only require effective leadership, but they also often emerge from a failure of leadership. Employee-centered crisis "develop over time and result from faulty or poorly administered management practices that result in [specific unfavorable perceptions that can emerge from] a collapse of sociopolitical systems or violation of formal management procedures, policies, and practices" (Pearson and Clair 1998) in Wooten and James (2008, p. 5). Regardless of the nature of a crisis or the direction of its impact a crisis inevitably produces change in an organization where the consequences of this change on the organization and its stakeholders is heavily impacted by leadership.

1.2 Total Quality Management (TQM)

Total quality management (TQM) is a systematic approach for better management of organization in general. Its process focusses on improving the quality of organization achievement including organization products and services, via continuous improvement of internal procedures and practices. TQM is mainly a customer-centered process that targets for continuous improvement of organization functions and operations. It struggles to guarantee all organization employee work to achieve the common goal of enhancing service or product quality which includes the improvement of internal production procedures. Although TQM was mainly created to improve the manufacturing sector, its principles can be applicable to other various sectors. It is intended to afford a consistent vision that ensures a systematic change via concentration on long-term change over short term goals. That's why TQM is applied in many sectors such as manufacturing, medicine and banking successfully. Moreover, its principles and techniques can be implemented within an organization's departments which allow guaranteeing that all employees are working together to achieve the common goals as well as improving the operational aspects of each department. Possible main Departments which can apply TQM principles within an organization are administration, production, employee training and marketing.

Recently quality in general has become the main interest and number one trend applied globally as a vital pillar of the new model of management which goes in line with worldwide innovation focus and adjust with international and local variables. Higher education is one of the sectors which recently applied TQM principles. Many of the universities have adopted and implemented comprehensive concepts of TQM due to the urge of continuous improvement and in order to enhance educational productivity and the outcome of the educational process in general. As TQM mainly aims to provide the proper tools and techniques which allow educational institutes to achieve its main goals and provide high quality educational services and ensure satisfaction for all stakeholders and concerning parties (Habbal and Jreisat 2018).

1.3 The Relationship Between Leadership and TQM

The quality management is used to be an overlooked part of organizations' practices in the past; but the idea about quality management process has been rapidly changed recently. Nowadays organizations depend on quality assurance departments to achieve their goals after they have realized the integral role of quality management in any business success. But it is well proved that leadership plays a vital role in proper application of the TQM process. A leader is the key person who puts TQM principles into actions, so without perfect leadership, the quality control process might not be effective. Only a leader with suitable leadership merits can apply quality management properly and take it to a level that put the organization in the best possible path to succeed.

Applying TQM requires a teamwork chaired by organization's leader and his team. Every person involved in change management has a defined role and responsibility and it is very important that everybody in the organization understand the vital role of leadership in implementing TQM to make it more effective and helpful for the organization benefit.

Crisis Leadership Competencies

In general, crisis management researchers have identified five phases that represent a typical business crisis: (a) signal detection, (b) preparation and prevention, (c) damage containment, (d) recovery, and (e) learning (Coombs 2014; Pearson and Mitroff 1993; Pheng et al. 1999).

The first phase, signal detection, requires leaders to feel early warning signals announcing a potential crisis. It also requires leaders to keep monitoring policies, procedures, and people which can stand and face current and upcoming threats, challenges, and opportunities. In the second phase, prevention and preparation, leaders should avoid crises and be well prepared whenever the crisis occur. They also should be responding promptly during significant disruptive events which change the usual organization functioning. In addition, planning tasks, processes, and resources wisely, without losing the ability to adjust plans on spot by attending to the way the teams do their work and helping them to make necessary adjustments.

The third phase entails containing damage by keeping the crisis from expanding to other parts of an organization or its environment. It needs leaders to make the right decisions about strategies, tactics and people judgments, to always have contingency plans and be able to change the plans quickly if required. They have to act timely and objectively during the process of decision making. In this phase it is always significant to be thinking outside the box, being creative and finding novel new solutions. Special merit to be added to leaders at this phase is performing with a sense of urgency; prioritizing and carrying out core tasks; focusing on achieving goals and pursuing projects and activities, identifying patterns and links between situations even if apparently unrelated (complexity management), having insight into how everything is internal and external components fit together and create important context for their team by attending to the way the teams do their work and helping them to make necessary adjustments whenever required.

The fourth phase: During the recovery phase, leaders are responsible for careful implementing short- and long-term plans, tasks, process and resources designed to help resume business functions. Keeping image and reputation of the organization should be one of the leader's priorities during the recovery phase by keenly working to build and maintain a positive reputation for the team/organization in order to keep the self-confidence a factor to reduce the time needed for a complete recovery.

Finally, in the fifth phase of crisis management, leadership encourages learning and examines the critical lessons from the crisis through providing insightful, timely, and essential developmental feedback; striving to help team members develop through experiences, mentoring, and training. Leadership competencies are described as specific personality merits, talents, qualities, values, knowledge, abilities that enables person's capability to implement leadership roles (Boyatzis 2008; Fernandez et al. 2010; Savanevi_cien_e et al. 2014).

Some scholars highlighted that advanced levels of leadership competencies facilitate and affect the efficiency of each team member's achievement acknowledged certain competencies of the leader, including decision-making, developing people and stakeholder management, creating and supporting organizational capabilities and culture, communication (Asree et al. 2010; Trivellas and Reklitis 2014). Wooten and James (2008). Leadership competencies are vital for proper management of crisis due to several reasons; they are needed to improve a decision-making strategy and indorse prompt, operative procedures to overwhelm the crisis while keeping mutual trust among the leader's teams and other stakeholders (James and Wooten 2010; Thach 2012).

In order to be able to adjust to the quick changes and any arising circumstances and to be able to influence and manage people during crisis, leaders need to have several competences which can be grouped under three categories: competencies related to self-management, competencies related to business management; and competencies related to people management.

Previous research has concentrated on four key leadership competencies important to crisis leadership: sense of urgency; creativity and problem-solving skills, proper communication and finally, crisis management and strong emotional intelligence (Betancourt et al. 2017; Tubin 2017).

Leaders' sense of urgency means that a leader is able to feel and prioritize tasks according to its urgency and importance which is vital for recognizing any evolving crisis and responding by taking the action as necessary (Betancourt et al. 2017; Kotter 2008); ; . Leaders must be skillful enough to distinguish the sense of urgency required through constant crisis management. Leaders with high sense of urgency are able to prioritize and execute essential responsibilities and daily jobs; constantly focusing on goal achievement and finish of projects and activities also, it allows leaders and their teams to follow the proper policies and procedures according to organization related rules and regulations. Moreover, it is required for facing different, complex and uncertain risks, like possibility of a natural disaster's occurrence. In extended crises, the role of sense of urgency might not be as effective as in the short term crisis since it might be weakening due to other causes like the leader's personal insight of risk, which can be inaccurate or defective in the case of some different kinds of risks (Then and Loosemore 2006). Therefore, this is not an unconnected factor as it is usually affected by other related factors (Wisittigars and Siengthai 2019).

Leadership's crisis management and emotional intelligence acts a fundamental role during different phases of crisis. Emotional intelligence allows team members to better harmonize and have mutual understanding during the crisis. Emotional intelligence is considered a way to motivate team members to do their assigned tasks more efficiently in order to face crisis arising issues (Holt and Wood 2017; Macaleer and Shannon 2002). Emotional intelligence helps leaders stay calm and adaptable to changes which means to be more flexible; moreover it enables them to regulate their own emotions to increase the team confidence and inspire positive emotional reactions in all of them (Madera and Smith 2009; Mahsud et al. 2010). Crisis management also help leaders to respond promptly during significant disruptive events which change the usual organization functioning (Hiller et al. 2016).

Creativity and problem-solving competency have a vital role throughout the crisis, leaders have to think in a systematic way to promptly and logically take necessary actions while dealing with the problems and make decisions during the crisis to avoid repetitive negative impacts. It is always significant to be thinking outside the box, being creative and finding novel new solutions (Hiller et al. 2016). Usually leaders with systematic skills are able to build up new precautionary measures and capable to improve performance creativity and novelty. Leaders who have high level of problem-solving skills usually perform critical thinking in reducing the negative conditions of the crisis by thinking outside the box (Wisittigars and Siengthai 2019).

Proper communication is very essential, before and during a crisis. Before a crisis it's so important that the crisis leaders understand and communicate timely and relevantly about crisis planning by evaluating the risk and its possible impact and accordingly setting disaster recovery plan. Communication permits leaders build up mutual trust among the team members and improve their commitments and sense of responsibility during crisis. Communication has a correlation with the swiftness of decision-making and taking necessary action. Moreover, leaders are required to promptly address issues and delegate authorities and distribute roles and assignments among the team during the crisis (Wisittigars and Siengthai 2019).

Upon the above discussion, herewith, the research we will focus on is the effect of the four mentioned crisis leadership competencies (a sense of urgency, crisis management and strong emotional intelligence, creativity and problem-solving skills and finally, proper communication) during the crisis phases to most achieve the TQM success factor.

TQM and Higher Education

Total quality management is a management theory meant to improve customer satisfaction and to enhance organizational performance. TQM principles are newly introduced and implemented in services like higher education in comparison with manufacturing sector which applied its principle long back. The implementation of TQM principles does not only result in impacting organizational structure or administrative process and resources utilization but also introduce changes to the basic values of business function. Integrating the value of quality into the culture, philosophy and organization identity is considered the initial step in reforming and maintaining it in its operational environment (Platis and Fragouli 2019).

TQM principles were introduced recently in HE due to the increasing competitions among different HE institutes and due to the market demand. The implementation of TQM in HE was initiated by US and UK due to the same reason to satisfy different categories of stakeholders (Bayraktar et al. 2008; Papanthymou and Darra 2017). However, TQM implementation in the field of HE is not widely applied in the developing countries, so it is not well studied. Accordingly, the need of having more researches about the effect of TQM success factors' application in the HE has emerged (Sousa and Voss 2001, 2008). Actually, there are conflicting ideas and findings about the applicability of TQM success factors in HE fields. Some authors assume that TQM principles and values are suitable in the manufacturing sector but not fitting the HE sectors due to several reasons such as the lack of agreement on defining the HEIs customers and the unique nature of academic process in general. While some other authors believe that TQM principles and values can be equally useful and implementable in both fields in the manufacturing sector and HE sector. Those who believe that TQM can fit the HE are two parties one who believes that all TQM values are equally applicable in the HE field, while the other party believes some TQM values are only supportive in the changing modern HE (Helms and Key 1994; Venkatraman 2007; Koch and Fisher 1998; Houston 2007).

Some studies have concentrated on the most vital TQM success factors like, Sanayei et al. (2008), Seetharaman et al. (2006), Sila (2007) and Sila and Ebrahimpour (2002). Sila and Ebrahimpour (2003) have found that Leadership commitment customer focus, information and analysis, human resources management, training, teamwork, supplier management, strategic planning, employee involvement,, process management, product and service design, process control, benchmarking, continuous improvement, employee satisfaction, employee empowerment, quality assurance,, and social responsibility were the most common factors in all these studies. Table 1 shows various TQM concepts from some elaborative examples. This table displays the common components in these studies such as (management commitment, customer focus, and process management) but it also shows that the critical success factors also vary across the studies. The table shows that there is no harmony among TQM success factors due to one possible reason that all these studies were conducted in different environments and various settings (Asif et al. 2013).

As shown in the below table, since environmental and other setting related factors differ widely, it makes it difficult to generalize the research findings in terms of the effect of TQM success factors in HE. This research is so specific, it focuses on a particular context (leadership during crisis): The effect of the Crisis Leadership Competencies on the TQM success factors (Leadership Performance, Process control and Improvement, Employee Involvement, Stakeholders Focus) in HE.

2 Research Problem and Conceptual Framework

As indicated earlier the effect of the leadership competencies in implementing the TQM component during crisis in the higher education sector remains a rich area of exploration and due to the urged need to further dig, many areas were studied carefully. In this section the main question of the research will be identified, the research hypotheses will be formulated and structure module that describes the problem will be explained.

Research Problem and Objectives

Problem to be addressed:

The problem of the study is to understand the essential leadership skills required for proper management of Quality in the teaching learning process in the event of the crisis situations by better understanding the roles of the employees and the stake holders. Thus, the study focuses on the basic requirement to understand the leadership competencies articulated along with the quality management and value driven delivery of the academic system that needs to be maintained during the crisis situations in institutions of Higher learning.

UAE provides facility for excellent education from diversified academic institutions across the globe. There exits best of the educational institutions from across the world like UK, US, India, Pakistan, Russia and to name from many nations. Like all other professional institutions, these academic institutions need authentic leadership which can better benefit to the value of academics in terms of quality education.

Table 1 Various TQM concepts from some elaborative examples

Saraph et al. (1989)	Anderson et al. (1994)	Flynn et al. (1994)	Black and Porter (1996)	Ahire et al. (1996)	Rao et al. (1999)	Joseph et al. (1998)	Bayraktar et al. (2008)	Asif et al. (2013)	Bernik, Merita; Sondari, Mery Citra; Indika, Deru (2017)
The role of top management leadership	Visionary leadership	Top-management support	Corporate quality culture	Top management commitment	Top management commitment	Quality policy	Leadership	Leadership	Leadership
						Organizational commitment	Vision of HEI	Vision	
	Customer satisfaction	Customer involvement	Customer satisfaction orientation	Customer focus	Customer orientation		Student focus other stakeholder focus	Other stakeholder's focus	
Process management	Process management	Process management	Strategic quality management	Design quality management			Process design and resources	Process control and improvement	Business processes
Product design service design		Product design		Product quality	Product/process design	Product design	Process design and resources	Program design and resources	
Quality data and reporting		Quality information	Communication of improvement information	Internal quality information usage	Quality information availability	Quality information system	Measurement and evaluation	Measurement and evaluation	Quality assurance
					Quality information usage	Operating procedures			
Employee relations	Employee fulfilment	Workforce management	People and customer management	Employee involvement		Human resources management	Employee involvement		
				Employee empowerment			Recognition and reward		
Supplier quality management		Supplier involvement	Supplier partnerships	Supplier quality management	Supplier quality	Supplier integration			
Training	Learning			Employee training	Employee training	Training	Education and training		
The role of quality department			Operational quality planning		Strategic quality planning	Role of quality department			
			Quality improvement measurement systems		Quality citizenship				
					Internal/external quality results				

(continued)

Table 1 (continued)

Saraph et al. (1989)	Anderson et al. (1994)	Flynn et al. (1994)	Black and Porter (1996)	Ahire et al. (1996)	Rao et al. (1999)	Joseph et al. (1998)	Bayraktar et al. (2008)	Asif et al. (2013)	Bernik, Merita; Sondari, Mery Citra; Indika, Deru (2017)
	Continuous improve-ment internal and external cooperation			Benchmarking	Benchmarking		Quality system improvement		Governance of academic and non-academic process
			External interface management						
			Teamwork structures	Statistical process control usage		Technology utilization			

Leadership is a direction that is provided to achieve better outcomes for the institution based on the quality management systems. Academic Institutions are in the event of transforming from traditional classroom education to net based online classes, while not compromising on the quality of the quality of the education. The emergence of the latest system of technology-oriented practices is addressed positively and professionally in this study to meet the demand of the situation, for everyone in the system may it be the management or the employee or the stake holder. The benefit of the quality management system needs to be clearly identified and well-organized to deliver quality academic requirements as well to organize the facilities in terms of including faculty, infrastructure, administrative and student support etc.

The Crisis faced by the academic institutions is diversified. This ranges from offering classes to the conduct of the exams, conduct admissions and graduation events, offer courses, establish academic schedules, conduct of exams, review, faculty co-ordination, and all other academic related activities. Considering this complexity of the academic system, the study tries to address the Quality management in delivery of the academics and the leadership concerns to be addressed in the process. From this study, the researcher is addressing the TQM and its influence in the crisis management process and the need of leadership efficiencies in the higher education sector.

Thus, the study looks into the basic research question to understand the *effect of leadership competencies during crisis in the implementation of TQM concepts in higher education sector.* In the current context successful TQM implementation is mainly affected by certain leadership competencies during crisis management. Based on the aforementioned research question the following are the research objectives:

1. To identify the effective specific leadership competencies during the crisis.
2. To identify the specific TQM success factors in the higher education sector.
3. To explore the effect of the leadership competencies in implementing TQM success factors during the crisis.

Based on the above discussions, the study focuses on the following four leadership competencies during the crisis phases that are considered to achieve the TQM success factors:

1. Sense of urgency
2. Crisis management and strong emotional intelligence
3. Creativity and problem-solving skills and finally
4. Sensitivity of communication

From the further discussions, it can be noticed that the most important TQM success factors to be addressed in the higher education sector includes:

1. Leadership performance
2. Process control and Improvement
3. Employee Involvement
4. Stakeholders Focus

Hypotheses for the Study:

To investigate the type and the strength of the relationship that reflect the effect of the leadership competencies during crisis in the implementation of TQM success factors the below hypotheses are introduced:

- H1: There exists a positive relationship between the leader sense of urgency during the crisis and the implementation of the TQM success factors.
- H2: There exists a positive relationship between leader emotional intelligence during the crisis and the implementation of the TQM success factors.
- H3: There exists a positive relationship between leader creativity skills during the crisis and the implementation of the TQM success factors.
- H4: There exists a positive relationship between leader communication skills during the crisis and implementation of the TQM success factors.

Accordingly, the structure of the conceptual framework illustrates the interrelationship between the two sets of variables is given in Fig. 1.

3 Methodology and Research Design

Population and Sample:—The population for the research included all Universities accredited to the CAA and the Ministry of Higher Education, UAE. From the above population, the sample for the study was suitably fixed, based on a set criterion namely more than five years in UAE as well as with at least three programs each at the undergraduate, and graduate level of education, and must have at least three colleges under the University. It can be a public or a private university.

Selection of Sample Size and Respondents for the Study:—There are 76 Universities or academic institutions accredited to CAA in UAE. The samples required for the study were fixed from this population. Nearly 30

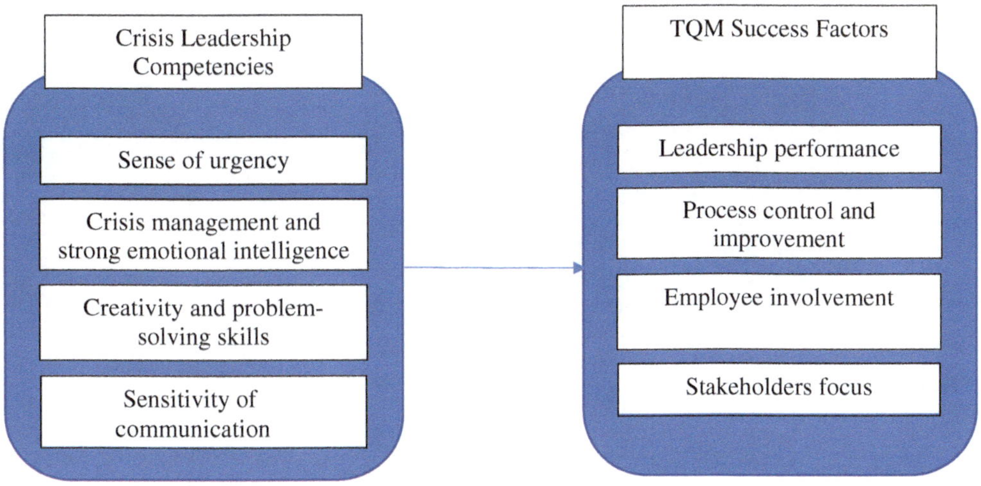

Fig. 1 The interrelationship between the crisis leadership competencies and the TQM success factor

institutions fixing into the category were selected as the sample for the study. The respondents to the study were selected from these institutions, who are enjoying leadership positions. The leadership positions included but not limited to Vice Chancellor, Vice President, College Deans, Associate Deans, Program Leaders, Course Co-ordinators and other academic positions. Nearly 160 respondents were identified, from which 125 respondents participated in the study. From the responses received, 100 responses were selected for the study for analysis and interpretation, as few of the responses were incomplete or not clear.

Data Collection Process:—Data needed for the study includes Primary and Secondary Data. The Primary data needed for the study were collected from the primary sources through questionnaires, as well as interview with respondents. Validation of the questionnaire was done through expert opinion, prior to the conduct of the study. Interview was carried out after fixing prior appointments. Qquestionnaires were distributed to the respondents, for the collection of the primary data required for the study.

Tools for Data Collection:—The tools for the primary data collection were questionnaires distributed through e-media to reach them on time, which benefitted the respondents to send their response without delay, which helped in proper conduct of the study. The questionnaire constituted closed ended questions covering questions based on the quality management and leadership initiatives.

Secondary data for the study included extensive search for historical data as available with the Universities, library references and publications. Few published journals, articles, library references, previous files/records as available and accessible with the respondents constituted as part of secondary source of information.

Data Analysis and Interpretation:—Data collected from all relevant sources were analyzed and systematically interpreted to arrive at a valid conclusion. The data collected through the questionnaire included quantitative data. Appropriate scientific as well as statistical data processing technique as appropriate were used to provide a valid information related to the study. Statistical techniques namely ccorrelation regression analysis, multivariate analysis and other related statistical tests were used for data analysis. SPSS was used for data analysis (see Table 2).

Data Analysis

The present section explores the results of the survey which were analyzed by SPSS.

Graphical analysis and descriptive statistics

We begin with the description of the sample with Fig. 2 Gender distribution table demonstrating the distribution by gender (60% male and 40% female).

Table 2 List of the considered variables in the proposed model

Discerption	Variables
Leadership performance	TQM1
Process control and improvement	TQM2
Employee involvement	TQM3
Stakeholders focus	TQM4
Sense of urgency	CLC1
Crisis management and strong emotional intelligence	CLC2
Creativity and problem-solving skills	CLC3
Sensitivity of communication	CLC4

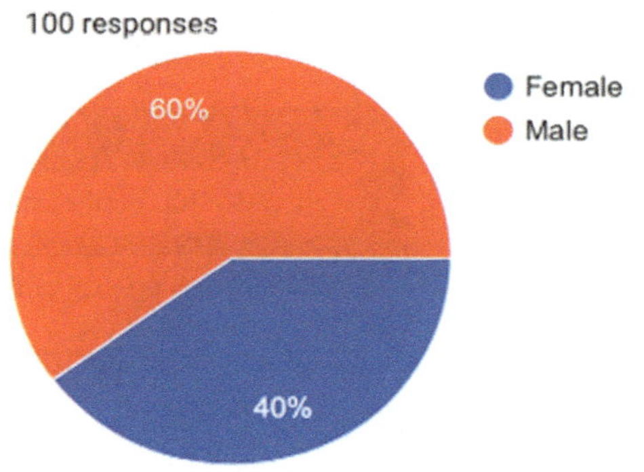

Fig. 2 Gender distribution

Gender					
		Frequency	Percent	Valid percent	Cumulative percent
Valid	1.00	60	60.0	60.0	60.0
	2.00	40	40.0	40.0	100.0
	Total	100	100.0	100.0	

Secondly in the description of the sample with Fig. 3 is the age of the respondents.

Age					
		Frequency	Percent	Valid percent	Cumulative percent
	1.00	2	2.0	2.0	2.0
Valid	2.00	14	14.0	14.0	16.0
	3.00	53	53.0	53.0	69.0
	4.00	25	25.0	25.0	94.0
	5.00	6	6.0	6.0	100.0
	Total	100	100.0	100.0	

In terms of years of experience, the Fig. 4 illustrate that a majority of the respondents have been present in their

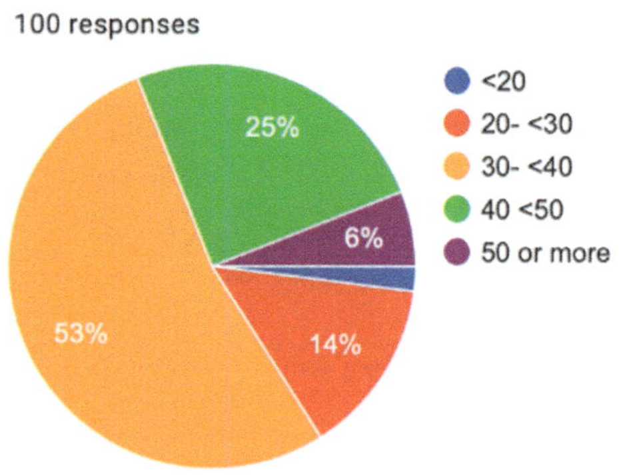

Fig. 3 Age of the respondents

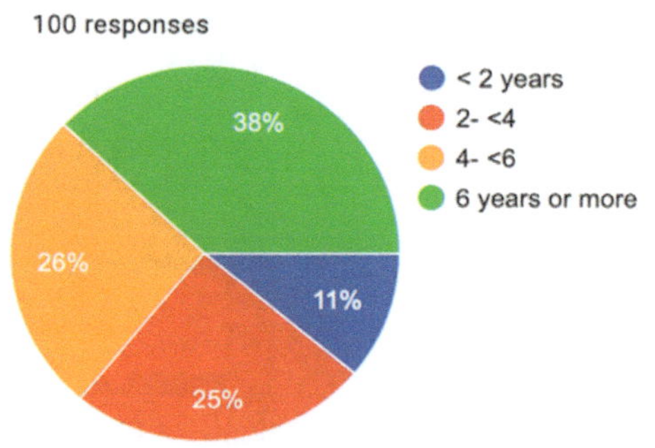

Fig. 4 Year of experience

universities in the range of 6 years and more. Hence, they are considerably experienced both possible in managerial positions and other stakeholders who witness the effect of leadership competencies alignment with TQM success factors.

Association and year of experience					
		Frequency	Percent	Valid percent	Cumulative percent
Valid	1.00	11	11.0	11.0	11.0
	2.00	25	25.0	25.0	36.0
	3.00	26	26.0	26.0	62.0
	4.00	38	38.0	38.0	100.0
	Total	100	100.0	100.0	

In terms of association Fig. 5 give the position in the university, and it's interesting to note that a majority of respondents were in the senior administrator and as staff closely followed by those in senior management positions. Hence the sample is well experienced with management's role and function in the context of crisis management. This is illustrated in the below figure.

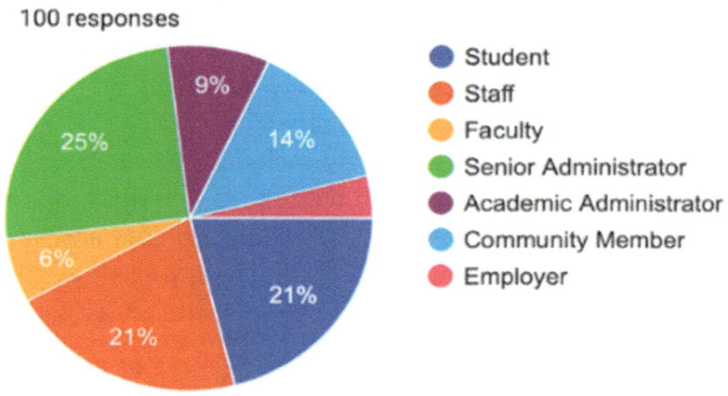

Fig. 5 Position in the university

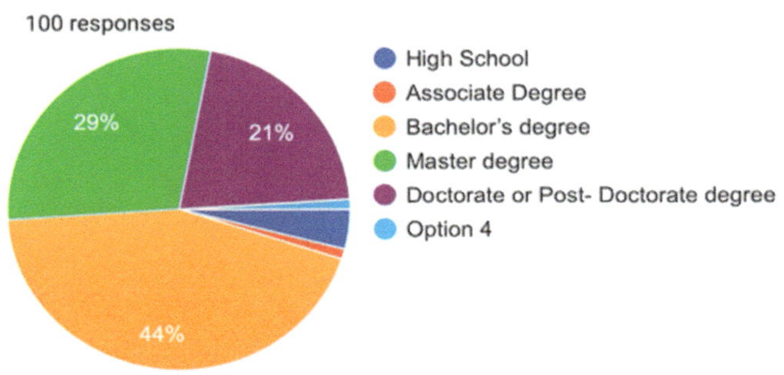

Fig. 6 Level of education

Position					
		Frequency	Percent	Valid percent	Cumulative percent
Valid	1.00	21	21.0	21.0	21.0
	2.00	21	21.0	21.0	42.0
	3.00	6	6.0	6.0	48.0
	4.00	25	25.0	25.0	73.0
	5.00	9	9.0	9.0	82.0
	6.00	4	4.0	4.0	86.0
	7.00	14	14.0	14.0	100.0
	Total	100	100.0	100.0	

In terms of education Fig. 6 indicate that a majority n of respondents hold graduate degrees (i.e. master's degrees or higher).

Education					
		Frequency	Percent	Valid percent	Cumulative percent
Valid	1.00	4	4.0	4.0	4.0
	2.00	45	45.0	45.0	49.0
	3.00	30	30.0	30.0	79.0
	4.00	21	21.0	21.0	100.0
	Total	100	100.0	100.0	

Cronbach Alpha for reliability test

TQM Reliability Test:

TQM1 reliability statistics	
Cronbach's alpha	N of items
0.972	36

RELIABILITY
/VARIABLES = TQM11 TQM12 TQM13 TQM14
/SCALE ('ALL VARIABLES') ALL
/MODEL = ALPHA

TQM2 reliability statistics	
Cronbach's alpha	N of items
0.830	4

RELIABILITY
/VARIABLES = TQM21 TQM22 TQM23 TQM24
/SCALE ('ALL VARIABLES') ALL
/MODEL = ALPHA

TQM3 reliability statistics	
Cronbach's alpha	N of items
0.765	4

RELIABILITY
/VARIABLES = TQM31 TQM32 TQM33 TQM34
/SCALE ('ALL VARIABLES') ALL
/MODEL = ALPHA

TQM4 reliability statistics	
Cronbach's alpha	N of items
0.831	4

RELIABILITY
/VARIABLES = TQM41 TQM42 TQM43 TQM44
/SCALE ('ALL VARIABLES') ALL
/MODEL = ALPHA

TQM reliability statistics	
Cronbach's alpha	N of items
0.872	5

RELIABILITY
/VARIABLES = TQM1 TQM2 TQM3 TQM4
/SCALE ('ALL VARIABLES') ALL
/MODEL = ALPHA

CLC Reliability Test:

CLC1 reliability statistics	
Cronbach's alpha	N of items
0.775	4

RELIABILITY
/VARIABLES = CLC11 CLC12 CLC13 CLC14 CLC15
/SCALE ('ALL VARIABLES') ALL
/MODEL = ALPHA

CLC2 reliability statistics	
Cronbach's alpha	N of items
0.794	5

RELIABILITY
/VARIABLES = CLC21 CLC22 CLC23 CLC24 CLC25
/SCALE ('ALL VARIABLES') ALL
/MODEL = ALPHA

CLC3 reliability statistics	
Cronbach's alpha	N of items
0.879	5

RELIABILITY
/VARIABLES = CLC31 CLC32 CLC33 CLC34 CLC35
/SCALE ('ALL VARIABLES') ALL
/MODEL = ALPHA

CLC4 reliability statistics	
Cronbach's alpha	N of items
0.865	5

RELIABILITY
/VARIABLES = CLC41 CLC42 CLC43 CLC44 CLC45
/SCALE ('ALL VARIABLES') ALL
/MODEL = ALPHA

CLC reliability statistics	
Cronbach's alpha	N of items
0.925	4

RELIABILITY
/VARIABLES = CLC1 CLC2 CLC3 CLC4
/SCALE ('ALL VARIABLES') ALL
/MODEL = ALPHA

The extent to which a set of items in a group are related thereby demonstrating internal consistency is measured by the Cronbach Alpha score. The Cronbach alpha score is at 0.70 implying an acceptable degree of internal consistency. Looking more closely to the above results of Cronbach alpha we can see that the minimum value is 0.765 which indicates that the internal consistency for both the TQM components collected answers and the CLC components collected answers are acceptable.

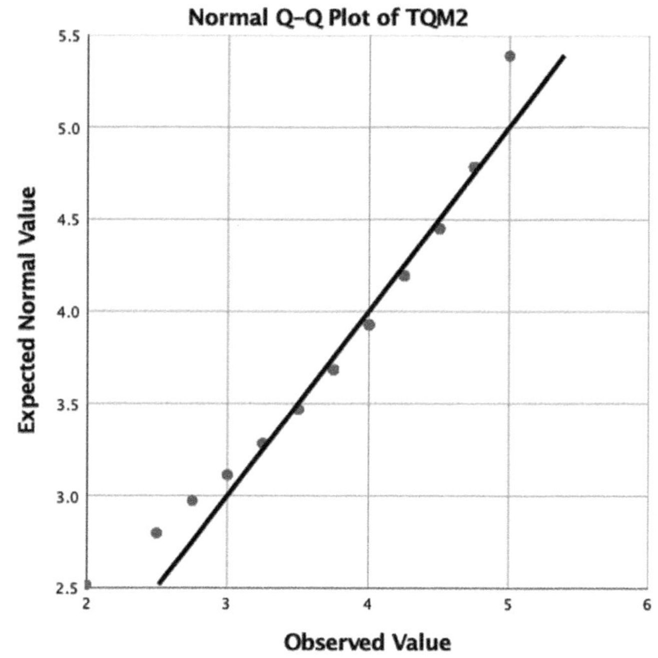

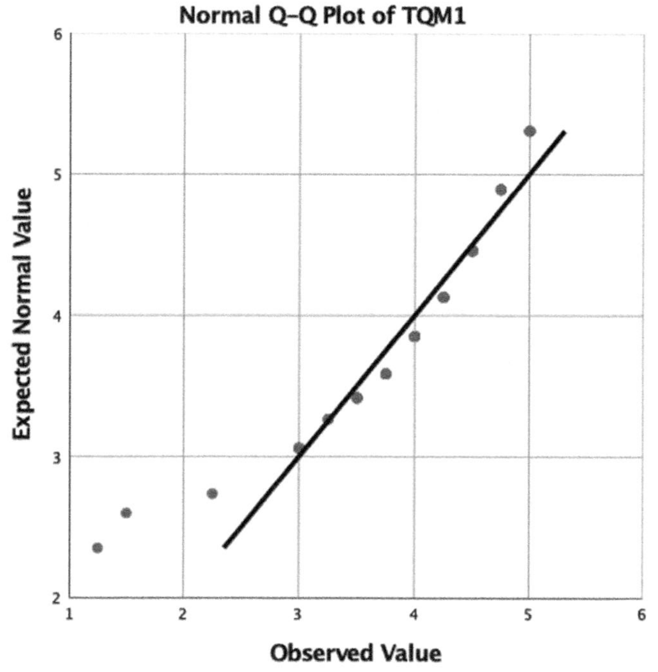

5-3 Normality Test of the Data (Kolmogorov–Smirnov normality test)

5-3-1 univariate normality test

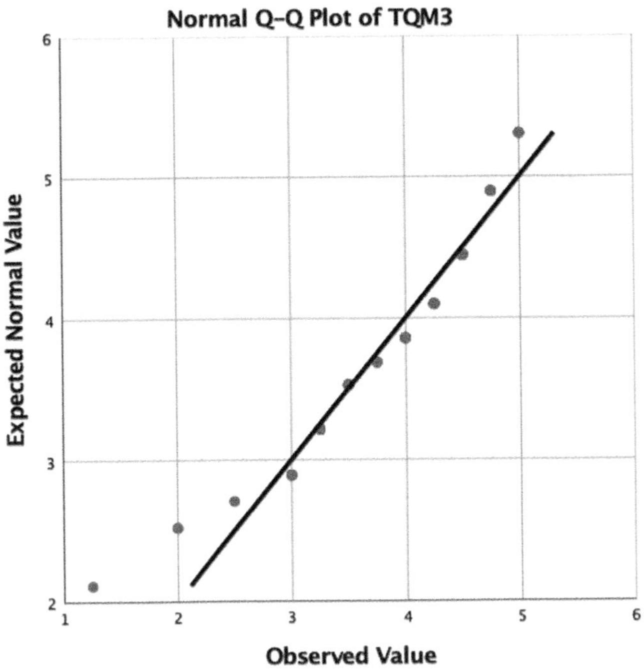
Normal Q-Q Plot of TQM3
Expected Normal Value
Observed Value
6
5
4
3
2
1
2
3
4
5
6

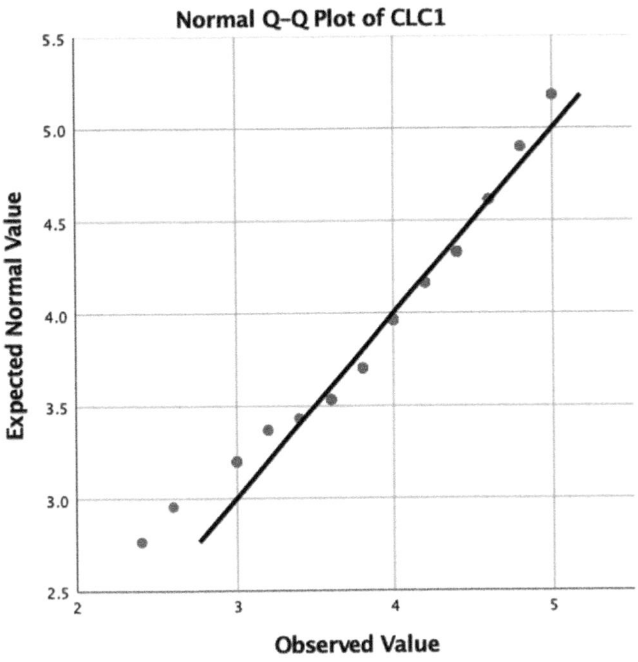
Normal Q-Q Plot of CLC1
Expected Normal Value
Observed Value
5.5
5.0
4.5
4.0
3.5
3.0
2.5
2
3
4
5

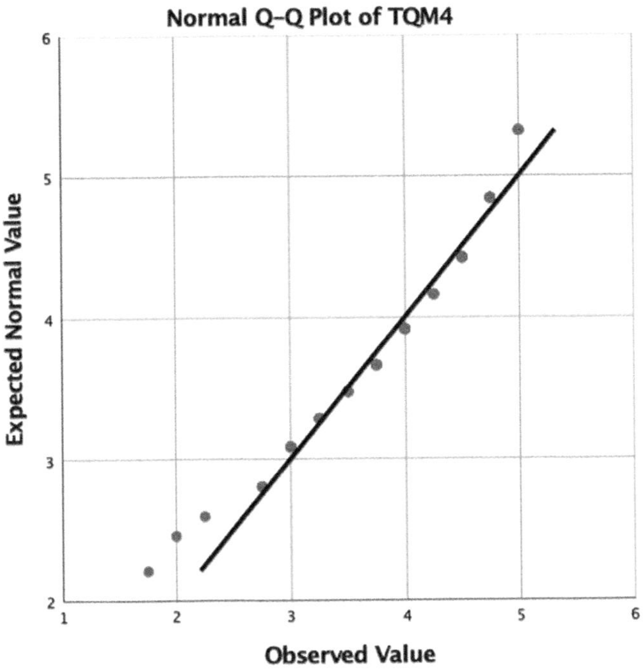
Normal Q-Q Plot of TQM4
Expected Normal Value
Observed Value
6
5
4
3
2
1
2
3
4
5
6

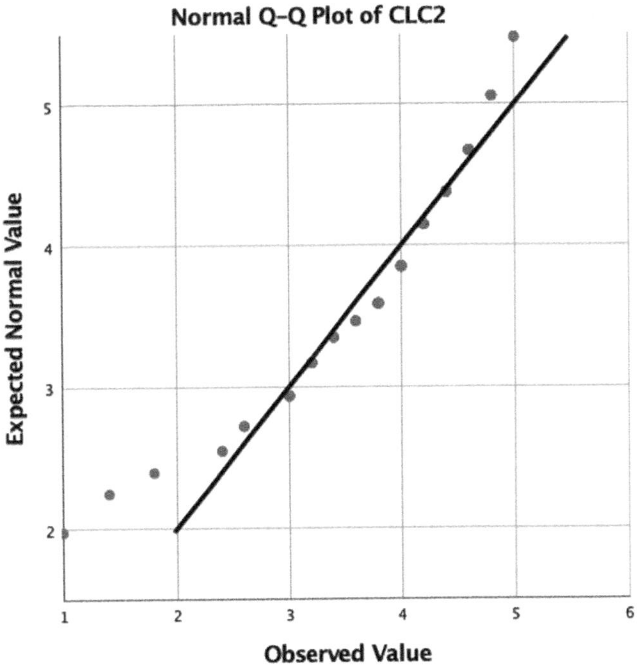
Normal Q-Q Plot of CLC2
Expected Normal Value
Observed Value
5
4
3
2
1
2
3
4
5
6

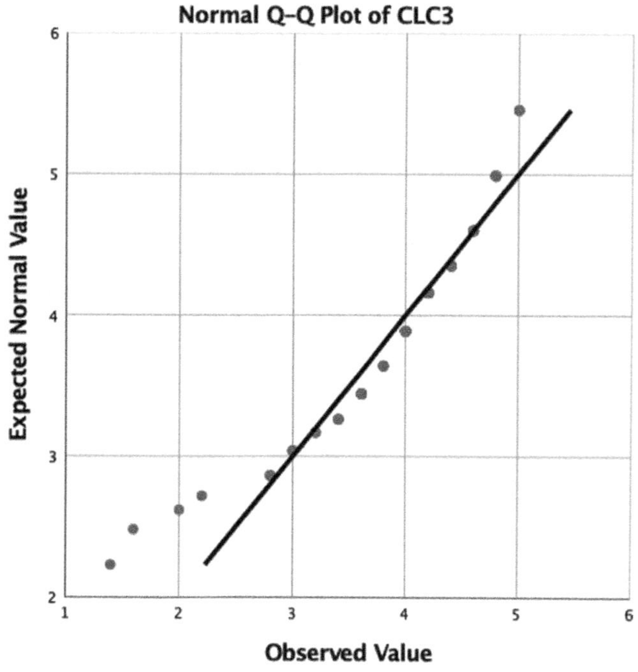

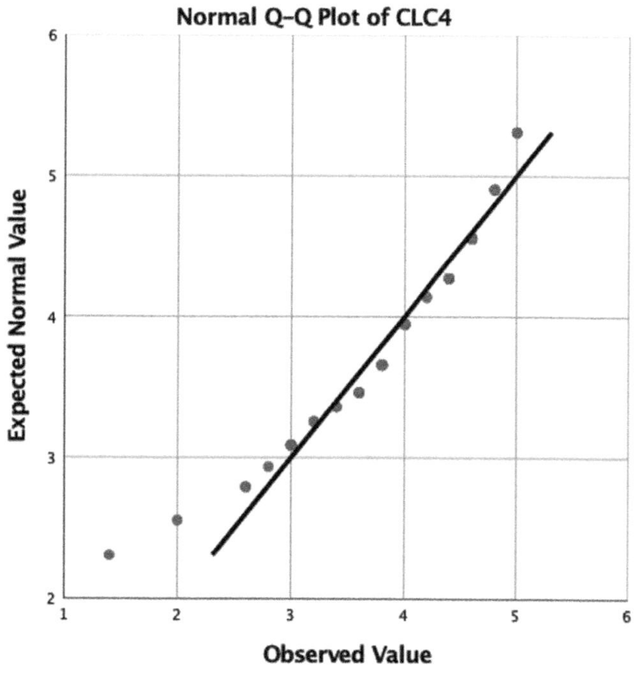

In general, the Q-Q plot reflects the normality of the investigated variables. If the residuals fall along the straight line at a 45-degree angle, after which the residuals are almost normally distributed. It is noticed from the above graphs all the residuals tend to deviated from straight lines specially at the tail ends and the some cases in head ends which may indicate that they are not normally distributed.

Multivariate normality test

The following graphs represent the results of the multivariate normality test for each dependent variable with all independent variables.

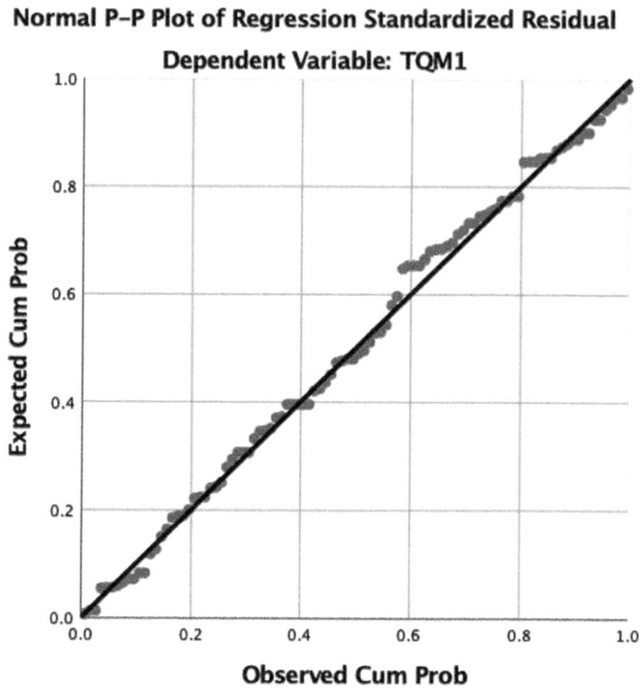

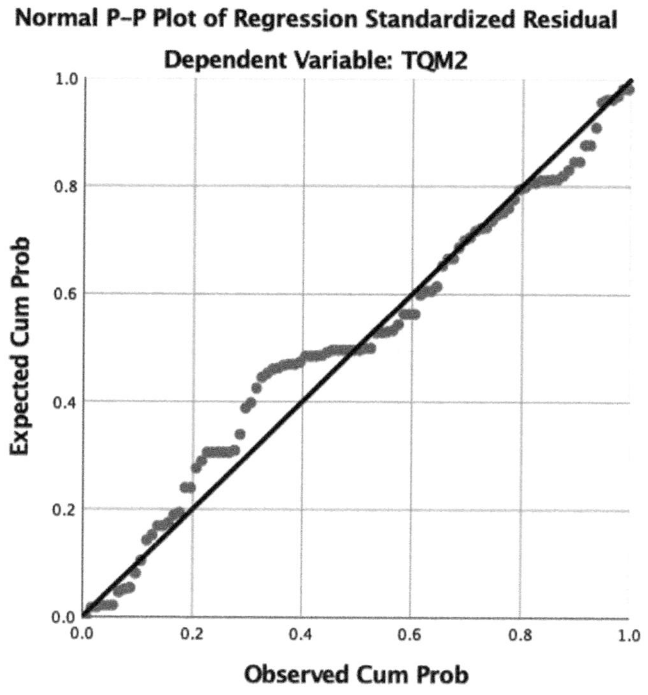

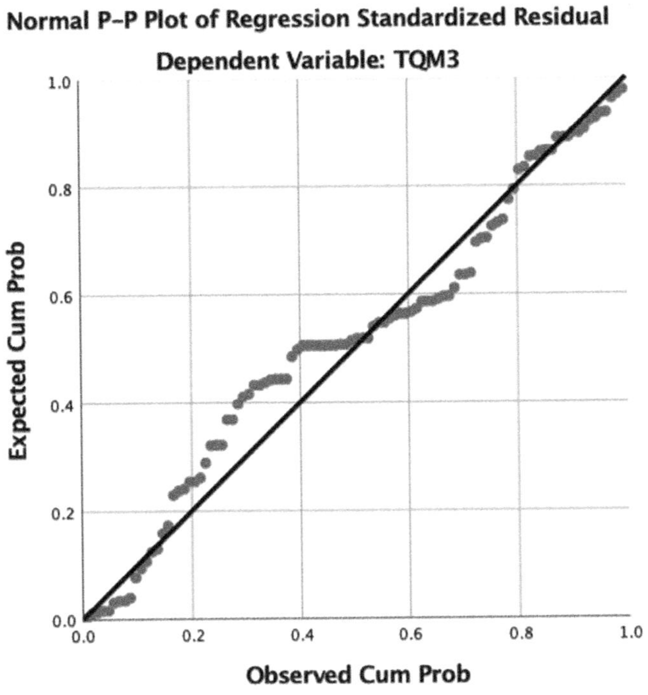

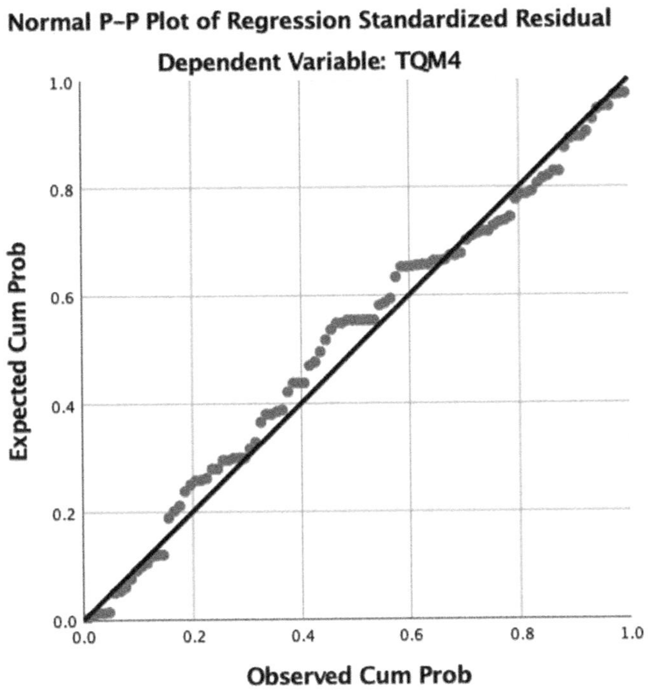

In general, the P-P plot reflects the normality of the investigated distribution. If the residuals fall along the straight line at a 45-degree angle, then the residuals are almost normally distributed. It is noticed from the above graphs all the residuals are distributed along the straight line.

Multicollinearity test VIF and tolerance:

Coefficients[a]

Model		Correlations	Collinearity statistics	
		Part	Tolerance	VIF
1	(Constant)			
	LD1	0.074	0.297	3.368
	LD2	0.154	0.273	3.659
	LD3	0.149	0.163	6.122
	LD4	0.042	0.185	5.403

Tolerance is a useful tool for diagnosing multicollinearity, which happens when variables are too closely related. These reported tolerance levels are sometimes called the tolerance statistics. Tolerance is associated with each independent variable and ranges from 0 to 1, while the Variance Inflation Factor (VIF) ranges from 1 to 10 but If the value of tolerance is less than 0.15 and, simultaneously, the value of VIF 8 and above, then the multicollinearity is problematic It is noticed in the above table that all the obtained values for the tolerance are greater than 0.15 and for VIF are less than 8 which indicates there is no collinearity between the independent variables.

Factor Analysis:

Correlation matrix[a]

		TQM1	TQM2	TQM3	TQM4	CLC1	CLC2	CLC3	CLC4
Correlation	TQM1	1.000	0.720	0.741	0.746	0.732	0.785	0.813	0.771
	TQM2	0.720	1.000	0.724	0.837	0.751	0.724	0.758	0.769
	TQM3	0.741	0.724	1.000	0.790	0.713	0.821	0.779	0.775
	TQM4	0.746	0.837	0.790	1.000	0.700	0.746	0.696	0.727
	CLC1	0.732	0.751	0.713	0.700	1.000	0.740	0.806	0.816
	CLC2	0.785	0.724	0.821	0.746	0.740	1.000	0.840	0.801
	CLC3	0.813	0.758	0.779	0.696	0.806	0.840	1.000	0.882
	CLC4	0.771	0.769	0.775	0.727	0.816	0.801	0.882	1.000
Sig. (1-tailed)	TQM1		0.000	0.000	0.000	0.000	0.000	0.000	0.000
	TQM2	0.000		0.000	0.000	0.000	0.000	0.000	0.000
	TQM3	0.000	0.000		0.000	0.000	0.000	0.000	0.000
	TQM4	0.000	0.000	0.000		0.000	0.000	0.000	0.000
	CLC1	0.000	0.000	0.000	0.000		0.000	0.000	0.000
	CLC2	0.000	0.000	0.000	0.000	0.000		0.000	0.000
	CLC3	0.000	0.000	0.000	0.000	0.000	0.000		0.000
	CLC4	0.000	0.000	0.000	0.000	0.000	0.000	0.000	

a. Determinant = 9.97E–005

Based on the obtained to Correlation Matrix there is no pair of values having a value less than 0.5, so it is not recommended to drop any of them from the analysis and there is no need to repeat the factor analysis with less number of variables. Since the values on the left and right side of the diagonal in the table below all are zeros it indicates the goodness of the model.

KMO and bartlett's test		
Kaiser–Meyer–Olkin measure of sampling adequacy		0.929
Bartlett's test of sphericity	Approx. chi-square	879.892
	Df	28
	Sig.	0.000

KMO test measures of sampling adequacy indicates the proportion of variance in the used variables that may be caused by underlying factors. From the above table the KMO value is 0.92 which indicates that the factor analysis might be helpful for our study.

Partial Correlations for CLC:

Correlations										
Control variables			CLC1	CLC2	CLC3	CLC4	TQM1	TQM2	TQM3	TQM4
CLC	CLC1	Correlation	1.000	−0.457	−0.324	−0.169	−0.060	0.118	−0.131	0.035
		Significance (2-tailed)		0.000	0.001	0.095	0.558	0.244	0.198	0.728
		Df	0	97	97	97	97	97	97	97
	CLC2	Correlation	−0.457	1.000	−0.315	−0.515	0.063	−0.082	0.241	0.136
		Significance (2-tailed)	0.000		0.002	0.000	0.533	0.420	0.016	0.181
		Df	97	0	97	97	97	97	97	97
	CLC3	Correlation	−0.324	−0.315	1.000	−0.173	0.091	−0.064	−0.105	−0.215
		Significance (2-tailed)	0.001	0.002		0.087	0.370	0.528	0.301	0.032
		Df	97	97	0	97	97	97	97	97
	CLC4	Correlation	−0.169	−0.515	−0.173	1.000	−0.103	0.040	−0.075	−0.014
		Significance (2-tailed)	0.095	0.000	0.087		0.312	0.695	0.459	0.893
		df	97	97	97	0	97	97	97	97
	TQM1	Correlation	−0.060	0.063	0.091	−0.103	1.000	0.137	0.135	0.283
		Significance (2-tailed)	0.558	0.533	0.370	0.312		0.175	0.183	0.005
		df	97	97	97	97	0	97	97	97
	TQM2	Correlation	0.118	−0.082	−0.064	0.040	0.137	1.000	0.153	0.567
		Significance (2-tailed)	0.244	0.420	0.528	0.695	0.175		0.132	0.000
		df	97	97	97	97	97	0	97	97
	TQM3	Correlation	−0.131	0.241	−0.105	−0.075	0.135	0.153	1.000	0.411
		Significance (2-tailed)	0.198	0.016	0.301	0.459	0.183	0.132		0.000
		df	97	97	97	97	97	97	0	97
	TQM4	Correlation	0.035	0.136	−0.215	−0.014	0.283	0.567	0.411	1.000
		Significance (2-tailed)	0.728	0.181	0.032	0.893	0.005	0.000	0.000	
		df	97	97	97	97	97	97	97	0

From the above table we can see that with the highlighted correlations there is a significant level of confidence with the t-tests indicating that there is a positive/negative correlation between TQM and CLC. Additionally, the above table demonstrates positive correlations like CLC2 and TQM3 and some other cases. Similarly, there are negative correlations like CLC2 and TQM4 and some other cases. Based on these results a regression test was conducted to further investigate the strength of the relationship between the independent and dependent variables.

Regression Analysis and Correlation

Regression/Correlations for TQM1

a. Dependent Variable: TQM1
b. Predictors: (Constant), CLC1, CLC2, CLC3, CLC4

Model summary				
Model	R	R square	Adjusted R square	Std. error of the estimate
1	0.812[a]	0.659	0.644	0.31787

ANOVA[a]

Model		Sum of squares	Df	Mean square	F	Sig.
1	Regression	18.519	4	4.630	45.822	0.000[b]
	Residual	9.599	95	0.101		
	Total	28.118	99			

Coefficients[a]

Model		Unstandardized coefficients		Standardized coefficients	t	Sig.
		B	Std. error	Beta		
1	(Constant)	1.177	0.222		5.295	0.000
	CLC1	0.236	0.077	0.305	3.077	0.003
	CLC2	0.358	0.101	0.404	3.546	0.001
	CLC3	0.171	0.077	0.234	2.213	0.029
	CLC4	−0.039	0.099	−0.051	−0.396	0.693

In terms of the relationship between TQM1 as the dependent variable and CLC1, CLC2, CLC3, and CLC4 as independent variables, the correlation shows a strong significant relationship R=0.812, in addition the independent variables explain 66% of TQM1($R^2 = 0.659$). From the table above we can see that there is a significant relationship between the dependent variable TQM1 and the independent variables CLC1 with a B value of 0.236, CLC2 with a B value of 0.358, CLC3 with a B value of 0.171 and CLC4 with B value of −0.039. The B values for CLC1, CLC2 and CLC3 are significant with P less than 0.05, however the P value for CLC4 is greater than 0.05.

Regression/Correlations for TQM2

a. Dependent Variable: TQM2
b. Predictors: (Constant), CLC1, CLC2, CLC3, CLC4

Model summary

Model	R	R square	Adjusted R square	Std. error of the estimate
1	0.867[a]	0.752	0.741	0.38347

ANOVA[a]

Model		Sum of squares	df	Mean square	F	Sig.
1	Regression	42.294	4	10.573	71.903	0.000[b]
	Residual	13.970	95	0.147		
	Total	56.264	99			

Coefficients[a]

Model		Unstandardized coefficients		Standardized coefficients	t	Sig
		B	Std. error	Beta		
1	(Constant)	−0.255	0.268		−0.953	0.343
	CLC1	0.359	0.093	0.328	3.877	0.000
	CLC2	0.164	0.122	0.131	1.347	0.181
	CLC3	0.477	0.093	0.463	5.128	0.000
	CLC4	0.029	0.120	0.026	0.242	0.810

In terms of the relationship between TQM2 as the dependent variable and CLC1, CLC2, CLC3 and CLC4 as independent variables, the correlation shows a strong significant relationship R=0.867, in addition the independent variables explain 75% of TQM2 ($R^2 = 0.752$). From the table above we can see that there is a significant relationship between the dependent variable TQM2 and the independent variables CLC1 with a B value of 0.359, CLC2 with a B value of 0.164, CLC3 with a B value of 0.477 and CLC4 with B value of 0.029. the B values for CLC1 and CLC3 are significant with P less than 0.05, however the P value for CLC2 and CLC4 are greater than 0.05.

Regression/Correlations for TQM3

a. Dependent Variable: TQM3
b. Predictors: (Constant), CLC1, CLC2, CLC3, CLC4

Model summary

Model	R	R square	Adjusted R square	Std. error of the estimate
1	0.876[a]	0.767	0.757	0.34319

ANOVA[a]

Model		Sum of squares	df	Mean square	F	Sig.
1	Regression	36.789	4	9.197	78.087	0.000[b]
	Residual	11.189	95	0.118		
	Total	47.978	99			

Coefficients[a]

Model		Unstandardized coefficients		Standardized coefficients	t	Sig
		B	Std. Error	Beta		
1	(Constant)	−0.028	0.240		−0.118	0.906
	CLC1	0.466	0.083	0.460	5.614	0.000
	CLC2	0.417	0.109	0.360	3.819	0.000
	CLC3	0.346	0.083	0.364	4.163	0.000
	CLC4	−0.239	0.107	−0.236	−2.229	0.028

In terms of the relationship between TQM3 as the dependent variable and CLC1, T CLC2, CLC3 and CLC4 as independent variables, the correlation shows a strong significant relationship R=0.876, in addition the independent variables explain 77% of TQM3(R^2 = 0.767). From the table above we can see that there is a significant relationship between the dependent variable TQM1 and the independent variables CLC1 with a B value of 0.466, CLC2 with a B value of 0.417, CLC3 with a B value of 0.346 and CLC4 with B value of −0.239. The B values for CLC1, CLC2, CLC3 and CLC4 are significant with P less than 0.05.

Regression/Correlations for CLC 4

a. Dependent Variable: TQM4
b. Predictors: (Constant), CLC1, CLC2, CLC3, CLC4

Model summary

Model	R	R square	Adjusted R square	Std. error of the estimate
1	0.854[a]	0.729	0.717	0.36590

ANOVA[a]

Model		Sum of squares	df	Mean square	F	Sig.
1	Regression	34.163	4	8.541	63.793	0.000[b]
	Residual	12.719	95	0.134		
	Total	46.882	99			

Coefficients[a]

Model		Unstandardized coefficients		Standardized coefficients	t	Sig.
		B	Std. error	Beta		
1	(Constant)	0.127	0.256		0.497	0.621
	CLC1	0.321	0.088	0.321	3.627	0.000
	CLC2	0.413	0.116	0.361	3.552	0.001
	CLC3	0.323	0.089	0.343	3.638	0.000
	CLC4	−0.085	0.114	−0.085	−0.748	0.456

In terms of the relationship between TQM4 as the dependent variable and CLC1, CLC2, CLC3 and CLC4 as independent variables, the correlation shows a strong significant relationship R=0.854, in addition the independent variables explain 73% of TQM4(R^2 = 0.729). From the table above we can see that there is a significant relationship between the dependent variable TQM4 and the independent variables CLC1 with a B value of 0.321, CLC2 with a B value of 0.413, CLC3 with a B value of 0.323 and CLC4 with B value of −0.085. The B values for CLC1, CLC2 and CLC3 are significant with P less than 0.05, however the P value for CLC4 is greater than 0.05.

4 Discussion

The results of the study reveal that there is a significant relationship between leadership competencies during crisis and the implementation of TQM concepts in the higher education sector. It is essential also to confirm that certain leadership competencies during crises management including (sense of urgency, crisis management and strong emotional intelligence, creativity and problem-solving skills and finally, proper communication) have a huge effect on higher education institutes through proper application of TQM principles in higher education.

Each leadership competency has its own effect on the implementation of TQM principles. Therefore, it was noticed that TQM1, TQM2 and TQM3 have positive regression with the selected crisis leadership competencies in higher education. However, the fourth component of the TQM success factor TQM4 has a negative correlation. According to the results received through the collected data from the distributed survey, it was found that the contribution of the leadership during the crisis toward involving the stakeholders did not support the implementation of the TQM success factors as expected.

According to correlation analysis its observed that the relationship between CLC components as independent variables and TQM components as dependent variables are strongly correlated with R values between 0.812 and 0.876, in addition the independent variables explain between 66 and 77% (R^2 values between 0.659 and 0.767) which supports the main motivation of the research and supports the assumption that leadership competencies during crisis directly affect the implementation of TQM success factors.

Cronbach alpha values show that the minimum value is 0.765 which indicates that the internal consistency for both the TQM components collected answers and the CLC components collected answers are acceptable. It is noticed from Q-Q plot all the residuals tend to deviate from the straight lines which may indicate that they are not normally distributed.

The results obtained from the above discussion are anticipated; indicating to the literature review leadership competencies during crisis have a direct effect on the implementation of TQM success factors to achieve the organization goals.

Limitations of the study:

The event of the crisis is unexpected. Hence the institutions were never prepared to face the same. It is the inevitable situation which made all organisations to be prepared to face the same diligently. Since the preparedness happened all of a sudden and all institutions tried to understand the same to its best possible manner, no one in the system was ready to address the negative instances or incidents as they believe might affect the institution. In addition, the reluctance of the respondents/or people to invest time and energy in better efforts stood as another difficulty in proper implantation of the Quality efforts in the academic institutions.

Expected future research from the study:

The study had basic focus on the leadership competencies during the crisis in aligning the TQM success factors in the higher education sector. The study was based on the four-quality management perspective namely leadership performance, process control and improvement, employee involvement and stakeholder focus. The study can better benefit in developing on each of the above pillars of the quality management process and enable the growth of the academic sector, without compromising on the quality of implantation of the teaching learning process.

5 Conclusion

The present research investigated the effect of the leadership competencies in implementing the TQM components during crisis in the higher education sector. More specifically the aim was to identify the effective specific leadership competencies during the crisis, the specific TQM success factors in the higher education sector and to explore the effect of the leadership competencies in implementing TQM success factors during the crisis. According to the results received through the collected data from the distributed survey, it was found that the contribution of the leadership during the crisis toward leadership performance, Process control and Improvement, Employee Involvement are positively affect the implementation of the TQM success factors, while involving the stakeholders did not support this implementation as expected. The relationship between CLC components (Sense of urgency, Crisis management and strong emotional intelligence, Creativity and problem-solving skills and, Sensitivity of communication) as independent variables and TQM components (Leadership performance, Process control and Improvement, Employee Involvement, and Stakeholders Focus) as dependent variables are strongly correlated and supports the main motivation of the research and supports the assumption that leadership competencies during crisis directly affect the implementation of TQM success factors. It's important to assert that it has contributed a window into an area that is under-investigated with potentially useful implications for researchers and practitioners alike.

References

Ahire SL, Golhar DY, Waller MW (1996)Development and Validation of TQM Implementation Constructs, Decision Sciences 27(1):23–56

Antonakis J, Day DV, Schyns B (2012) Leadership and individual differences: at the cusp of a renaissance

Asif M, Awan MU, Khan MK, Ahmad N (2013) A model for total quality management in higher education. Qual Quant 47(4):1883–1904

Bayraktar E, Tatoglu E, Zaim S (2008) An instrument for measuring the critical factors of TQM in Turkish higher education. Total Qual Manag 19(6):551–574

Barbu M, Nastase M (2010) Change leadership and the worldwide crisis. Rev Int Comp Manag 2(1)

Betancourt JR, Tan-McGrory A, Kenst KS, Phan TH, Lopez L (2017) Organizational change management for health equity: perspectives from the disparities leadership program. Health Aff 36(6):1095–1101

Black SA, Porter LJ (1996) Identification of the critical factors of TQM. Decision sciences 27(1):1–21

Coombs WT (2014) Ongoing crisis communication: planning, managing, and responding. Sage Publications

Day D, Antonakis J (2012) The nature of the leadership, 2nd ed. Sage Publications

Fiedler FE (1971) Validation and extension of the contingency model of leadership effectiveness: a review of empirical findings. Psychol Bull 76(2):128

Fernandez S, Cho YJ, Perry JL (2010) Exploring the link between integrated leadership and public sector performance. Leadersh Q 21(2):308–323

Flynn BB, Schroeder RG, Sakakibara S (1994) A framework for quality management research and an associated measurement instrument. Journal of Operations management 11(4):339–366

Hassan A (2018) The influence of project managers' competencies on the delivery of successful innovation in projects. Thesis, The British University in Dubai

Habbal FM, Jreisat A (2018) Implications of successful implementation of total quality management in UAE universities. Calitatea 19(165):56–62

Holt SS, Wood A (2017) Leadership and emotional intelligence. In: Leadership today. Springer, Cham, pp 111–138

Hiller N, Novelli SÖ, Ponnapalli AR (2016) Leadership competency builder

Helms S, Key CH (1994) Are students more than customers in the classroom? Qual Prog 27(9):97

Houston D (2007) TQM and higher education: a critical systems perspective on fitness for purpose. Qual High Educ 13(1):3–17

Kotter JP (2008) A sense of urgency. Harvard Business Press

Koch JV, Fisher JL (1998) Higher education and total quality management. Total Qual Manag 9(8):659–668

Liikamaa K (2015) Developing a project manager's competencies: a collective view of the most important competencies. Procedia Manuf 3:681–687

Macaleer WD, Shannon JB (2002) Emotional intelligence: how does it affect leadership? Employ Relat Today 29(3):9

Madera JM, Smith DB (2009) The effects of leader negative emotions on evaluations of leadership in a crisis situation: the role of anger and sadness. Leadersh Q 20(2):103–114

Mahsud R, Yukl G, Prussia G (2010) Leader empathy, ethical leadership, and relations-oriented behaviors as antecedents of leader-member exchange quality. J Manag Psychol

Pearson CM, Clair JA (1998) Reframing crisis management. Acad Manag Rev 23(1):59–76

Pearson CM, Mitroff II (1993) From crisis prone to crisis prepared: a framework for crisis management. Acad Manag Perspect 7(1):48–59

Pheng LS, Ho DK, Ann YS (1999) Crisis management: a survey of property development firms. Prop Manag

Platis C, Fragouli E (2019) TQM in higher education institutions: the case of HSJ. Int J High Educ Manag 6(1):21–46

Papanthymou A, Darra M (2017) Quality management in higher education: review and perspectives. High Educ Stud 7(3):132–147

Pereira AES, Sandoval-Herrera IE, Zavala-Betancourt SA, Oliveira HC, Ledezma-Pérez AS, Romero J, Fraceto LF (2017) γ-Polyglutamic acid/chitosan nanoparticles for the plant growth regulator gibberellic acid: characterization and evaluation of biological activity. Carbohyd Polym 157:1862–1873

Sanayei A, Mousavi SF, Abdi MR, Mohaghar A (2008) An integrated group decision-making process for supplier selection and order allocation using multi-attribute utility theory and linear programming. J Franklin Inst 345(7):731–747

Saraph JV, Benson, PG, Schroeder RG (1989) An instrument for measuring the critical factors of quality management. Decision sciences 20(4):810–829

Sila I (2007) Examining the effects of contextual factors on TQM and performance through the lens of organizational theories: an empirical study. J Oper Manag 25(1):83–109

Sila I, Ebrahimpour M (2002) An investigation of the total quality management survey-based research published between 1989 and 2000. Int J Qual Reliab Manag

Sila I, Ebrahimpour M (2003) Examination and comparison of the critical factors of total quality management (TQM) across countries. Int J Prod Res 41(2):235–268

Sousa R, Voss CA (2008) Contingency research in operations management practices. J Oper Manag 26(6):697–713

Thach L (2012) Managerial perceptions of crisis leadership in public and private organizations: an interview study in the United States. Int J Manag 29(2):712

Then SK, Loosemore M (2006) Terrorism prevention, preparedness, and response in built facilities. Facilities

Venkatraman S (2007) A framework for implementing TQM in higher education programs. Qual Assur Educ

Wooten LP, James EH (2008) Linking crisis management and leadership competencies: the role of human resource development. Adv Dev Hum Resour 10(3):352–379

Wisittigars B, Siengthai S (2019) Crisis leadership competencies: the facility management sector in Thailand. Facilities

Managing Impact of "Shock Value" News on the Millennial Generation

Marina Arnaut and Amina Arnaut

Abstract

Media and news outlets have the innate ability to convey certain messages that are packaged to various demographic audiences in order to manipulate or reaffirm the standing dogmas in regard to current global events. This paper analyses the profound innovation in social media such as 'shock value' news and its impact on millennial generation. Employing quantitative and qualitative methodology, the research uses the cross-case examination between the frequency of 'shock value' sememe and the connotations they hold. Based on the content and semiotic analysis, it was found that not only the use of shocking motifs within daily global news have a significant impact on millennial audiences, but the frequency at which it is delivered may contribute to the notion of Millennials being 'lost' and 'existential'. The study reveals the correlation between Millennials' media portrayals and millennial existentialism. The findings of the study provide a platform for discourse and corroboration to the new theoretical process of 'Millennial Existentialism' and propose a new paradigm for social media managers with regard to contemporary society.

Keywords

Media · Innovation · Millennial existentialism · Shocking news · Society

M. Arnaut (✉)
University of Dubai, Dubai, UAE
e-mail: marnaut@ud.ac.ae; marina.arnaut@aue.ae

American University in the Emirates, Dubai, UAE

A. Arnaut
University of Reading, Reading, England
e-mail: a.arnaut@pgr.reading.ac.uk

1 Introduction

Shocking stories and visuals that are perpetrated by news outlets may offer an unconventional perception on news events within the contemporary time frame of the twenty-first century. However, some audiences may unequivocally view certain reportages of stories as unorthodox. This can be evaluated through the analysis of the coverage of shocking events such as the September 11th incident (2001), the Japanese Earthquake and Tsunami of 2011 and the Syrian Civil War (since 2012). As Seaton (2003, p. 46) states "normality broken by violence is always poignant", this garners mass audience attention. However, within the new millennia, the overabundance of these shocking depictions may have inoculated individual audiences to lack "true compassion" (Höijer 2004, p. 514), possibly as a result of the influence power of the media in its coverage of lugubrious global events. Moreover, various theorists have deliberated the innumerable ways in which agencies in the mediatic paradigm have the ability to influence audience observations, ideologies and routines (Dayan and Katz 1994, p. 5). Notwithstanding the notion that the "production of meaning through texts…illuminate[s] the relationship between media and society" (Burton 2010, p. 44), the encapsulation of news for audience acuity can elevate 'shocking' reportages to a platform of discourse. Though a myriad of motives lying behind the reasoning of such delivered information, albeit to garner mass audience attention for capitalist, educational or cautionary purposes, is inherent to acknowledge the mass media's subconscious authoritarianism over the public sphere. Through this, not only does the use of shocking motifs within daily global news have a significant impact on audiences, but the frequency at which it is delivered may contribute to the notion of Millennials being "lost" (SuccessStory 2018) and 'existential'.

In corroboration to this, an aspect of existentialist philosophy dictates that the disclosure of shocking news events, that illustrate human suffering, may precondition audiences

A. Salman and A. Tharwat (eds.), *Smart Designs for Business Innovation*,
Advances in Science, Technology & Innovation, https://doi.org/10.1007/978-3-031-49313-3_4

to question their "phenomenon of being" (Sartre cited in Flynn 2006, p. 7) as a result of "the continual exposure to mass media" (Barnes 1968, p. 170). Furthermore, individuals among target audiences may experience existentialist perceptions on society that may emerge due to the continual exposure to the reportage of dramatic events over the course of 17 years. This can precondition mediatic perceptions of Millennials as 'apathetic', thus possibly 'falsely portraying' the age-group as "bored and selfish" (Kaklamanidou and Tally 2014, p. 3). However, this media representation is arguable as Millennials are stratified as a 'Hero' generation "because they resolve that crisis" (Howe cited in Mauldin 2016) depicted in global media events. Thus, it can be suggested that these portrayals of the discussed generation may be due to their growth and acclimatisation within an environment oversaturated by 'shock value' news that result in the media's incongruous understanding of Millennials.

The research question of the present study is: *What is the influence of 'shocking value' news on Millennial Existentialism in correlation to the portrayal of Millennials in the media?*

To address this question we have explored the theoretical 'influence power' of the media in delivering an abundance of 'shock value' news and Millennial mediatic portrayals as apathetic and an intolerant demographic in regard to compassion. Incorporating quantitative and qualitative research methods, and using the data gathered through the cross-case examination between the frequency of 'shock value' *semes* (Stokes 2003, p. 24) and the connotations they hold, we have evaluated news events among various media texts. Given acclimatisation to technological advancements and access to a variety of sources on disastrous events, the current research has taken the step of addressing the knowledge gap identified in the literature in regard to the adverse effect of shocking value news on Howe and Strauss's 'Hero' generation (Mauldin 2016) that experiences an existentialist outlook, and therefore, owing to their "fictional representations" (Kaklamanidou and Tally 2014, p. 6). Based on political and sociological agendas of media outlets to "get inside the collective public mind" (Soules 2015, p. 12) through negatively sensationalist coverage, the purpose of this study is to provide a platform on which global and local media agencies may incrementally innovate a different mechanism or model to attract viewership while maintaining empathy and news longevity.

2 Literature Review

Using a variety of sources within the chosen domain, this article strives to reach a judgment which can offer a perspective on the extent that 'shock news' has an influence on the Millennial existentialist ideology in an inverse correlation to their portrayal within the media.

2.1 Influential Power of the Media

The magnitude of impact that international media outlets have on the deliverance of transnational news stories may be justifiable through the analysis of current criticisms regarding the notion. Clausen (2003, p. 60) states that news agencies "manage meaning and the interpretations of events…they are powerful actors in the creation of social knowledge". This is corroborated by McLuhan (cited in Soules 2015, p. 12) who suggests the influence of media outlets "assist the public to observe consciously the drama which is intended to operate upon it unconsciously". Thus, it is tangible to propose that media-related corporations, though perceived to be unbiased, are suggested to manage the construction of social conventions and ideologies within various strata, in relation to not only shocking events, but portrayals of certain societal demographics such as Millennials. However, this suggestion is marginally opposed by Burton (2010, p. 84) who advocates that "it is also difficult to define or prove this influence". This is refuted by the notion that a plethora of analysis, into the ways in which the mass media garners influence over its audiences, has been undertaken.

This is further supported by the statements that outlets "acknowledge emotions as an important motivation for watching news" and that to "negotiate a story successfully depends on their ability to 'frame' international information" (Clausen 2003, pp. 76–83). This is further justified by Le Bon (cited in Soules 2015, p. 50) who states, "the most persuasive words and images are often…prone to deceptive abstraction and mystification" among global news events. While McLuhan and Le Bon offer a rationalisation to Clausen's perspective on the influence power of the media, it is this influence that is not only acquired through the 'framing' of certain news stories, but the inoculative traits that certain reportages may contain (Burton 2010, p. 102). This suggests that not only are international media occurrences "cognitively engaging and immersive, especially when they embed a moral, myth or belief salient to audiences" (Soules 2015, p. 34), but when used to package and release "'shocking' subject matter which arouses intense emotional responses" (Barker 2013, p. 204). It is tangible to support that media management measures and judges the perceived newsworthyness of events based on what they imagine their audiences find newsworthy (Bednarek 2016) and use it as the power of influence that the media retains to induce the notion of 'compassion fatigue'.

2.2 'Shock Value' News Theory

When analysing the discourse around the reportage of global events, that are depicted with shocking imagery or lexis, it may be important to consider the ways in which these depictions are manipulated or, to an extent raw, to accommodate or refute audience ideologies that can impact the portrayal of various aspects in society. While Barker (2013, p. 200) mentions that "shocking images can always find a receptive market", this may prove counterproductive in allowing mediatic institutions to "evoke a renewal of loyalty to the society and its legitimate authority" (Dayan and Katz 1994, p. 9). It can be suggested that shocking news and imagery overabundance stagnates viewer response and thus, can cause a possible aversion to a media outlet due to compassion fatigue. Notwithstanding this, Gowing (2003, p. 231) acknowledges that the "significant changes in covering conflict…because of the overwhelming nature of what happened on 9/11" aroused a "pivotal moment in news coverage, [where] 9/11 was the most graphic example of a trend". Thus, it can be corroborated that, with the arrival into a new millennium, and the change in which news agencies report events in an unfiltered and shocking manner, the "contrast between comfort" of the audience's surroundings and the "horror" viewed on television screens (Seaton 2003, p. 46) or digital platforms may impact an audience's philosophical dogma.

Hence, this notion is prominent in supporting the theory of the way shock news may affect individual thinking. Benjamin (cited in Barker 2013, p. 200) further extends this discourse by stating broadcasters "convert not just human misery but also the struggle against it into an object of consumption". Though Seaton (2003, p. 54) argues that "if the news pleases us too much it may fail to alert us properly", Benjamin's statement revokes this dispute as media agencies may lack equilibrium in the coverage of emotionally disruptive and non-disruptive news stories. This can be furthered into a discussion regarding how certain exposure to media events may not only 'shock' audiences but can "exploit them" as "the 'moral responsibilities of practitioners…and the 'rights' of viewers" are "mutable parts of a greater sum of capital arrangements" (Barker 2013, p. 204). Owing to this, extensive theoretical observations of the portrayal of Millennials in society may be deliberated to have a connection on how shocking news may catalyse existential thought in the respective demographic generation, thus possibly depicting the age group in an inaccurate falsehood within the media.

2.3 Millennials and the Media

As a cohort, Millennials seem to be suspected of retaining characteristics dissimilar to those of preceding generations. This is comprehensive in the way in which these individuals interact and react with illustrations of news events and their generational representation within the mediatic paradigm. Subramanian (2014) debates "the spectre of 9/11…has turned into a more frightening reality" (p. 76). This in turn corroborates to the Millennial generation's development in a media environment that tends to expend graphic imagery and stories "for the sake of circulation" (Barker 2013, p. 197). Given that media pays close attention to the habits of news consumers it becomes obvious that the editorial prioritisations promote news stories dealing with themes influenced by statistics for news sharing (Kalsnes and Larsson 2018). Therefore, it can be evaluated that Millennials have been under the exposure of 'shock value' agendas throughout the progression of their lives, which may have inadvertently affected their philosophical outlook. This may have exacerbated the "ubiquitous detractions levelled at Millennials" as "lazy" within the media (Casey 2016). Moreover, Gitlin (cited in Kaklamanidou and Tally 2014, p. 4) supports the concept that the "torrent of images and sounds overwhelms our [Millennials'] lives". Hence, with Gitlin's statement, Millennial responses to 'shock value' news and media can be argued to be a defensive response to the "pressure" (Coomes and De Bard 2004, p. 93) faced as a "hero generation…during a time of crisis" (Mauldin 2016) when exposed to shock-worthy news that they have no control over.

Therefore, it is possible to assume that the mythic depictions of Millennials as lackadaisical may be a "fictional representation" (Kaklamanidou and Tally 2014, p. 6). Accordingly, their perceived apathy may be a result of 'compassion fatigue', taking into consideration the Millennials' exposure and upbringing in a graphically 'shock value' media environment, which has transgressed into a philosophical thought process of existentialism. Though Casey (2016) states "journalists love to…make generalisations" when characterising the Millennial generation, this may be due to the media's uninformed understanding of how the use of sensationalism and shock, when delivering news stories, can influence the generation toward an existentialist stance.

2.4 Existentialism

When combining media and philosophical concepts into a single paradigm, the basis of evaluations and judgements may be forged through a theoretical approach. As the philosophy of existentialism is an abstract concept in how it relates to the media and its audiences, it is inherent to remember that it can be applicable to the ways in which 'shock value' news may affect Millennial outlooks, and thus their false portrayal in the media. While Millennials are often portrayed as apathetic, it may be as a result of the overexposure to shocking depictions in the news that induce "suffering, pain and despair" which may precondition the contemporary generation to be within "a world he cannot face, or a world he does not want to face" (Barnes 1968, p. 77). Thus, it can be argued that the 'accused' apathy of Millennials is rather a misinterpreted assumption of their existentialist process by the portrayers of the generation, in the media. Though Singer (2007, p. 5) mentions that "Sartre said journalists should choose to use freedom to disclose social patterns and weaknesses", news agencies may abuse this privilege, where the overabundance of reportage of tragic news can influence existentialist thought "through the continual exposure to the media" (Barnes 1968, p. 170).

Moreover, it can be said that the Millennial's instinctive use of hermeneutics induces "implicit awareness" (Sartre cited in Flynn 2006, pp. 120–121) when exposed to shock-worthy news stories, where their seemingly apathetic reaction may be a bi-product of 'compassion fatigue' as a result of "feelings of despair, agony and crisis" (Barnes 1968, p. 76) when exposed to the 'shock value' news trend over a period of time. Therefore, it is arguable that though "Nietzsche was more concerned with the formation of individuals" (Flynn 2006, p. 85) than society, the accusatory effigy of Millennials as uncompassionate causes to question "to what extent are they themselves a social construction of media?" (Kaklamanidou and Tally 2014, pp. 3–6). In collaboration to this, the use of semiotic and content analysis methods may offer insight into how this process, which can be named 'Millennial Existentialism', may be rectified through in-depth analysis of various media texts relating to 'shock-worthy' news events.

2.5 'Millennial Existentialism'

Through the amalgamation of the extant literature, it is palpable to argue that: due to the supposed influence power of the media, 'shock value' news is delivered in an efficient manner that may cause an interactive discourse within an audience's ideological stance or philosophical thought process. Thus, for example, youth in MENA region 'have grown up within social, cultural and political circumstances where distrust of state-controlled media is the logical outcome of their own or their parents' experiences' (Moreno-Almeida and Banaji 2019). Owing to this, as Millennials may have been under the exposure of receiving shocking media over an extended period of time, the generation may have adopted a more existentialist philosophy. There are many socio-historical phenomena that explain why millennials are drawn to lower involvement escapist life. Millennials have grown up in a "world that promised them everything but neglected to deliver" (Koltun 2018, p. 102). Facing economic instability and experiencing institutional uncertainty during chaotic and anxiety-inducing environment of Information Era, millennials are heavily impacted by the psychological effects of stressful factors in their lives (Koltun 2018). As existentialism may influence the age-group to "be free from a world he cannot face" as a result of "feelings of agony…and crisis" (Barnes 1968, pp. 76–77), this may contribute to the "collective 'compassion fatigue' or a cultural climate based on a total loss of idealism" (Moeller, Eng and Kazanjian cited in Sedmak 2009, p. 72). Hence, it is ostensible that the "dominant culture" (Subramanian 2014, p. 31) of portraying Millennials as 'apathetic' may contribute to the "fictional representations of this generation" as "selfish or bored" (Kaklamanidou and Tally 2014, pp. 3–6). This process of overexposure to shocking news that influences existentialist thought, and which is perceived as apathy or carelessness, is illustrated by the Fig. 1

In the present paper we defined this process by the term 'Millennial Existentialism'.

3 Methods

This section discusses and examines how the reportage of shocking news events precondition the ways in which audiences may interpret current situations.

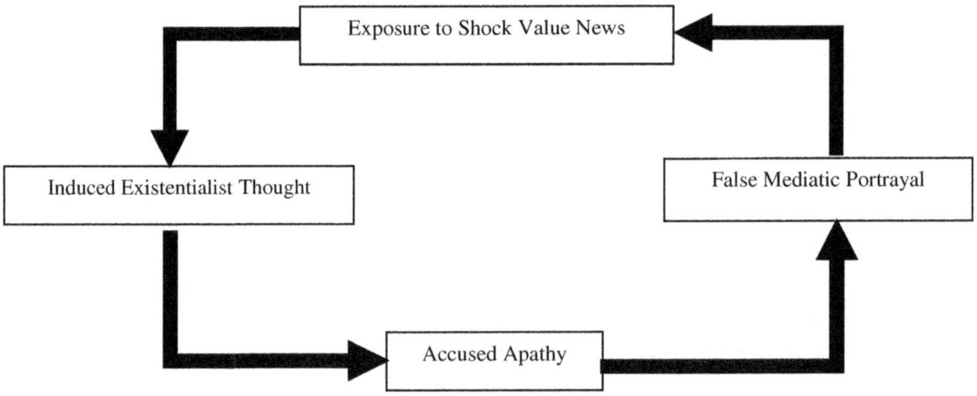

Fig. 1 Theoretical process of Millennial Existentialism

3.1 Content Analysis

Through the use of content analysis, textual objects were categorised and the frequency was deliberated. This was executed through the evaluation of a total of 30 articles (10 articles from each news event: 9/11, the Japanese Earthquake and Tsunami of 2011, and the Syrian Civil War). Following this, Tables 1, 2 and 3 present an interpretation of the frequency of the empirical data was carried out. As "82% of Millennials get most of their news from online sources" (American Press Institute 2015), the analysis of these news events through digital articles offers insight into how the ease of access to the frequency of 'shock value' news may affect the respective generation and their mediatic portrayals.

Moreover, a semiotic analysis was undertaken to analyse the denotations and connotations of the categorised objects. Figure 2 summarises occurrences of the combination of analysing numerical data with the interpretations of the categorised *semes*.

It became conclusive to understand how often certain interpretational objects were delivered to audiences, specifically Millennials. We undertook content analysis of ten articles spanning from 2001 to present that revealed evidence of the frequency at which these 'false' portrayals are delivered.

While Table 4 supports the concept of undesirable Millennial's depictions within the media, Fig. 3 depicts the notion of how 'shock value' news may influence existential thought. The occurrences of stereotypical millennial *semes*

Table 1 Articles on the 9/11 Attack (2001)

Seme per news outlet	'Survive' No	'Horror' No	'Tragedy' No	'Chaos' No	'Death/ Kill' No	'Life' No	'Devastating' No	No. imagery of destruction	No. death/ injury imagery	No. individual accounts
Washington Post	0	0	0	1	0	0	0	0	0	11
U.S. News	1	0	0	1	4	2	2	0	0	13
Time Magazine	5	2	3	4	7	4	0	3	2	40
CNN	0	0	1	0	0	0	0	3	1	3
The Guardian	2	1	0	3	0	1	1	0	0	15
FOX NEWS	2	1	1	1	3	0	0	0	0	14
The Telegraph	0	0	0	0	2	0	1	1	0	4
New York Times	1	3	2	0	5	1	0	0	0	18
BBC	0	1	0	2	1	1	3	2	1	6
The New Yorker	0	0	1	0	3	2	1	0	0	14
Total	**11**	**8**	**8**	**12**	**25**	**8**	**8**	**9**	**4**	**148**

Table 2 Articles on the Japanese Earthquake and Tsunami (2011)

Seme per news outlet	'Survive' No	'Horror' No	'Tragedy' No	'Chaos' No	'Death/ Kill' No	'Life' No	'Devastating' No	No. imagery of destruction	No. death/ injury imagery	No. individual accounts
CNN	2	0	0	0	6	0	3	9	1	10
BBC	1	0	0	0	1	0	2	2	1	1
RT	0	0	0	0	7	1	2	10	2	11
Independent	1	1	0	0	2	1	2	13	4	6
The Telegraph	0	6	5	1	15	4	7	22	3	33
New York Times	3	0	0	0	2	2	6	5	1	8
NHK	2	0	0	0	0	2	0	6	1	5
The Guardian	1	0	0	0	1	0	2	1	0	3
CBS	0	1	0	0	10	0	0	3	0	7
The Atlantic	5	0	0	0	1	0	4	19	9	0
Total	**15**	**8**	**5**	**1**	**45**	**10**	**28**	**90**	**22**	**84**

Table 3 Articles on the Syrian Civil War (2012—present)

Seme per news outlet	'Survive' No	'Horror' No	'Tragedy' No	'Chaos' No	'Death/Kill' No	'Life' No	'Devastating' No	No. imagery of destruction	No. death/ injury imagery	No. individual accounts
Gulf News	0	1	0	1	17	0	0	1	0	3
The Independent	0	0	0	0	8	0	0	1	2	8
The Telegraph	0	0	0	0	12	0	0	1	1	1
CNN	0	0	0	0	6	0	0	2	0	10
BBC	1	0	0	0	2	0	0	1	1	6
RT	0	0	0	0	1	0	0	1	1	6
The Guardian	0	1	3	1	3	4	0	1	2	6
New York Times	1	0	0	0	5	0	0	1	0	4
The National	1	0	0	0	2	0	0	0	0	2
Sky News	0	0	0	0	5	0	0	2	1	7
Total	**3**	**2**	**3**	**2**	**61**	**4**	**0**	**11**	**8**	**53**

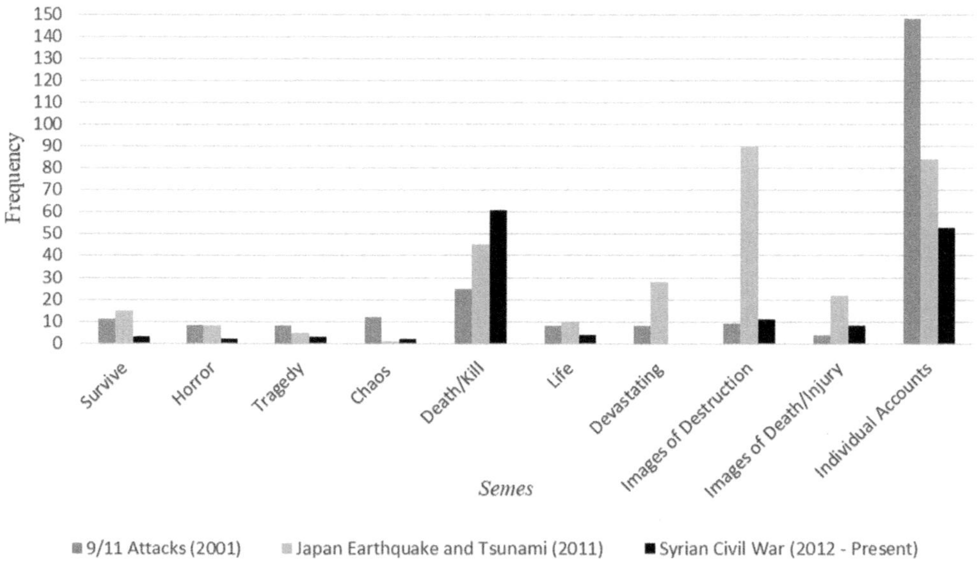

Fig. 2 Occurrences of 'Shock Value' *Semes* across 30 Articles (2001—present)

result in an accusatory apathetic depiction within the media. Thus, compassion fatigue may be construed in correlation to the theoretically constructed process of 'Millennial Existentialism'.

3.2 Semiotic Analysis

After the use of content analysis on articles about the 9/11 Attacks (2001), the Japanese Earthquake and Tsunami (2011) and the Syrian Civil War (2012—present), the frequency at which the ten categorised words and images occurred was established. However, the chosen *semes* have denotations and connotations as well as sign interactions. Through semiotics, connotations of these signs may be determined and thus, the frequency at which these meanings and imbued emotions reach audiences can be concurred. This can be corroborated by the notion that a "balance between the objective and implied aspects of textual data" (Roberts 1989, p. 148) may offer insight into how the frequency of 'shock value' news *semes*, that hold myths and meanings, are delivered to news audiences. Along with the occurrence of these interpretations, in combination with existing literature, it can be analysed to determine whether or not the overexposure to signs with negative associations may induce the Millennial audience's existential response that results in misinterpreted apathy and thus a false mediatic portrayal.

3.2.1 Semiotic Analysis of 'Individual Accounts'

Across all three major news events, the use of quotes and accounts from witnesses or affected individuals is

Table 4 Articles on Millennials (2001—present)

'Semes' per news outlet	'Lazy' No.	'Bored' No.	'Apathetic' No.	'Careless' No.	'Entitled' No.	'Depressed' No.	'Existential' No.	'Millennial' No.	'Social Media' No.	'Politics' No.
The Atlantic	0	1	0	0	0	3	0	0	4	1
The Entrepreneur	1	0	0	0	4	0	0	41	2	0
BBC	0	0	0	2	2	0	0	0	0	1
The Telegraph	1	0	0	1	7	2	0	1	0	1
CBC	0	5	0	0	0	5	0	12	1	0
Time Magazine	3	1	0	0	5	0	2	53	3	1
The Guardian	2	0	0	0	2	2	0	8	2	0
Odyssey	1	0	6	5	0	0	0	1	1	1
Elite Daily	0	0	3	1	0	0	0	1	3	2
METRO	1	17	0	0	0	1	0	1	1	0
Total	**9**	**24**	**9**	**9**	**20**	**13**	**2**	**118**	**17**	**7**

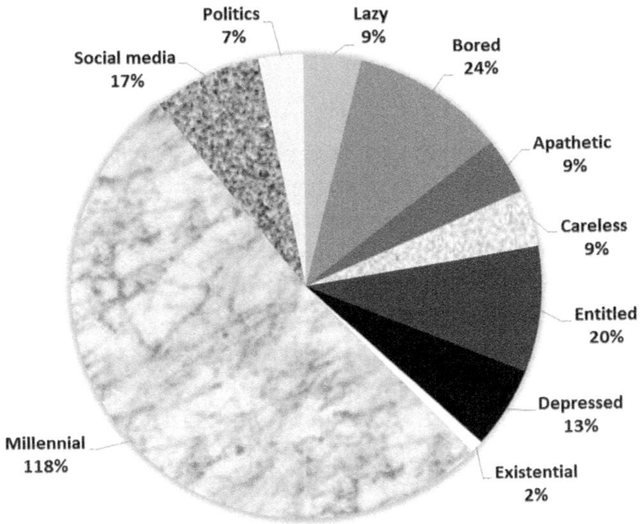

Fig. 3 Occurrences of Stereotypical Millennial *Semes* across 10 Articles (2001—present)

suggested to be the categorised object which is the highest across 30 articles. When denoting the notion of these 'Individual Accounts' or quotes relating to the aforementioned disastrous news events, it can be considered as a conventional journalistic approach that adds substance to a news story through a recorded personal description of an event and the news actor's experiences with it. References to "ordinary people" as news actors "construct Personalization" (Bednarek and Caple 2017, p. 89) while the prominence of 'official' accounts create the notion of "spatial proximity" (Berglez 2011, p. 144) and justify the significance of the news event. However, there can be a plethora of connotations, ones which may impact viewer response and emotions through pragmatics. While audiences may view this news technique as the media's influential power to derive an emotional response, the use of quotes as signs from 'ordinary' individuals may connote to the idea that the news actors are connected to or have experienced the event in an emotional or physical sense. In audience meaning systems, this can further imbue, in relation to the tragic events, a sense of sympathy and compassion for individuals involved.

3.2.2 Semiotic Analysis of the Words 'Death or Kill'

The high frequency *seme* is 'Death or Kill' that follows 'Individual Accounts'. Having the second highest occurrence across 30 articles, this object's representation and impact through the audience's meaning systems can be determined through textual analysis. Initially, audiences may denote these words as an act of ceasing to exist, failing to survive and/or the act of ending someone's life. Conventionally, this object could connote to morbidity, ruthlessness and eventual finality. By extension, 'Death or Kill' can be associated with anxiety, the grotesque, blood and vulnerability which can induce a "fight/flight reflex" (Potter 2012, p. 95). As a result, it is possible to interpret that media outlets use these words in relation to coverage of events such as 9/11, the Japanese Earthquake and Tsunami and the Syrian Civil War, to evoke a sense of sympathy and impact, where the lexical and structural interactions of 'Individual Accounts' juxtaposes with the notion of casualties.

Table 5 Summary of *semes* Total *semes* 696

'Individual Accounts'	'Death/Kill'	'Images of Destruction'	'Devastating'	'Images of Death/ Injury'	'Survive'	'Life'	'Horror'	'Tragedy'	'Chaos'
285	131	110	36	34	29	22	18	16	15

3.2.3 Semiotic Analysis of the Use of 'Images of Destruction'

Bednarek and Caple (2012, p. 132) state "image/verbiage complexes" create "intersemiotic relations". Through the interaction of lexical and visual signs, this may offer more connotations to the audience's system of meanings. The categorised object, 'Images of Destruction', is depicted as the third highest *seme* frequency. The denotation of this categorised object is similar across all three news events: destroyed buildings. The imagery of the destroyed buildings and rubble may connote to the idea of chaos or a prevalent threat. In combination with this, audiences may interpret these buildings as inhabited homes and workplaces. Moreover, across the 30 articles a plethora of imagery was of buildings that caught fire. The imagery of fire may subconsciously represent an untameable element, thus acting as a sign that induces a sense of hopelessness, sympathy and compassion for the individuals who were once present in these spaces. Thus, the images that depict a 'disastrous' tenor may induce a further emotional response from viewers.

3.2.4 Semiotic Analysis of Millennial Related Semes

Along with the content analysis of the three news events that took place between 2001 and 2018, the representations of Millennials in the media was analysed in a similar fashion in order to evaluate the frequency of categorised objects used to describe the age group. The denotation of this content analysis is that there were a multitude of times that the sign 'Millennial' was used to interact with the 'lazy', 'bored', 'entitled' and 'apathetic' *semes*. This may connote to the notion of child-like behaviour or to individuals that do not accept societal conventions and expectations (see Fig. 3). For some audiences, these sign interactions may produce a prejudiced outlook on the generation, which reasserts the media's false portrayal of Millennials as apathetic.

4 Summary of the Content and Semiotic Analysis

Content and semiotic analysis offers a deliberation on the notion that the influential power of the media enthrals audiences through a high frequency of *semes* that can be deconstructed to connote to negative meanings which may cause audiences to emotionally "evaluate its relevance" (Rosenthal and Visetti cited in Bondi and La Mantia 2015, p. 12). The results of the content analysis are presented by Table 5.

Ten articles on each of the three transnational news stories show that the use of 'Individual Accounts', the use of the words 'Death or Kill' and the use of 'Images of Destruction' had the highest frequencies. Table 5 suggests that the level of occurrences of these *semes* across three news events over the course of seventeen years is abundant (total number of *semes* is 696). Not only can the frequency of the categorised objects be interpreted, moreover semiotic analysis provides the possibility to determine the meanings behind the verbal signifiers and their emotive effects.

5 Findings

Based on the results from the content and semiotic analysis, it is palpable to stipulate the extent of which the 'Fourth Estate's' influence over the deliverance of 'shock value' news that stimulates existential thought among Millennial audiences. By extension, this sequence can be argued to have adverse effects on the generation's portrayals in the media where the theoretical process of 'Millennial Existentialism' is an arguably conclusive hypothesis. By analysing news articles on 9/11 (2001), the Japanese Earthquake and Tsunami (2011) and the Syrian Civil War (2012—present), the frequency at which their respective *semes* are packaged for audience consumption is evident. Moreover, semiotics reveals the connotations that each *seme* provides to an audience's meaning systems, which arouse an emotional response with every occurrence. Additionally, the analysis of Millennial portrayals, within each time frame of the analysed news stories, corroborates to the extent of which the 'shock value' media environment excites the oversaturation of typically expected compassionate responses. Thus, the findings show how Millennial viewers and readers of transnational news stories are exposed to a high frequency of signifiers and their emotive effects, which may not only induce compassion fatigue, but existential thought through "the continual exposure to the media" (Barnes 1968, p. 170), when inundated and grown within a saturated 'shock value' media environment over the course of seventeen years.

With regard to the media's influence in exposing audiences to textual objects that can be deemed of 'shock value', content analysis reveals the occurrence of 696 denotatively 'negative' *semes* across the 30 articles analysed. The objects with the highest frequencies are the use of 'Individual Accounts', the words 'Death or Kill' and 'Images of Destruction'. In relation to Fig. 2, it is possible to assume that the innate use of these categorised objects is to promote an archetypal empathic response from audiences as "elements of media messages often act on us as if they were occurring in the real world" (Potter 2012, p. 95). Moreover, the intertextual interactions between the abovementioned *semes* with arguably less impactful objects such as 'Life' and 'Survive', that have a frequency of 51, creates a juxtaposition that may facilitate an "intense emotional responses" (Barker 2013, p. 204).

Semiotic analysis suggests that the abovementioned textual objects connote to negative, disastrous and emotion provoking imagery such as the suffering perceived in the 9/11 Attacks, the level of destruction by the Japanese earthquake and tsunami as well as shocking acts and reference to children in the Syrian Civil War. This finding corroborates with Benjamin's (cited in Barker 2013, p. 200) suggestion of how "human misery but also the struggle against" is employed as "an object of consumption". However, it can be deliberated that the high frequency at which audiences make these interpretations, which provoke an emotional response and induce emotions of compassion, may be of an "overwhelming nature" (Gowing 2003, p. 231).

Enduring continual exposure to 'shock value' *semes* and their emotionally evocative interpretations may eventually result in "collective 'compassion fatigue'" (Moeller, Eng and Kazanjian cited in Sedmak 2009, p. 72). Through the "pivotal moment in news coverage, [where] 9/11 was the most graphic example of a trend" (Gowing 2003, p. 231), it can be said that the respective generation has been acclimatised to the current emotionally fatiguing media environment. Furthermore, the constant 'shock value' news messages absorbed by Millennial audiences, with regards to their appropriated perspectives on the contemporary news milieu, not only establishes compassion fatigue but may transcend into an existential thought process that may cause the generation to refute conventional media attitudes and be free from "a world he cannot face, or a world he does not want to face" (Barnes 1968, p. 77). In relation to this, content and semiotic analysis of mediatic Millennial portrayals between 2001, the time of 9/11, and the present day reveal an 'accusatory' trend that media outlets deliberate to be the reasoning behind the generation's lifestyle and attitudes.

Content analysis of *semes* relating to Millennials' discourse showed 228 occurrences. Media outlets interpret the theoretical 'existential' subconsciousness as uncompassionate through objects such as 'Entitled', 'Lazy' and 'Bored' (see Fig. 3). In addition, the content analysis of 10 articles shows how 37% of *semes* that are used to describe the age group and interact with the 'Millennial' *seme* at 52%, may precondition audiences to the supposition that the generation is detached and passive. Over the course of seventeen years, it can be said that through high frequencies of apathetic connotations, a mythic representation of Millennials is built which can reinforce their false mediatic portrayal.

6 Discussion

It is unequivocal that the media has reasserted itself as an institution that has the power to manipulate the framing and packaging of news events and its respective objects of interpretation in order to not only inform but influence ideological standpoints and arouse conventional responses from audiences. It is important to note that this incitation has the ability to inoculate modern news consumers and create social constructs that can affect perceptions of events, journalistic practices and society as a whole. Within the contemporary context, it can be said that news deliverance practices, along with its consumers, are evolving. Digitalisation and technological advancements have affected the frequency at which information creates a "contrast between comfort" (Seaton 2003, p. 46) and 'shock value' news to evoke a dogmatic impact on audience.

However, it is arguable that with the continual overexposure to shock news, an existential outlook is produced through "feelings of despair, agony and crisis" (Barnes 1968, p. 76). Hence, we propose that through Millennial's "implicit awareness" (Sartre cited in Flynn 2006, pp. 120–121) of these shock news methods, their subliminal refutation to succumb to continuous emotional responses is exacerbated to suggest that the generation themselves are "a social construction of media" (Kaklamanidou and Tally 2014, pp. 3–6).

In corroboration to our findings, theorists have highlighted that exposure to 'shock value' news may have "media-influenced effects" (Potter 2012, p. 56) on audiences in order to arouse "consciousness about elements of existence" in correlation to emotive responses (Gebner cited in Potter 2012, p. 73). Though Barker (2013, p. 84) states that media messages are strategically framed "for the sake of circulation", it is difficult to identify the media's true agenda in exciting overabundance of compassionate retorts. Nevertheless, theorists such Barnes (1968, p. 170) suggests that audiences may adopt existentialist philosophies as a result of "the continual exposure to the media". In parallel, Kaklamanidou and Tally's (2014, p. 6) observation of the "fictional representation" of Millennials and their "ubiquitous detractions" as "lazy" (Casey 2016) in the media is also evident. However, the research's findings illustrate an element of which has yet to be fully discoursed by the previously synthesised literature: *the extent of 'shock value' news' influence on the notion of 'Millennial Existentialism' in correlation to the portrayal of Millennials in the media.* As a result, the findings have synthesised the literature to be localised around Millennials' portrayals that reflects 'the essentialist notions of human beings, seeing them instead as amalgams of ever-changing, dynamic, lively data points' (Fisher and Mehozay 2019) and their "formation [as] individuals" (Flynn 2006, p. 85). Owing to the theoretical response to the overexposure to shock news, their acclimatisation to a compassion inducing media environment may become inoculative to the generation, which can influence existentialist behaviour and their falsely portrayed apathy as a result.

Overall, the analysis of findings corresponded to the initial speculations deliberated by the literature review and the results of the methodology. The comparison between *seme* frequencies, *seme* interactions and their connotations with regard to the 9/11 Attacks (2001), the Japanese Earthquake and Tsunami (2011), and the Syrian Civil War (2012—present) can be a rectification of the notion that the media has a hand in influencing an age group's conscious observation of "the drama which is intended to operate upon it unconsciously" (McLuhan cited in Soules 2015, p. 12). In combination with this, the analysis of Millennials' media portrayals in the contextual time frames, coagulated with compassion fatigue and existentialist theory, can now facilitate the argument of how the overexposure to 'shock value' news brings about a potential existential realisation through a "climate based on a total loss of idealism" (Moeller, Eng and Kazanjian cited in Sedmak 2009, p. 72). By extension, shocking events and their exacerbated reportages can adversely affect the respective generation's mediatic portrayal.

7 Implications for Research and Practice

The literature had revealed a multitude of theories relating to the research conducted, such as the influential power of the media, its regurgitation of 'shock value' news and "their ability to 'frame' international information" (Clausen 2003, pp. 76–83). Additionally, the synthesis of the theory on compassion fatigue, existentialist philosophy, Millennials and their misrepresentations in the media (Kaklamanidou and Tally 2014, p. 6) has presented the palpability of the theoretical process of 'Millennial Existentialism' in coagulation with 'shock value' news. This produced a platform for further methodological research.

The methodology concurred that the combination of qualitative and quantitative research methods can "yield more insights" (Spurk and Lublinski 2014, p. 14). This methodological approach proved to be beneficial in sowing results that answer the extent to which 'shock value' news may influence audiences and media portrayals as a result of the theoretical process of 'Millennial Existentialism'. Though the combination of content and semiotic analysis as research methods may help quantitative data "to reveal patterns of signification which qualitative data help[s] to explain" (Csikszentmihalyi and Rochberg-Halton cited in Chandler 2004, p. 142), extensive research through interviews, surveys or focus groups may be suggested to offer primary insight into how "media-influenced effects" (Potter 2012, p. 56) on Millennials can be determined to induce existential thought. Through further content and semiotic analysis of Millennial portrayals in the media, their accused apathy and false mediatic portrayal over the course of seventeen years may provoke a reimbursing of shock worthy news in attempts to curb the perceived uncompassionate responses. Thus, it can be suggested that the methodological techniques used may offer a platform for discourse and corroboration to the theoretical process of 'Millennial Existentialism'.

The contemporary stratum has made it inherent for journalists and media outlets to possibly modify the encapsulation of news in ways that do not allow the acclimatisation to interpretatively negative textual objects, but to also prevent the manifestation of apathetic media perceptions of the 'Hero' generation (Mauldin 2016). The research undertaken can be considered beneficial in reiterating the effects of "media messages" (Potter 2012, p. 95) through the constant influx of disastrous event coverage. With regard to Millennials and the gestation of their philosophical outlook over the course of 17 years, the accustomisation to the overabundance of shock news suggests the compassion fatigue that may be experienced by some precursory generations has transcended into an existential phenomenon among Millennial audiences. This can be dignified as a biproduct that influences their false mediatic portrayals. It can be suggested that the saturated 'shock value' media environment needs reformation through institutional interference in order to prevent socio-marginalisation through mediatic means.

Having considered the effects of 'shock value' news in the induction of the 'Millennial Existentialism' process, the notion that the Millennial generation are "themselves a social construction of media" (Kaklamanidou and Tally 2014, pp. 3–6) is apparent through the power of the 'Fourth Estate'. In light of this, the current research can elevate the discourse around media effects onto a platform for further exploration in relation to a possible reform of journalistic practices with the consideration of Millennials as evolving contemporary news consumers.

References

American Press Institute (2015) How millennials get news: inside the habits of America's first digital generation. American Press Institute. https://www.americanpressinstitute.org/publications/reports/survey-research/millennials-news/single-page/. Accessed 16 Mar

Barker J (2013) 'Shock': the value of emotion. In: Barry D (ed) Ethics and media culture: practices and representations, 2nd ed. Focal Press, Burlington

Barnes W (1968) The philosophy and literature of existentialism. Barron's Educational Series, Inc., New York

Bednarek M, Caple H (2012) News discourse. Bloomsbury, London

Bednarek M (2016) Voices and values in the news: news media talk, news values and attribution. Discourse Context Media 11:27–37

Bednarek M, Caple H (2017) The discourse of news values: how news organizations create newsworthiness. Oxford University Press, New York. https://books.google.ae/books?id=FHsLDgAAQBAJ&pg=PA89&dq=quotes+from+ordinary+people+bednarek+and+caple&hl=en&sa=X&ved=0ahUKEwiEzaz_09PaAhXH1RQKHb56DkcQ6AEINDAC#v=onepage&q=quotes%20from%20ordinary%20people%20bednarek%20and%20caple&f=false

Berglez P (2011) Global journalism: an emerging news style and an outline for a training program. In: Franklin B, Mensing D (eds) Journalism education, training and employment. Routledge, New York

Bondi A, La Mantia F (2015) Phenomenology and semiotics: crossing perspectives. Int Stud Phenomenol Philos 3(1):7–18

Burton G (2010) Media and society: critical perspectives, 2nd edn. Open University Press, New York

Casey L (2016) Minding the generation gap: investigating media portrayals of millennials and 'Gen Z'. The New York Times. https://www.nytimes.com/2016/10/28/learning/lesson-plans/minding-the-generation-gap-investigating-media-portrayals-of-millennials-and-gen-z.html. Accessed 31 Oct

CBC Radio (2016) Video: millennials are bored, stressed and sad. CBC. http://www.cbc.ca/radio/spark/335-the-lonely-generation-and-more-1.3853837/video-millennials-are-bored-stressed-and-sad-1.3853847. Accessed 21 Nov

Chandler D (2004) Semiotics: the basics, 3rd edn. Routledge, New York

Clausen L (2003) Global news production. Copenhagen Business School, Denmark

Coomes MD, De Bard R (eds) (2004) Serving the millennial generation, new directions for student services, vol 1, no 106

Dayan D, Katz E (1994) Media events: the live broadcasting of history. First Harvard University Press, USA

Fisher E, Mehozay Y (2019) How algorithms see their audience: media epistemes and the changing conception of the individual. Media Cult Soc, 0163443719831598

Flynn TR (2006) Existentialism: a very short introduction. Oxford University Press, Oxford

Gowing N (2003) Journalists and war: the troubling new tensions post 9/11. In: Thussu DK, Freedman D (eds) War and the media: reporting conflict 24/7. Sage, London, pp 231–240

Höijer B (2004) The discourse of global compassion: the audience and media reporting of human suffering. Media, culture & society. Sage, London

Kaklamanidou B, Tally M (eds) (2014) The millennials on film and television: essays on the politics of popular culture. McFarland and Company, Inc. Publishers, North Carolina

Kalsnes B, Larsson AO (2018) Understanding news sharing across social media: detailing distribution on Facebook and Twitter. Jism Stud 19(11):1669–1688

Koltun K (2018) Rick, Morty, and absurdism: the millennial allure of dark humor. In: The forum: journal of history, vol 10, no 1, p 12

Mauldin J (2016) Millennials are doomed to face an existential crisis that will define the rest of their lives. Forbes. https://www.forbes.com/sites/johnmauldin/2016/06/24/millennials-are-doomed-to-face-an-existential-crisis-that-will-define-the-rest-of-their-lives/#3ba98d1c75b0. Accessed 24 Jun

Moreno-Almeida C, Banaji S (2019) Digital use and mistrust in the aftermath of the Arab Spring: beyond narratives of liberation and disillusionment. Media Cult Soc 41(8):1125–1141

Potter WJ (2012) Media effects. Sage, London

Roberts CW (1989) Other than counting words: a linguistic approach to content analysis. Soc Forces 68(1):147–177

Seaton J (2003) Understanding not empathy. In: Thussu DK, Freedman D (eds) War and the media: reporting conflict 24/7. Sage, London, pp 45–54

Sedmak C (2009) Christian ethics and the challenge of absolute poverty. In: Mack E, Schramm M, Klasen S, Pogge T (eds) Absolute poverty and global justice: empirical data—moral theories—initiatives. Routledge, New York, pp 69–78

Singer JB (2007) The socially responsible existentialist: a normative for journalists in a new media environment. Jism Stud 7(1):2–18

Soules M (2015) Media, persuasion and propaganda. Edinburgh University Press Ltd., Edinburgh

Spurk C, Lublinski J (2014) Content analysis: measuring the success of journalism capacity building, DW Akademie, 10, pp 1–8. https://issuu.com/dwakademie/docs/dw_akademie_measuring_the_success_o

Stokes J (2003) How to do media and cultural studies. Sage, London

Subramanian J (2014) The mind project: south Asians and television multiculturalism. In: Kaklamanidou B, Tally M (eds) The millennials on film and television: essays on the politics of popular culture. McFarland and Company, Inc. Publishers, North Carolina

SuccessStory (2018) Existential crisis of millennials. https://successstory.com/inspiration/existential-crisis-of-millenials

A Snapshot of Socio-Economic Impact of COVID-19 on the Sultanate of Oman: Measures and Coping Strategies

Venkat Ram Raj Thumiki and Hesham Magd

Abstract

COVID-19 is an economic shock that has been causing disruption at a drastic level and faster pace than a normal crisis, leaving less time for social and organizational systems to respond. This crisis has negatively impacted the socio-economic factors of the world by infecting millions of people, causing hundreds of thousands of deaths, closure of businesses and job losses. Sultanate of Oman, one of the key economies in the Middle East is not an exception and has been facing socio-economic problems due to the COVID-19 pandemic. This paper attempts to evaluate the socio-economic impact of COVID-19 on Oman's economy, along with the coping strategies and measures taken by the Government to mitigate the risk arising out of this crisis. Extensive research of published data in newspapers, World Bank reports, and other secondary sources has been collected and reviewed in articulating this paper. COVID-19 impacted Oman's social life—deaths, state budget—cuts, market consumption—decreased purchases, employment—job loss, tourism—cancellation of Salalah Tourism Festival 2020, logistics—reduced port operations, aviation—reduced revenues, real estate—decline in property deals, etc. However, the Government of Oman through its professional approach, has undertaken measures and coping strategies such as, lockdown to control the spread of virus, Bayan digital platform to support logistics sector, tax reliefs, financial package and continuation of developmental projects to fuel the economic activity in Oman. Thus, through the retroactive decisions made by the Government, Omani economy has proved itself as the best performing market during the ongoing COVID-19 crisis.

V. R. R. Thumiki (✉) · H. Magd
Faculty of Business and Economics, Modern College of Business and Science (MCBS), Muscat, Sultanate of Oman
e-mail: venkat@mcbs.edu.om

H. Magd
e-mail: hesham.magd@mcbs.edu.om

Keywords

COVID-19 · Dual-crisis · Economic shocks · Socio-economic factors · Mitigation · Coping strategies

1 Introduction

Crises is not uncommon; they occur from time to time in countries across the world. The world has been facing crises of time immemorial. Each time—there is a crisis—organizational mechanisms and systems emerge as stronger than before as people learn how to deal with difficult situations during and after the crisis (Mitroff et al. 1987; Augustine 1995). According to Hart et al. (Hart et al. 1993) different types of crises include; natural crises caused by cyclones such as Emma in 2018, that disrupted the retail sector across the United Kingdom (Woods 2018), technology crises such as Y2K in 2000 which posed a great threat to the banking sector (Li et al. 1999; Appelbaum et al. 2012) and economic crises caused by the real estate fallout in 2007 (Aziz 2012) and falling oil prices in 2014 that effected almost all sectors of the global economy (Omoregie 2015). Similarly, the current health crisis a.k.a. COVID-19—that started at the end of December 2019 in Wuhan city and quickly spread across the world— is known as 'shock' (Carlsson-Szlezak et al. 2020). The difference between crisis and shock is that, while a crisis causes gradual disruption, shock is much faster and gives very little or no time to create safety systems (Roubini 2020).

COVID-19 shock has impacted the socio-economic factors of human life. Across the world, more than 435,000 people have died. Whilst there are more than 7.9 million registered cases as of 15th June 2020. Several service sectors (including, travel, tourism, education, and entertainment) that play a supporting role in many economies have been disrupted due to movement restrictions imposed by

A. Salman and A. Tharwat (eds.), *Smart Designs for Business Innovation*,
Advances in Science, Technology & Innovation, https://doi.org/10.1007/978-3-031-49313-3_5

governments. The manufacturing sector suffered major losses due to the halting of work and even resulted in closure for several factories and workshops. Millions of daily wage earners lost their jobs, not only in poorer countries but also in developed economies such as the USA and England. The Middle East is not an exception and has been facing socio-economic problems due to the COVID-19 pandemic. The Middle East is the home to nearly 4% of the global population and contributes nearly 8% of global sea trade, 37% of the world's oil and 18% of global gas production. The Middle East and central Asian countries contributed nearly $4 trillion to the global GDP in 2019 (International Monetary Fund 2019). The Sultanate of Oman, one of the key economies in this part of the world, has been suffering from COVID-19 with its first 2 cases detected on 20th February 2020 leading to a steep rise in the number of positive cases going up to 13,000 by the end of May 2020. This paper attempts to evaluate the current situation with reference to the socio-economic impact of COVID-19 on the economy of the Sultanate of Oman.

2 Impact of COVID 19

2.1 Public Health

Though huge repositories are available with constantly updating COVID-19 data, researchers on this paper have compiled specific data to make it convenient for readers to take a stock of the situation as it is related to GCC as well as Oman, as of 15th June 2020. The data was collected on 17th June 2020 from the European Centre for Disease Prevention and Control-ECDC (Centre and for Disease Prevention and Control 2020), a highly reliable source for global health data. This pandemic has been rapidly spreading with an average of 1.43 million positive cases and 78,775 deaths per month from January 2020 to 15th June 2020 giving little time for the governing mechanisms to react. The below section presents the exponential spread of COVID-19 cases and deaths across the GCC countries (Figs. 1 and 2) from the 31st December 2019 to 15th June 2020 and will further narrow down to the situation in Oman (Figs. 3 and 4).

It can be seen in Figs. 1 and 2 that Saudi Arabia—the largest state in the GCC in terms of population—has recorded a greater number of COVID-19 cases and deaths as of 15th June 2020. Though the death rate in GCC countries (Bahrain: 0.24, Kuwait: 0.82, Oman: 0.45, Qatar: 0.1, Saudi Arabia 0.77 and UAE: 0.68) is lower than the global average of 3.4%, it has still become a serious concern for the respective governments. Figures 3 and 4 clearly present the situation in Oman that has been struggling with the increased number of cases as well as deaths. Particularly, a steep rise from 1st June 2020 onwards has become a major concern for the government. The number of cases and deaths doubled from 31st May to 15th June 2020. According to the Ministry of Health, the main reasons for increasing cases are due to family gatherings (Covid-19: Family gatherings main cause of increasing cases in Oman 2020).

2.2 Oman Economy

COVID-19 began with the oil crisis is going on, hence, it can be called a crisis-in-crisis or dual crisis. As an impact of the oil crisis, the Government of Oman has already been informed of the downward trend in GDP by 1.6% in first quarter of the year (Mendoza 2019), real estate by 13.9% in the first five months (Decline in real estate deals in Oman 2019), automobile by 12.5% in total annual sales (Oman 2020) and other sectors of the economy. Thus, when the COVID-19

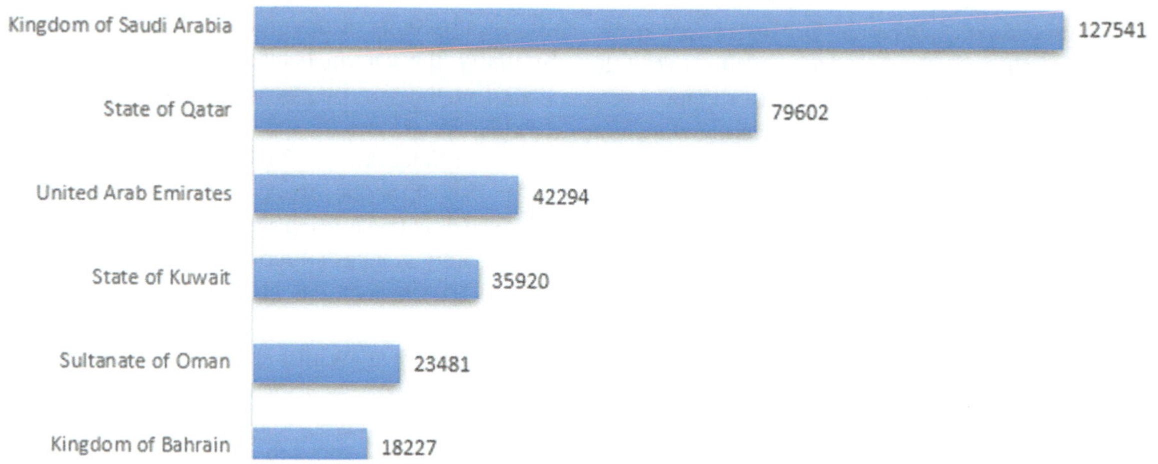

Fig. 1 GCC country-wise distribution of COVID-19 cases as of 15 June 2020 (*Source* Compiled by the authors)

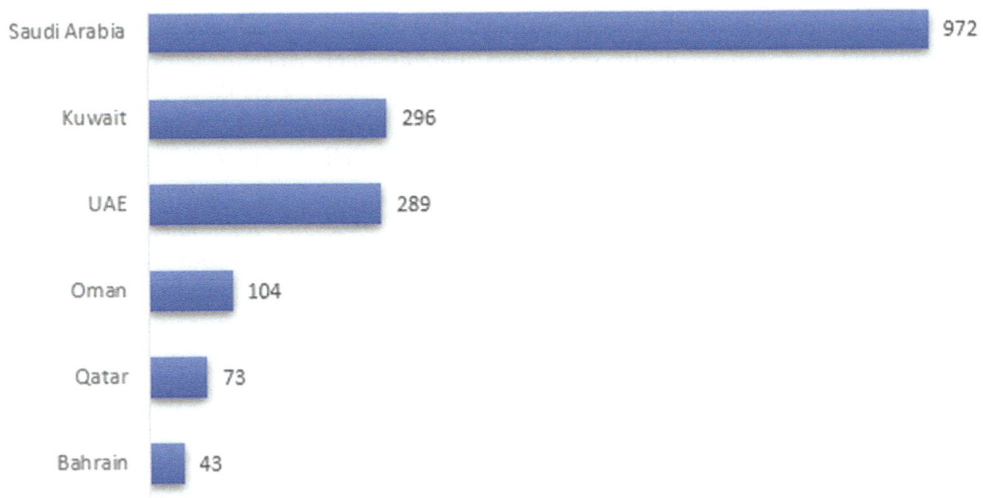

Fig. 2 GCC country-wise distribution of COVID-19 deaths as of 15 June 2020 (*Source* Compiled by the authors)

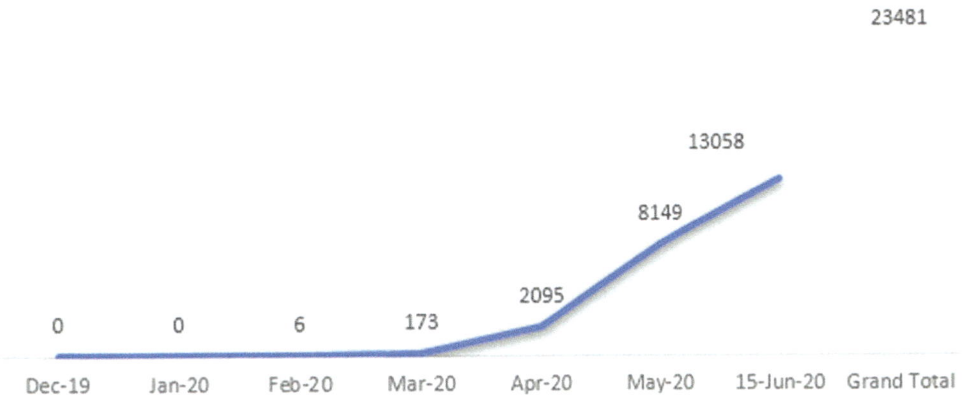

Fig. 3 COVID-19 cases in Oman as of 15 June 2020 (*Source* Compiled by the authors)

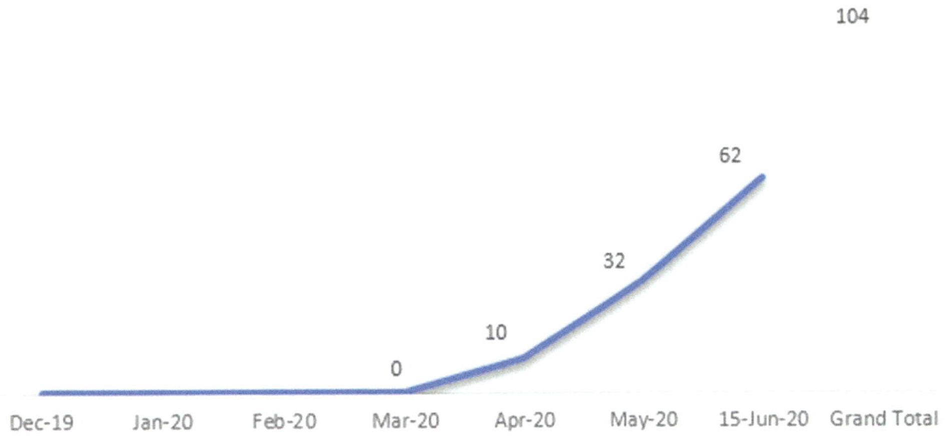

Fig. 4 COVID-19 deaths in Oman as of 15 June 2020 (*Source* Compiled by the authors)

crisis began, it was an extension of the current crisis for policy makers rather than a new crisis. The difference was that it was beyond a crisis, it was a 'shock' that left very little time to respond.

Though COVID-19 impacted several aspects of the country, its major impact was on the state budget which was cut by 10% (Oman government orders more budget cuts 2020). This is notable because most of the major projects in Oman are driven by Government spending which influences employment and other macroeconomic variables in the country. For example, the Government of Oman awarded approximately OMR 250 million worth of contracts in the 2019 financial year (Coronavirus: tens of thousands of foreign workers lose their jobs in Oman 2020). Thus, the

Omani economy that survives on government spending to a large extent has suffered due to cuts in government budget caused by COVID-19.

Further, in terms of sectoral dependence, Oman's economy continues to rely on petroleum as it is a sector which contributes 87% of Oman's budget revenues, 51% to its GDP and 60% of the country's total exports (Oman GDP Annual Growth Rate (n.d)). It seems that Oman's economic diversification into manufacturing, tourism, and other non-oil sectors (The National Program for Enhancing Economic Diversification (Tanfeedh) (n.d.)) aimed at avoiding dependence on the petroleum sector and Government spending helped the Omani economy absorb the shocks from this dual crisis to certain extent. As World Bank clearly mentioned, despite reduced economic growth in MENA in 2020, Oman's economy provides a positive outlook (Economic and Update: How Transparency Can Help the Middle East and North Africa, 2020). Various reports also clearly indicate that Oman is the best performing market during the current COVID-19 crisis (Ubhar Capital Report 2020).

COVID-19 made a clear impact on the national budget of the Sultanate of Oman. The budget released on 1st January 2020 indicated a total government spending of OMR 13.2 billion (USD 34.3 billion) which is 2% higher compared to OMR 12.9 billion spent in 2019 (Oman budget 2020). However, the government changed its decision due to the current situation and adjusted its spending. As part of the new measures to cut expenditure in the Sultanate, the Ministry of Finance has decided to reduce the 2020 budget by OMR 500 million (Oman State Budget 2020), which is approximately a 10% cut to the budgets of ministries and government units (Oman government orders more budget cuts 2020).

While the global GDP has recorded a declining trend in the last few years due to the oil crisis, COVID-19 has further pulled the curve down and brought the global GDP growth rate annual percentage change to negative figures (International Monetary Fund 2020).

It's evident from the data presented in Table 1 that the economy of Oman bounced back in 2018 and achieved a greater growth rate than the global and GCC average. This development is due to diversification during 2018 into manufacturing, logistics & supply chain, travel & tourism, agriculture & fisheries and mining. The economic diversification strategy was supported by well-articulated programs such as, the set-up of the National Center for Employment and National Youth program aiming to empower youth through knowledge sharing for the purpose of developing workable skills and to create job opportunities. The program also aimed to create awareness among key stakeholders in society about the diversification and Vision 2040 through a well-planned, 'All of Oman' campaign, and to further the solid implementation of activities mentioned in the Social Action Strategy 2016–2025 (Review and of The Sultanate of Oman, 2019).

Due to this planned economic diversification, the Sultanate could make considerable improvements which can be evidently seen in the share of oil revenues decreasing from 66.7% of the GDP in 2000, to 40.8% in 2017 (*ibid*). 2019 witnessed a smaller growth rate than the global and GCC average due to the oil crisis and even before the current COVID-19 crisis began. Thus, from the gloomy picture presented in Table 1 regarding a declining GDP growth rate, it cannot be concluded that the decline in GDP is solely due to the ongoing COVID-19 pandemic but has been around even before the health crisis began.

According to the World Economic Outlook of International Monetary Fund (International Monetary Fund 2020), inflation in Oman was 0.1% in 2019 and is forecast to increase to 1.0% in 2020 and further to 3.4% in 2021. While these projections were made before COVID-19, the pandemic has added to the current situation and further increased the inflation rate. Hence, it cannot be concluded that the rise in inflation is exclusively due to COVID 19.

Household consumption expenditure which refers to all household expenses made by people—including, food, rent, clothing, energy, transportation, durables such as home appliances and cars, health, leisure, etc. —is impacted due to COVID-19. While food is bought for the purpose of survival, people's spending on product categories such as automobiles and electronics recorded a steep fall due to the COVID-19 crisis. The market was optimistic about the

Table 1 Global, GCC and Omani GDP in US$ in the last three years

Region	2017		2018		2019		2020 as of 7th June	
	GDP in US$	GDP growth rate	GDP in US$	GDP growth rate	GDP in US$	GDP growth rate	GDP in US$ (approx.)	GDP growth rate
Global	80.963 Trillion	0.5	85.931 Trillion	0.8	87.263 Trillion	2.98	38.421 Trillion	−3.0
GCC	1.464 Trillion	0.2	1.645 Trillion	1.95	1.67 Trillion	2.1	1.669 Trillion	–
Oman	70.78 Billion	−0.9	79.29 Billion	2.1	79.5 Billion	1.1	74 Billion	−2.84

Source Compiled by the authors from various sources

future of automobile sales in 2020 (Oman automobile sales in top gear 2019) and now experts have started showing concern due to the Coronavirus situation (Oman's automobile sector concerned over Coronavirus impact on industry 2020) as China is one of the major suppliers of spare parts. According to an automotive market study by FitchSolutions (Oman Autos Report (n.d.)), sales of commercial vehicles is going to be affected more than the sales of passenger vehicles. Thus, it can be understood that COVID-19 has negatively impacted public expenditure and consumption.

According to the National Centre for Statistics and Information (NCSI), 53,332 expatriates worked in the government sector until the end of March 2020, with the total number of foreign workers in the country standing at 1,321,753 workers (53,332 expats employed in Oman's government sector 2020). COVID-19 has directly impacted the employment and labor market with nearly 27,000 workers losing their jobs (Coronavirus: tens of thousands of foreign workers lose their jobs in Oman 2020).

2.2.1 Impact on Sectoral Performance

Unlike some of its regional counterparts, Oman is a multifaceted economy with dependence on agriculture and fisheries along with oil production. Proactive measures of the Ministry of Agriculture and Fisheries in the form of adopting new projects (Ministry of Agriculture and Fisheries adopts new project 2020) increased fish farming from 33 tons in 2016 to 192 tons at the end of 2019. Thus, Oman stood as one of the largest fish producers in the Gulf region with capture of 580,000 fish in 2019. Despite its strength, COVID-19 is expected to disrupt this market (Macro poverty Outlook Oman 2020) in the form of lack of buyers due to closure of the retail market.

COVID-19 has less impact on cement manufacturing in Oman as the Omani cement manufacturers braced up to encounter this difficult situation. Omani cement manufacturers are self-sufficient in raw materials. As global supply chains are affected, the movement of raw materials within the country have not been disrupted due to COVID-19 (Ubhar Capital Report 2020). The Omani cement manufacturers used innovative low-cost and eco-friendly strategies to fight the difficult situation. One such instance comes from converting expired tires into fuel that can be used in cement production operations, as part of sustainable waste management (Expired tyres to drive cement production 2020). Medical equipment manufacturers in Oman started using 3D-printing technology to manufacture personal protective equipment a.k.a. PPEs (Omani companies use 3D printing to make COVID-19 protective gear 2020).

Like many other nations across the world, the tourism sector in Oman has been suffering severely as movement is restricted due to COVID-19. This pandemic has negatively impacted Oman's tourism as Salalah Tourism Festival and Kharif season in Salalah which are expected to attract around 8 million tourists has been cancelled due to COVID-19. The impact can be understood by looking at the 2019 data published by the National Centre for Statistics and Information–NCSI (Festival and concludes with 723, 720 visitors, 2019). According to NCSI, a total of 723,720 tourists visited the Salalah Tourism Festival (STF-2019) up to the end of August 2019, out of which 71.3% are Omanis and 17% are GCC nationals. It is evident from this data that even domestic and regional tourism has suffered due to COVID-19. While there was a decrease in terms of the number of visitors compared to 2018, the income generated from STF-2019 was OMR 78 million, an increase from OMR 76.9 Million in 2018 (More than 750, 000 visited Oman's Salalah Tourism Festival in 2019). This potential income is lost due to the cancellation of STF-2020 (Salalah Tourism Festival 2020).

MICE tourism (meetings, incentives, Conferences and exhibitions) has been given a boost by the development of a world-class convention center, the Oman Convention and Exhibition Centre (OCEC) opened in 2016 (Sultanate first choice for MICE tourism 2018). Since then OCEC has been contributing to the sprawling tourism sector by attracting the MICE potential participants long with the conventional tourism segments. Yet, this sector has also suffered the negative effects of COVID-19. OCEC which was expected to host an average of 30 events per year, has cancelled all activities and events planned between March and July 2020 until further notice.

Oman's Ministry of Tourism has identified cruise tourism as one of the top contributors to the national tourism sector by attracting global tourists (Castelier 2020). This is important because, events such as the Salalah Tourism Festival have been attracting local and regional tourists. Thus, due to special focus, Oman has grown as a cruise hub in the Middle East with a significant rise in the number of cruise ships visiting different ports during the 2018–2019 tourism season (Nair 2019a). According to the Ministry of Tourism, 283,488 cruise ship tourists visited Oman in 2019 which is around a 44% increase compared to 2018 (Bridge 2020). A total of 284 cruise ships were scheduled to visit different ports during the 2019–2020 tourism season which has now been affected by COVID-19 (Cruise tourists to Oman up 4.6pc in 2019 2020). This sector is badly affected as most of the visitors come from China, Italy and Iran. The number of visitors from these three countries reached 125,000, a four-fold increase between 2011 and 2018 (Castelier 2020).

The hospitality industry is greatly impacted by COVID-19 as the occupancy rates and subsequent revenue has been falling drastically. Hotels in Oman received 1.77 million guests in 2019 and garnered an attractive revenue of OMR 229.5 million (Omani hotel revenue takes \$122m hit 2020), most of it is lost in 2020 due to lockdown measures and the cancelling of major events across the country. Hotels ranging from 3 to 5 stars have recorded only OMR 54.2 million by the end of March 2020, which is around 25% less in revenue compared to the same period in 2019 (Oman hotel revenues fall 25% in months ahead of Covid-19 pandemic 2020).

Oman's higher education sector is mildly affected by COVID-19 as all higher educational institutions have transitioned to function online. The Government Communication Centre has decided to suspend the National Program for Postgraduate Studies for a year considering the ongoing global COVID-19 pandemic (National Program for Postgraduate Studies suspended in Oman 2020). Schools in Oman have reduced fees as a show of support to the parents, which has totaled to approximately OMR 1.1 million (Indian schools give relief worth over OMR1 million to students, families 2020) which could affect their future operations (Asif 2020).

The logistics sector in Oman becoming the transportation and logistics hub of the region. The logistics sector has contributed an attractive amount of OMR 1091 million in 2019 which is 3.73% of the GDP (Logistics GDP (n.d.)). Such an attractive sector has been affected by COVID-19 due to restrictions on the movement of people and goods. Despite the negative effects of COVID-19, the performance of Omani ports has been positive with around 2500 vessels visiting Omani ports in the first quarter of 2020 (Results and in Handling, Cargo, Export, 2020). It is only local trade and not international trade as Omani maritime trade is moderately impacted by COVID-19 (Prabhu 2020a).

COVID-19 has severely affected the aviation sector. According to an estimate, in Oman, the flight disruptions could result in a 2 million loss in passenger volume (Covid-19 impact: 16, 000 flights cancelled, 347, 000 jobs at stake in GCC aviation industry 2020). Airports in Oman have been major contributors to government exchequer in the form of non-tax revenues. Revenues from airports to the Oman Government were OMR 68.8 Million in 2018 (Nair 2019b). The number of flights landing and departing from the three major airports in Oman, viz., Muscat, Salalah and Sohar reached 104,830 up to the end of November of 2019 - serving 16.21 million passengers (million passengers use Oman airports 2020). The aviation sector has grown three times between 2010 and 2019. Hence, it has become imperative to pursue the recovery plan to resume flights in the Sultanate (COVID-19: Ministry prepares recovery plan for resuming flight services in Oman 2020).

Even before COVID-19, the oil crisis had impacted the real estate sector due to which property deals sharply fell by over 10% by the end of September 2019 (Oman eyes key real estate areas amid low rents and occupancy rates (n.d.)). Despite this, the situation took a turn for the better from the beginning of 2020. Wherein, the first two months of total value of property transactions increased by 24% compared to the same period in 2019 (Oman sees real estate deals hit $1.63bn in first two months of 2020 2020). Then, the introduction of COVID-19 worsened the situation as property deals and real estate transactions have been affected due to the restriction on the movement of people. The real estate sector also suffered in terms of rent collection, as the tenants were unable to pay due to jobs being affected by COVID-19 (Kutty 2020).

3 Coping Strategies and Measures

The government and private sectors have been undertaking coping strategies to combat the ongoing COVID-19 crisis. Hence, relief measures are being undertaken by the Government of Oman to mitigate not only the effect of COVID-19 but also the spillover effect of its coping strategies. Number of relief measures such as relaxation of regulatory compliance for certain businesses and requesting landlords to reduce or postpone rent (MOSD urges landlords to exempt nurseries from rent 2020), are being utilized. The following section attempts to present the coping strategies and relief measures undertaken by the Government and business sector(s) to mitigate the risk of COVID-19 on the economy of the Sultanate of Oman.

The Government of Oman has been actively pursuing stringent measures for controlling the spread of active cases as well as deaths. Starting from the first implementation of lockdown from 10th April 2020 in the Muscat Governorate (Muscat lockdown from Friday, schools suspended until further notice 2020) until the recent lockdown in the Duqm and Dhofar regions including various tourist areas such as Jabal Shams, Jabal Akhdar and Masirah islands (Lockdown begins in Dhofar, tourist destinations 2020). The Government of Oman has been trying its best to control the spread of the deadly virus. In addition, the Government has been opening multiple COVID-19 testing centers across the country (Fourth COVID-19 testing centre opens in Seeb 2020) with world-class testing facilities. The Ministry of Tourism has urged hotel owners to contribute a few of their rooms towards the institutional quarantine as part of their contribution to this national cause (Hotel owners urged to provide free rooms for COVID-19 measures 2020). Oman has always been at the forefront of research and development and has been utilizing global and national data to identify patterns that could be helpful in finding solutions to control the spread of the virus (Oman identifies three local strains of COVID-19 2020). Furthermore, the Ministry of Health developed a health app, known as Tarassud Plus that could help people identify the COVID-19 patients around them (Kothaneth 2020) and this usage of a tracing system not only helps to control the spread of COVID-19 but also assists in generating useful data that could help with decision making (New Covid-19 tracking system launched 2020).

As part of positioning Oman as an attractive logistics hub in the region, and transform Oman into the central gateway to India, Africa and Middle East, the Government has been focusing on improving and upgrading the ports despite COVID-19. Its efforts not to bring the industry stand-still are evidence of its commitment to make Oman a preferred logistics partner for global traders. For example, the Transportation Ministry brought into effect new rules for ship repairing (Transport ministry clarifies rules for ship repairs in Oman 2020) and adopts the best global practices in shipping sector operations through a single shop window, Bayan (Transport ministry adopts best global practices in shipping sector operations 2020).

The digital platform, Bayan, has drastically reduced the clearance time to complete export documentation procedures from 47 to 7 h (The logistics of performance. How Oman is supporting businesses and driving global trade (2020) Logistics Middle East. 2020). Similarly, several actions have been taken by public and private parties to support the logistics sector during the current COVID-19 crisis. Such measures include the physical closure of One Stop Shop at Sohar Port and continuation of the business electronically in order to avoid physical contact (Dealing with Covid-19 situation 2020). One of the leading logistics companies, Hutchison Ports Sohar announced a 20% discount on all containers discharged at Sohar port after 20th March 2020 as part of its support to encourage port activities. In addition to the private sector, the Government holding company, Oman Aviation Group has responded by reducing the air cargo handling prices for medicines and food from 26 baizas per kilogram to 15 baizas per kilogram (Newsflash–Dealing with Covid-19 situation 2020).

The Central Bank of Oman (CBO), the custodian of the Omani banking sector announced a liquidity incentive package of nearly OMR 8 billion to keep the economic activities moving in the country during the ongoing dual crisis. In addition, CBO announced tax relief measures such as allowing a deferred filing of tax returns and the payment of tax up to 3 months from the due date, tax deductions for all donations related to the COVID-19 pandemic, exemption of tourist and municipality tax of 4% to restaurants and 5% to commercial establishments until 31 August 2020 (Hariharan 2020). In addition, it has decided to support the tourism sector by postponing the collection of various charges from tourism establishments until the first quarter of the next financial year, 2021, to mitigate the impact of COVID-19 crisis (Al Sherbini 2020). Furthermore, the government has decided to allow the affected private sector firms to defer electricity and water bills for three months (Policy responses to COVID-19 2020). Most importantly, the Omani government's acceptance and approval of development projects to the tune of OMR 300 million is certainly expected to support the national economy during the current dual crisis (HM gives Royal Directive to execute projects worth RO300mn 2020).

The government's focus on encouraging youth to be job creators instead of job seekers leads to a conducive entrepreneurial ecosystem in the Sultanate of Oman. The Government of Oman announced several measures to support entrepreneurship in the country. Some of the measures implemented include, loan payments postponed, exemption of rent of small factories (Hariharan 2020) etc., The government has liberalized the import of medical products by reducing tariffs on medical products designated for the Oman Ministry of Health in order to combat COVID-19. At the same time, the export of masks and hand sanitizers is prohibited to avoid any shortages during a period of crisis (COVID-19 Temporary Trade Measures (n.d.)).

The adaptation of digitally innovative technology by the Ministry of Agriculture and Fisheries has supported Omani fish markets allowing them to flourish during difficult times. When the fish market in Oman encountered supply chain problems due to COVID-19, the technology initiative of the Ministry of Agriculture and Fisheries, Behar, an integrated online platform helped Omani fishermen to compete globally and escape the negative impact of COVID-19 (From bustling Omani fish markets to online auctions 2020). The Telecommunications Regulatory Authority (TRA) of Oman permitted use of Voice Over Internet (VoIP) platforms, Skype, Google Meet and Zoom during the current crisis which enabled organizations and institutions to conduct official meetings seamlessly (Coronavirus: Skype for Business, two other apps legal to use in Oman 2020).

Petroleum Development Oman (PDO), the leading oil and gas production company in Oman supported the education sector by supplying equipment and 3D printers to technical colleges aiming at building skills related to 4.0 industrial revolution (Oman and to provide 3D printers to technical and vocational colleges, 2020). In addition to voluntary measures, the Government has been taking up mitigation efforts in the cement industry by introducing anti-dumping measures that are expected to work as a neutralizer of the COVID-19 effect (Prabhu 2020b). The Government has decided to focus more on gas (LNG) production to mitigate the effects of the dual crisis (Oman's Economic Update 2020) and recover from the financial losses occurred during the current year. The Government of Oman has been trying to reduce the expenses by 43% in the aviation sector, anticipating a revival within four years (Nair 2020).

Table 2 below provides a snapshot of key socio-economic variables of Oman impacted by COVID-19. The

Table 2 Impact of COVID-19 on economy of Oman and coping strategies by the government of Oman

Variable	Description of the impact	Coping strategies and measures for mitigating the risk
Spread of COVID-19 cases and deaths	• Cases increased from 8149 on 31st May to 13,058 on 15th June i.e., the cases doubled in 15 days	• Lockdown starting in Muscat governorate on April 10 till end of May • New lockdown in in Duqm and Dhofar regions including various tourist areas, Jabal Shams, Jabal Akhdar and Masirah islands • Opening COVID-19 testing centers and quarantine centers • Inclusive approach by urging hotels to contribute to the institutional quarantine facilities in the country • R & D utilizing the global as well as national data to identify patterns Tarassud plus health app and health tracking system
Macroeconomic variables	• Oman state budget: cut by OMR 500 million • GDP: negative growth of −2.84 is forecast • Inflation: from 0.1 in 2019 to 1.0 in 2020 and further to 3.4 in 2021 • Consumption & expenditure: automobile spare parts market will suffer as China is the major supplier • Commercial vehicles' sales are going to be affected more than passenger vehicles • Employment: nearly 27,000 workers losing their jobs	• OMR 8 million liquidity incentive package • Approval of development projects to the tune of OMR 300 million • Allowing a deferred filing of tax returns and payment of tax up to 3 months from the due date • Tax deductions for all donations related to the COVID-19 pandemic • Exemption of tourist and municipality tax of 4% to restaurants and 5% to commercial establishments until 31 August 2020 • Allow the affected private sector firms to differ electricity and water bills for three months • Postpone loan instalments and fees payable by SMEs to Al Raffd fund to six months • Exemption of rent to small factories in the industrial cities for three months from April to June 2020 • Liberalized the import of medical products by reducing tariff on medical products designated for the Oman ministry of health • Prohibited the export of masks and hand sanitizers
Agriculture and fisheries	• Lack of buyers due to closure of retail market	• Behar, an integrated online platform helped Omani fishermen to compete globally and thus escape the negative impact of COVID-19
Manufacturing	• Moderate impact on cement manufacturing due to self-sustainability in raw materials • Moderate impact on medical equipment manufacturing due to using innovative 3D printing technology	• Introduction of anti-dumping measures in the cement industry • Focus more on gas (LNG) production
Tourism and hospitality	• Salalah tourism festival (STF) 2020: lost around estimated 8 million tourists • MICE tourism: Oman convention and exhibition centre-OCEC cancelled all events planned during March and July 2020 • Cruise tourism: 284 cruise ships were scheduled to visit Omani ports during 2019–2020 tourism season • Hotel revenues fell by 25%	• Postponing collection of various charges from tourism establishments to the first quarter of financial year, 2021

(continued)

Table 2 (continued)

Variable	Description of the impact	Coping strategies and measures for mitigating the risk
Education	• Moderate impact as the industry moved on to online mode • OMR 1.1 million tuition fee was reduced by Indian schools which could impact their operations and other decisions	• Petroleum development Oman (PDO) the leading oil and gas production company in Oman supported the education sector by supplying equipment and 3D printers to technical colleges aiming at building skills related to 4.0 industrial revolution
Transportation and logistics	• Moderate impact as Salalah port could receive 20% less volume of cargo	• Closure of one stop shop at Sohar Port and continue the business electronically in order to avoid physical contacts • Digital platform, Bayan, has drastically reduced the clearance time to complete export documentation procedures from 47 to 7 h • Hutchison Ports Sohar announced 20% discount on all containers discharged at Sohar port after 20th March 2020 • Oman aviation group reduced the air cargo handling prices for medicines and food from 26 baizas per kilogram to 15 baizas per kilogram
Aviation	• 2 million loss in passenger volumes	• Reduce expenses by 43% in aviation sector and anticipating the revival within four years
Real estate	• Low rental recovery from tenants	• Owners called on to reduce or postpone rent

Source Compiled by the authors

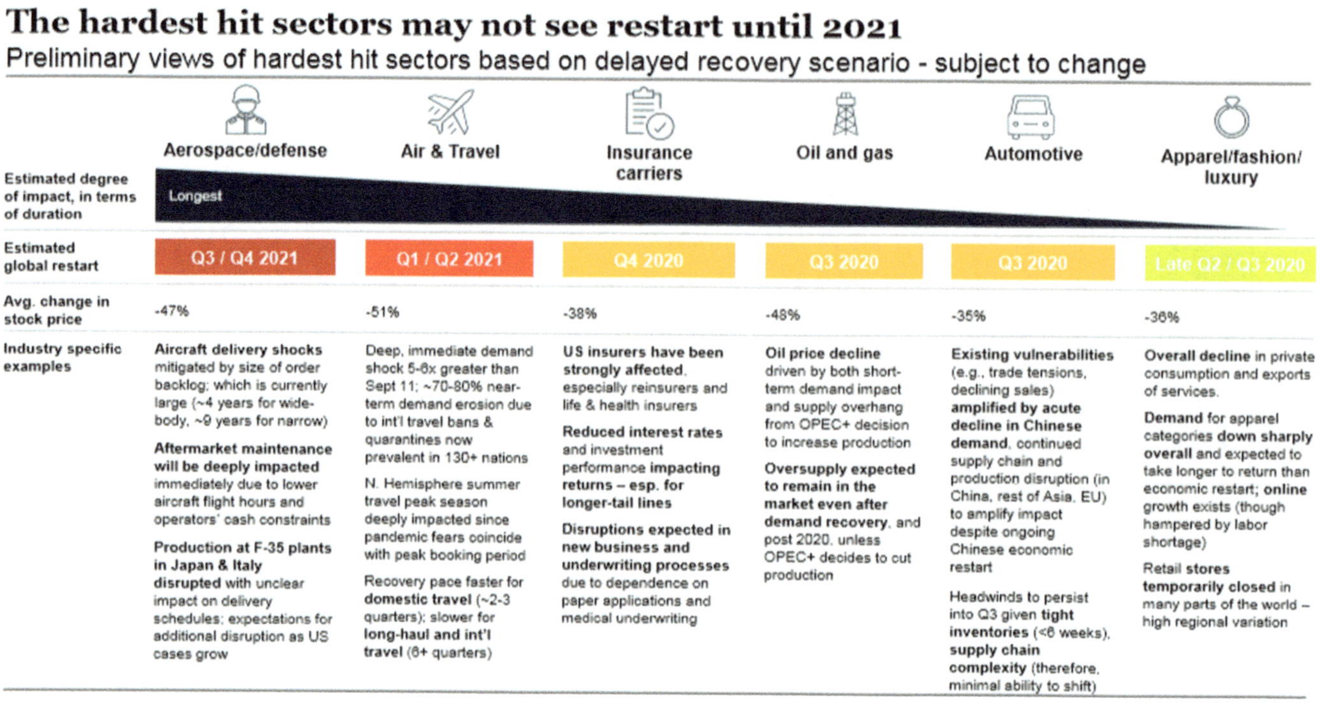

Fig. 5 Impact of COVID-19 on aerospace/defense and air & travel. *Source* (Surico and Galcotti 2020)

chart explains each of the affected variables, their description along with related measures and coping strategies undertaken by the Government of Oman for mitigating the risks arising out of COVID-19 crisis.

These sections have highlighted the strategies and measures taken in Oman to reduce the risk and the impact of COVID-19. Therefore, it is important to recognize the sectors that will be hit much longer for the policy makers to consider strategies to avoid economic recession. Figure 5 illustrates the fact that Aerospace/defense and Air & travel will be the hardest hit sectors, which may take longer to recover from the COVID-19 pandemic and as a result governmental support will be needed to ensure economic sustainability within these sectors.

4 Conclusion

These coping strategies could help businesses and regulatory authorities to normalize the situation but may also have side effects. For example, the Government's decision to cut the budget could have a spillover effect on other sectors of the economy as it is the major economic booster for the economic cycle in this country. Several measures taken by the Government of Oman even before the strike of COVID-19 helped the regulations to either neutralize or moderate the effect of the crisis on various sectors. The government's strategies to safeguard citizens' interests during the dual crisis is laudable. Innovative approaches such as Behar and Bayan have successfully resulted in boosting the two main non-oil sectors in the country, viz. fisheries and logistics respectively. The government's approval of OMR 300 million in projects reflects the thrust on developmental activities as the government is aware its spending can fuel the economy. Thus, a mature and professional approach by the Government has enabled the Omani economy to mitigate the associated risks and withstand the most severe effects of COVID-19.

References

2 million passengers use Oman airports (2020) Oman Observer. https://www.omanobserver.om/16-21-million-passengers-use-oman-airports-till-nov-2019/

53,332 expats employed in Oman's government sector (2020) Zawya, Times of Oman. https://www.zawya.com/mena/en/economy/story/53332_expats_employed_in_Omans_government_sector-SNG_173414058/

Al Sherbini R (2020) COVID-19: Oman to levy 4% fee on hotel clients. Gulf News. World Gulf. https://gulfnews.com/world/gulf/oman/covid-19-oman-to-levy-4-fee-on-hotel-clients-1.71989632

Appelbaum S, Keller S, Alvarez H, Bédard C (2012) Organizational crisis: lessons from Lehman brothers and Paulson & company. Int J Commer Manag 22(4):286–305. https://doi.org/10.1108/10569211211284494

Asif M (2020) Schools cut fees to help reduce COVID-19 impact on families. Times of Oman. https://timesofoman.com/article/3014281/oman/education/schools-cut-fees-to-help-reduce-covid-19-impact-on-families

Augustine NR (1995) Managing the crisis you tried to prevent. Harv Bus Rev 73(6):147–158. https://hbr.org/1995/11/managing-the-crisis-you-tried-to-prevent

Aziz B (2012) Financial crisis 2007–2009. How real estate bubble and transparency and accountability issues generated and worsen the crisis. Estudios Fronterizos, nueva época 13(26):201–221. http://www.scielo.org.mx/pdf/estfro/v13n26/v13n26a8.pdf

Bridge S (2020) How Oman is growing its cruise tourism sector. Arabian Business. Industries. https://www.arabianbusiness.com/travel-hospitality/439195-how-oman-is-growing-its-cruise-tourism-sector

Carlsson-Szlezak P, Reeves M, Swartz P (2020) Understanding the economic shock of coronavirus. Harv Bus Rev. https://hbr.org/2020/03/understanding-the-economic-shock-of-coronavirus

Castelier S (2020) Coronavirus: Oman's tourism sector takes a hit. The New Arab. https://english.alaraby.co.uk/english/indepth/2020/3/12/coronavirus-omans-tourism-sector-takes-a-hit

Coronavirus: Skype for Business, two other apps legal to use in Oman (2020) Times of Oman. https://timesofoman.com/article/2924018/business/technology/coronavirus-skype-for-business-two-other-apps-legal-to-use-in-oman

Coronavirus: tens of thousands of foreign workers lose their jobs in Oman (2020) The National. https://www.thenational.ae/world/gcc/coronavirus-tens-of-thousands-of-foreign-workers-lose-their-jobs-in-oman-1.1025061

Covid-19 impact: 16,000 flights cancelled, 347,000 jobs at stake in GCC aviation industry (2020) The Arabian Stories. https://www.thearabianstories.com/2020/03/20/covid-19-impact-16000-flights-cancelled-347000-jobs-at-stake-in-gcc-aviation-industry/

COVID-19 Temporary Trade Measures (n.d.) ITC Market Access Map. https://www.macmap.org/covid19. Accessed 16th June 2020

Covid-19: family gatherings main cause of increasing cases in Oman (2020) Times of Oman. https://timesofoman.com/article/3015984/oman/covid-19-family-gatherings-main-cause-of-increasing-cases-in-oman

COVID-19: Ministry prepares recovery plan for resuming flight services in Oman (2020) Times of Oman. https://timesofoman.com/article/3015723/oman/covid-19-ministry-prepares-recovery-plan-for-resuming-flight-services-in-oman

Cruise tourists to Oman up 4.6pc in 2019 (2020) Trade Arabia. http://www.tradearabia.com/news/TTN_363635.html#:~:text=The%20Ministry%20said%20a%20total,Salalah%20(47%20cruise%20ships)

Dealing with Covid-19 situation (2020) Oman Logistics Center. https://asyad.om/docs/default-source/default-document-library/tf_newsflash_20200325.pdf?sfvrsn=1fda979f_0

Decline in real estate deals in Oman (2019) Times of Oman. https://timesofoman.com/article/1553137/oman/decline-in-real-estate-deals

European Centre for Disease Prevention and Control (2020) https://www.ecdc.europa.eu/en/publications-data

Expired tyres to drive cement production (2020) Muscat Daily. https://muscatdaily.com/Oman/386091/Forbes-list:-Nine-from-Oman-in-top-100

First Voluntary National Review of The Sultanate of Oman 2019 (2019) United nations high-level political forum on sustainable development. https://www.scp.gov.om/PDF/2030Report.pdf

Fourth COVID-19 testing centre opens in Seeb (2020) Oman Observer. https://timesofoman.com/article/3016025/oman/fourth-covid-19-testing-centre-opens-in-seeb

From bustling Omani fish markets to online auctions (2020) Food and agriculture organization of the United Nations. http://www.fao.org/fao-stories/article/en/c/1278611/

Hariharan A (2020) Oman government measures to address COVID-19. KPMG Insights. https://home.kpmg/om/en/home/insights/2020/04/Oman%20Government%20measures%20to%20address%20COVID-19.html

Hart P, Rosenthal U, Kouzmin A (1993) Crisis decision making: the centralization thesis revisited. Adm & Soc 25(1):12–45. https://doi.org/10.1177/009539979302500102

HM gives Royal Directive to execute projects worth RO300mn (2020) Muscat Daily. https://muscatdaily.com/Oman/386944/HM-gives-Royal-Directive-to-execute-projects-worth-RO300mn

Hotel owners urged to provide free rooms for COVID-19 measures (2020) Oman Observer. https://www.omanobserver.om/hotel-owners-urged-to-provide-free-rooms-for-covid-19-measures/

Indian schools give relief worth over OMR1 million to students, families (2020) Times of Oman. https://timesofoman.com/article/3015927/oman/indian-schools-give-relief-worth-over-omr1-million-to-students-families

International Monetary Fund (2019) World economic outlook, global manufacturing downturn, rising trade barriers. Washington, DC. www.imf.org/~/media/Files/Publications/WEO/2019/October/English/text.ashx

International Monetary Fund (2020) World economic outlook: The Great Lockdown. https://www.imf.org/~/media/Files/Publications/WEO/2020/April/English/Ch1.ashx?la=en

Kothaneth L (2020) MoH develops app that alerts about Covid positive people around you. Times of Oman. https://www.omanobserver.om/moh-develops-app-that-alerts-about-covid-positive-people-around-you/

Kutty S (2020) Tenants struggle to pay rent. Oman Observer. https://www.omanobserver.om/tenants-struggle-to-pay-rent/

Li F, William H, Bogle M (1999) The 'Millennium Bug': its origin, potential impact and possible solutions. Int J Inf Manage 19(1):3–15. https://doi.org/10.1016/S0268-4012(98)00043-7

Lockdown begins in Dhofar, tourist destinations (2020) Oman Observer. https://www.omanobserver.om/lockdown-begins-in-dhofar-tourist-destinations/

Logistics GDP (n.d.) Oman logistics the MEA hub. https://logistics.om/industry_statistic/logistics-gdp/

Macro poverty Outlook Oman (2020) World Bank. http://pubdocs.worldbank.org/en/124071554825491319/mpo-omn.pdf

MENA Economic Update (2020) How transparency can help the middle east and North Africa. The World Bank. https://www.worldbank.org/en/region/mena/publication/mena-economic-update-april-2020-how-transparency-can-help-the-middle-east-and-north-africa

Mendoza J (2019) Oman's GDP contracts 1.6pc in Q1 2019, weighed down by slump in oil prices: CBO. Oman Observer. https://www.omanobserver.om/omans-gdp-contracts-1-6pc-in-q1-2019-weighed-down-by-slump-in-oil-prices-cbo/

Ministry of Agriculture and Fisheries adopts new project (2020) Times of Oman. https://timesofoman.com/article/3014420/oman/government/ministry-of-agriculture-and-fisheries-adopts-new-project

Mitroff II, Shrivastava P, Udwadia FE (1987) Effective crisis management. Acad Manag Exec 1(3):283–292. https://doi.org/10.5465/AME.1987.4275639

More than 750,000 visited Oman's Salalah Tourism Festival in 2019 (2020) Zawya, Times of Oman. https://www.zawya.com/mena/en/life/story/More_than_750000_visited_Omans_Salalah_Tourism_Festival_in_2019-SNG_165797497/

MOSD urges landlords to exempt nurseries from rent (2020) Oman Observer. https://www.omanobserver.om/mosd-urges-landlords-to-exempt-nurseries-from-rent/

Muscat lockdown from Friday, schools suspended until further notice (2020) Oman Observer. https://www.omanobserver.om/muscat-supreme-commitee/

Nair V (2019) Oman to be developed as 'cruise' hub in Middle East. Oman Observer. https://www.omanobserver.om/cruise-hub-in-middle-east/

Nair V (2019) Water, airports top in non-tax revenues. Oman Observer. https://www.omanobserver.om/water-airports-top-in-non-tax-revenues/

Nair V (2020) Oman may open airports soon: supreme committee. Oman Observer. https://www.omanobserver.om/oman-may-open-airports-soon-supreme-committee/

National Program for Postgraduate Studies suspended in Oman (2020) Times of Oman. https://timesofoman.com/article/3015016/oman/education/national-program-for-postgraduate-studies-suspended-in-oman

New Covid-19 tracking system launched (2020) Oman Observer. https://www.omanobserver.om/new-covid-19-tracking-system-launched/

Newsflash–Dealing with Covid-19 situation (2020) Oman logistics the MEA Hud. https://logistics.om/news/newsflash-dealing-with-covid-19-situation/

Oman (2020) Despite postponing VAT introduction, the market signed the 6th annual fall in a row (2020) Focus2move. https://www.focus2move.com/oman-auto-market/

Oman automobile sales in top gear (2019) Times of Oman. https://timesofoman.com/article/2473380/oman/oman-automobile-sales-in-top-gear

Oman Autos Report (n.d.) FitchSolutions. https://store.fitchsolutions.com/oman-autos-report

Oman budget 2020 (n.d.) KPMG Insights. Retrieved from https://assets.kpmg/content/dam/kpmg/om/pdf/oman-budget-2020.pdf

Oman eyes key real estate areas amid low rents and occupancy rates (n.d.) Oxford Business Group. https://oxfordbusinessgroup.com/overview/pockets-opportunity-environment-low-rents-and-occupancy-rates-identifying-areas-hold-promise-key

Oman GDP Annual Growth Rate (n.d.) Trading economics. https://tradingeconomics.com/oman/gdp-growth-annual

Oman government orders more budget cuts (2020) Times of Oman. Retrieved from https://timesofoman.com/article/3014863/oman/government/oman-government-orders-more-budget-cuts

Oman hotel revenues fall 25% in months ahead of Covid-19 pandemic (2020) Arabian business. https://www.arabianbusiness.com/travel-hospitality/447837-oman-hotel-revenues-fall-25-in-months-ahead-of-covid-19-pandemic

Oman identifies three local strains of COVID-19 (2020) Times of Oman. https://timesofoman.com/article/3015726/oman/health/omani-researchers-analyse-covid-19-gene-sequencing

Oman sees real estate deals hit $1.63bn in first two months of 2020 (2020) ifp info. http://www.ifpinfo.com/oman-sees-real-estate-deals-hit-1-63bn-in-first-two-months-of-2020/

Oman State Budget 2020 slashed by RO 500 million (2020) Oman Observer. https://www.omanobserver.om/oman-state-budget-2020-slashed-by-ro500-million/

Oman's automobile sector concerned over Coronavirus impact on industry (2020) The Arabian stories. https://www.thearabianstories.com/2020/02/23/omans-automobile-sector-concerned-over-corona-virus-impact-on-industry/

Oman's Economic Update—April 2020 (2020) The World Bank. https://www.worldbank.org/en/country/gcc/publication/oman-economic-update-april-2020

Omani companies use 3D printing to make COVID-19 protective gear (2020) Times of Oman. https://timesofoman.com/article/3015661/oman/omani-companies-use-3d-printing-to-make-covid-19-protective-gear

Omani hotel revenue takes $122m hit (2020) Hotelier Middle East. https://www.hoteliermiddleeast.com/business/117694-omani-hotel-revenue-takes-122m-hit

Omani Ports Post Positive Results in Handling, Cargo, Export (2020) Oman News Agency. http://omannews.gov.om/description_bkp/ArtMID/867/ArticleID/13234/Omani-Ports-Post-Positive-Results-in-Handling-Cargo-Export

Omoregie U (2015) The oil price crash of 2014: implications for a multi-billion dollar LNG project. Nat Resour 6:577–582. https://doi.org/10.4236/nr.2015.612055

Petroleum Development Oman to provide 3D printers to technical and vocational colleges (2020) Times of Oman. https://timesofoman.com/article/3015891/oman/education/petroleum-development-oman-to-provide-3d-printers-to-technical-and-vocational-colleges?utm_campaign=layout&utm_source=article_page&utm_medium=layout_related_articles

Policy responses to COVID-19 (2020) Policy tracker, International monetary fund. https://www.imf.org/en/Topics/imf-and-covid19/Policy-Responses-to-COVID-19#O. Accessed 12 June 2020

Prabhu C (2020) Oman's cement industry welcomes anti-dumping measures. Oman Observer. https://www.omanobserver.om/omans-cement-industry-welcomes-anti-dumping-measures/

Prabhu C (2020) COVID-19 impacts: Salalah port foresees 20% decline in local trade volumes. Oman Observer. https://www.omanobserver.om/covid-19-impacts-salalah-port-foresees-20-decline-in-local-trade-volumes/

The National Program for Enhancing Economic Diversification (Tanfeedh) (n.d.) Omanuna. https://omanportal.gov.om/wps/portal/index/interact/tanfeedh/!ut/p/a1/hc9Nb4JAEAbgX8OVmV0IQW9TPwENpWsV92LQrCsJsAa38velxksTrXN7J8-bzICEHGRTXEtd2NI0RfWbZbBLMxaweYpJuM4mSF8kMmKcI_o92PYAXwzhu_4G5J2IOPkQkc8xnQqGEUXz0YhWnH0HD-DhDDEdRMtktSTk3noaDxaBNx77D_DPDTFIXZn9_Z8tNXsv1CBbdVStat2ftl-frD1fhg462HWdq43RlXIPpnbwWeVkLhbyvxKEauBc51h1pvQhnQDZBSlIQ!!/dl5/d5/L0lKQSEvUUt3TS80RUkhL2Vu/

Roubini N (2020) Coronavirus pandemic has delivered the fastest, deepest economic shock in history. The Guardian. https://www.theguardian.com/business/2020/mar/25/coronavirus-pandemic-has-delivered-the-fastest-deepest-economic-shock-in-history

Salalah Tourism Festival 2020 cancelled (2020) Zawya, Times of Oman. https://www.zawya.com/mena/en/life/story/Salalah_Tourism_Festival_2020_cancelled-SNG_172753407/

Salalah Tourism Festival concludes with 723,720 visitors (2019) Oman Observer. Retrieved from https://www.omanobserver.om/salalah-tourism-festival-concludes-with-723720-visitors/#:~:text=Salalah%3A%20A%20total%20of%20723%2C720,with%205.3%20per%20cent%20decrease

Sultanate first choice for MICE tourism (2018) Oman observer. https://www.omanobserver.om/sultanate-first-choice-for-mice-tourism/

Surico P, Galcotti A (2020) The economics of a pandemic: the case of COVID-19, London Business Scholl, Lecture Series. https://icsb.org/theeconomicsofapandemic/

The logistics of performance. How Oman is supporting businesses and driving global trade (2020) Logistics Middle East. https://www.logisticsmiddleeast.com/34910-the-logistics-of-performance?utm_source=Jarvis&utm_medium=logisticsmiddleeast.com&utm_campaign=recommended

Transport ministry adopts best global practices in shipping sector operations (2020) Times of Oman. https://timesofoman.com/article/3015502/oman/transport/ministry-adopts-best-global-practices-in-shipping-sector-operations

Transport ministry clarifies rules for ship repairs in Oman (2020) Times of Oman. https://timesofoman.com/article/3015888/oman/government/transport-ministry-clarifies-rules-for-ship-repairs-in-oman

Ubhar Capital Report (2020) Coronavirus impact on global, GCC & Oman market. Ubhar Capital. https://www.u-capital.net/pdf/Coronavirus%20Impact%20-%20March%202020.pdf

Woods B (2018) Snow to melt high street sales as retailers brace for more pain. World News Edition, Independent.ie, 1st March. https://www.independent.ie/world-news/snow-to-melt-high-street-sales-as-retailers-brace-for-more-pain-36658839.html

Impact of Covid-19 on the Financial Regulatory Framework in ASEAN

Asma Salman, Qaisar Ali and Muthanna G. Abdul Razzaq

Abstract

Even though ASEAN governments have considerably flattened the Covid-19 curve through stringent containment measures however, these measures have resulted in deep economic and financial disruptions. Consequently, there is a need to investigate the economic and financial impacts of Covid-19 so that relevant policies may be developed by the ASEAN member states (AMS). This study outlines the major economic and financial consequences of Covid-19 and the strategies to minimize these impacts. The findings reveal that the current situation of Covid-19 and the characteristics of AMS have broad impacts on the GDP growth, trade, tourism, supply chains, MSMEs, and the financial market. This study forecasts that these risks can be mitigated provided regulators and policymakers in AMS focus on developing a comprehensive and holistic approach by incorporating functional response strategy, effectively mobilizing policy tools, preserving production capacities, preventing leaning supply chains, and switching to digital trade. Our study contributes to the ongoing research on the current pandemic outbreak and elucidates implications to reduce economic and financial risks amidst Covid-19 in ASEAN.

Keywords

Covid-19 · ASEAN · Economic & financial risks · Policy implications

A. Salman (✉) · M. G. A. Razzaq
College of Business Administration, American University in the Emirates (AUE), Dubai, United Arab Emirates
e-mail: asma.salman@aue.ae

M. G. A. Razzaq
e-mail: dr.muthanna@aue.ae

Q. Ali
Faculty of Islamic Economics and Finance,
University Islam Sultan Sharif Ali, Darussalam, Brunei

1 Introduction

Countries around the globe are battling to curtail the spread of novel Coronavirus (Covid-19), a contagious respiratory disease caused by Sars-Cov-2 initially reported in Hubei (Wuhan) China on 31 December 2019 (World Health Organization (WHO) 2020). It has already affected more than 16.55 million people and claimed 656,093 lives in 203 countries (World Health Organization (WHO) 2020). Following its alarming growth, the World Health Organization (WHO) declared it as a global pandemic on 11 March 2020. American region has become the next epicenter of Covid-19 with more than 8.84 million confirmed cases and 342,635 deaths (World Health Organization (WHO) 2020). As the virus continues to surge, scientists and global health officials have warned that the world is yet to face the worse due to the lack of global solidarity and political differences among countries (Martin 2020). The exponential growth of Covid-19 is forcing governments to impose lockdowns and safety measures to halt its spread which is burning the economic activities to nearly a standstill (The World Bank 2020). The pandemic has arrived at the times when the global economy was scrambling towards a downturn (International Monetary Fund (IMF) 2020). The unprecedented disruptions asserted by the pandemic have overturned everyday live patterns and many economists are convinced that the world has formally entered into a recession (Times 2020).

The regional economies, businesses, and investments across the world were reasonably optimistic while entering into 2020 despite lingering fears of the US-China trade war (Mikic et al. 2020). 'World Economic Outlook' published in April 2020 projected a 2.9% growth in the global economy however, the uncertainties associated with the pandemic due to lack of medical interventions and slow economic recovery overturned these projections (Crisis Like No Other and Recovery 2020). IMF released another 'Economic Outlook' report in June 2020 and warned the contraction

A. Salman and A. Tharwat (eds.), *Smart Designs for Business Innovation*,
Advances in Science, Technology & Innovation, https://doi.org/10.1007/978-3-031-49313-3_6

of global economic growth by 4.9%. Many other economic platforms such as 'The Economist' (The Economist 2020) and The World Bank (The World Bank 2020) forecasted the contraction of the global economy by 1.3% within the first quarter of 2020 and the decline of global GDP by 5.2%. The popular stock markets such as DOW Jones Industrial Average (DJI), FTSE, and Nikkei substantially contracted following the start of the outbreak (Bloomberg 2020). Pandemic has an irreversible effect on travel, tourism, retail, service, manufacturing, labor industries, and global supply chains. Recent studies on pandemic mortality and morbidity impacts describe it as the worst disaster in over a century (Crisis Like No Other and Recovery 2020; Ferguson et al. 2020; Jorda et al. 2020).

The pandemic was first reported in China however, due to trade and tourism propinquity and enhanced interconnections Covid-19 disease soon spread to the neighboring countries such as South Korea, Japan, Iran, and the countries in the Southeast Asian Nation (ASEAN) (OECD 2020a). Initially, the outbreak was controlled in countries such as Singapore and Indonesia however, the uncertainties affiliated with the pandemic and an increase in the infection rate prompted governments to further tighten the safety protocols. Besides fears of an increase in the mortality rate, the economic impacts of a pandemic will be irreversible even if the countries control the spread of infection (The Economist 2020). Covid-19 is expected to hit hard MSMEs in emerging economies and most of the ASEAN economies are characterized as emerging economies. The pandemic impact and government response to economic recovery also interest the scholars due to the facts associated with the ASEAN region; it is one of the regional cooperation bodies in the world which provides a discrete platform to enhance cooperation, health, and security since 1980 (Association of Southeast Asian Nations (ASEAN) 2020).

While the pandemic continues to claim lives, its serious consequences have suppressed demand and supply channels particularly, countries dependent on the integrated global value chains are exposed to the shocks of demand and supply connectivity lost. China is the largest external trade partner of the economies in ASEAN, about 17.1% of ASEAN's total trade and 6.5% of total foreign direct investment flows rely on the supply chain integration (ASEC 2020). Covid-19 is expected to contract international trade by 13 to 32% by 2020 which is projected to have a deep impact on ASEAN economies (World Trade Organization 2020). ASEAN community was established on the mutual pillars of Political-Security Community, ASEAN Economic Community and ASEAN Socio-Cultural Community (ASCC) which used to mutually combat epidemics during SARS, H1N1, and MERS-CoV. ASCC's vision is to ensure a healthy, caring and sustainable ASEAN community which was a key to the ASEAN Post-2015 Healthier Development Agenda in 2018. However, the nature of the current crises entails a different holistic approach to ensure the safety and health of the ASEAN community.

Furthermore, the decline in GDP growth, revenues, and discretionary support has added to the debt and deficits of governments. IMF reported that the global public debt will soar to 101% of GDP in 2020–21 which is havoc for the ASEAN community. (Crisis Like No Other and Recovery 2020) The rise in public debt and fiscal deficit raises concerns over the capacity of the governments to provide support to the regional communities in ASEAN. Another report on financial sector response to Covid-19 concluded that it is impossible to estimate pandemic's impact on macroeconomic and financial markets (Ernst and Young 2020). We argue that despite economists' prediction of negative GDP growth in 2020, businesses, economies, and the banks are at a higher risk of devastating impacts. This has already been witnessed in China, despite governments' efforts to restart and reopen businesses there is a decline in demand and generally people are reluctant to spend which is further slowing down economic recovery. Therefore, we aim to investigate the following two research questions;

1. What are the economic and financial consequences of Covid-19 faced by AMS?
2. How AMS can mitigate the economic and financial impacts of Covid-19?

To answer the above research questions, this study attempts to categories the impacts of Covid-19 through a descriptive analysis by reviewing the collective response strategies of ASEAN society which will contributes to the ongoing research on Covid-19 impacts and policy development. In addition to the economic challenges ushered by Covid-19, we also analyse the discrete capacity of each ASEAN country to continue providing support for the regional communities which contributes to mapping economic resilience and developed capacities such as health, financial, and economic response strategies to minimise pandemic's impacts. Lastly, we analyse the financial sector contribution to facilitate the general public, businesses, and governments in restarting the recovery process which contributes in analyzing the strength and response strategies developed by the banks.

The rest of the paper is organised as follows; section two review the literature and outlines the current situation of Covid-19 in ASEAN and the response to the pandemic outbreak. The third section discusses the adopted research methods to analyze the collected data. Section four outlines the findings and discussion which comprise of various economic and financial challenges faced by AMS. The last section concludes this study and suggests policies to further improve the health, economic and financial situation in ASEAN regions.

2 Literature Review

2.1 Current Situation of Covid-19 in ASEAN

ASEAN is a regional body in Southeast Asia comprised of 10 member states having a population of more than 649 million and a GDP of US$2.8 trillion (Development and Bank 2020). ASEAN member states (AMS) are effectively coordinating and cooperating to control the spread of the virus in the region, ever since the first case of Covid-19 was reported in the six-member states in late January 2020 (Association of Southeast Asian Nations (ASEAN) 2020). As of 02 August 2020, there are about 267,534 confirmed cases and 7,375 Covid-19 related deaths in ASEAN (World Health Organization (WHO) 2020). Table 1 shows the current situation of Covid-19 and the timelines of the first reported case in AMS.

The above statistics indicate that the number of Covid-19 cases is still escalating in the Philippines, Indonesia, Singapore, and Vietnam. Most of the ASEAN countries continue to impose safety measures such as partial lockdowns, travel restrictions, contact tracing, and mandatory social distancing to ensure the safety and health of the public. While, other countries such as Brunei Darussalam, Malaysia, Thailand, and Vietnam have gradually relaxed the lockdowns and restriction of movements which has facilitated the start of economic activities. The situation remains highly uncertain as the people are yet to acquire immunity against Covid-19 due to the lack of medical intervention. The nature of the current crises demands the ASEAN community to render a holistic approach and cooperation surpassing the traditional protocols and models to warrant a timely, effective, and strategic response to minimize the spread of disease.

2.2 ASEAN Response to Covid-19

2.2.1 Regional Response

Historically, ASEAN has mitigated several disasters and health crises such as SARS, H1N1, and HIV through frameworks developed in response to the epidemics. Currently, there are a few robust mechanisms under the umbrella of ASCC which ensure the development of a response strategy in ASEAN during Covid-19 (Association of Southeast Asian Nations (ASEAN) 2020). The ASEAN Health Ministers, ASEAN Plus Three Health Ministers, ASEAN plus Three Senior Officials Meeting for Health Development (APT SOMHD). Establishment of the ASEAN Emergency Operations Centre (EOC) network to facilitate public health emergency and the visualization of big data analytics is made possible through the ASEAN BioDiaspora Virtual Centre (ABVC). Another framework is the ASEAN Coordinating Council Working Group (ACCWG) to cater to public health emergencies (Association of Southeast Asian Nations (ASEAN) 2020).

All AMS implemented significant safety measures to safeguard the health and welfare of its people. At the regional level, significant measures are the 26th ASEAN Economic Ministers (AEM) on 10 March 2020 stating to render shared action to minimize the spread of Covid-19 infection by leveraging technology and digital trade to retain the connectivity of the supply chains and sustainability. The leaders of ASEAN member States issued another statement after the Special ASEAN Summit on Covid-19 on 14 April 2020 calling for a post-pandemic recovery plan and proposed to establish Covid-19 ASEAN response

Table 1 Current situation of Covid-19 in AMS (As of, 02 August 2020)

Country	First case reported	Confirmed cases	Last 24 h	Deaths	Tests	Recovered
Brunei Darussalam	March 10, 2020	141	0	3	29,841	138
Cambodia	January 27, 2020	234	0	0	12,378	164
Indonesia	March 02, 2020	108,376	2,040	5,131	866,539	65,907
Lao PDR	March 24, 2020	20	0	0	27,106	19
Malaysia	January 25, 2020	8,976	12	125	955,133	8,644
Myanmar	March 23, 2020	353	0	6	115,701	295
Philippines	January 30, 2020	93,354	7,868	2,023	1,497,313	65,178
Singapore	January 23, 2020	52,205	396	27	1,321,094	46,308
Thailand	January 13, 2020	3,310	6	58	703,001	3,125
Vietnam	January 23, 2020	545	81	1	261,004	373

Source WHO; Health ministries of ASEAN member states

Fund (OECD 2020a). WHO issued a warning after noticing the increase in infection rate in ASEAN and suggested to scale up the efforts to curtail the spread of infection as there were significant differences in the capacity to provide PCR (Polymerase Chain Reaction) tests (World Health Organization (WHO). 2020). This warning increased the policy convergence and triggered a united regional response as the 36th ASEAN Summit in Vietnam in April 2020 was postponed to June 2020.

2.2.2 Domestic Response

The domestic response strategy is a key to contain the spread of Covid-19 in any country as domestic capacities are the first-line defense against the current pandemic (Anderson et al. 2020). Each AMS took substantial measures according to the safety and health charter of WHO. Brunei Darussalam managed to control the spread of infection through its strategic response, outstanding health facilities, and generous government support. All the infected patients were treated freely at the National Isolation Centre. The government immediately canceled all the flights, imposed travel bans, cancellation, and of all religious events and imposed nationwide social distancing measures. However, Brunei did not impose curfew as the infection, and the mortality rate was under control. To ensure the community welfare the government announced the early opening of the Temburong bridge for the general public and introduced a stimulus package of BND450 million to support the financial sector and MSMEs in private business (KPMG 2020a). Banks in Brunei deferred the loan payments of the private businesses affiliated with hospitality, travel, event management, and food beverage. The government also announced to contribute 25% to the salaries of private-sector employees affected due to the pandemic. Additionally, the Ministry of Finance and Economy (MOFE) established a virtual platform to unite the community and help local businesses (Ministry of Finance and Economy (MOFE) 2020).

The infection and mortality rate in Cambodia are relatively low as well as there are no deaths and new cases in the country it is inferred that despite lack of Covid-19 testing capacity the country has controlled the virus outbreak through its distinguished safety measures. These measures include mandatory quarantine, cancellation of the New Year (Khmer) celebration and the government announced to issue an economic stimulus package focused on the welfare of the general public (KPMG 2020b). The government announced to compensate workers with 5 days of public holidays during an appropriate time. However, Cambodia did not impose any lockdowns, restriction of movements at public places, and cancellation of flights or travel ban. The government also announced to provide financial assistance for employees whose jobs were suspended due to Covid-19.

Indonesia had the highest infection rate among ASEAN due to an inappropriate mechanism to combat Covid-19. Indonesia announced to enhance restrictions on entry and transit of foreign travelers and canceled its visa exemption policy for short stay visits. The government declared a state of national emergency on 31 March 2020 and imposed large scale restrictions, closures of public places such as schools, religious places, and non-essential workplaces. Other large-scale measures include cancellation of religious, public entertainment events, and limited public transportation (OECD 2020b). The government announced a stimulus package of US$26.5 billion to be used as a financial relief amid Covid-19.

The Infection rate in Lao PDR is nominal however, the local government and international bodies such as the United Nations Country Team (UNCT) and WHO kept the situation under control. The government continuously assisted the businesses affected due to the pandemic by implementing tax breaks and delay tax payments for certain types of businesses. The World Bank-supported Lao PDR to release the stimulus package of US$18 million and local banks are encouraged to reclassify their debt and provide interest rate incentives (KPMG 2020c). Many businesses, servicing, and trade agencies were exempted from paying annual fees. Additionally, the government established 17 hotlines to provide psycho-social support and counseling to the public.

The spike in Covid-19 cases in Malaysia originated from a mass religious gathering in Malaysia (Kuala Lumpur) on 27 February 2020. The event was attended by more than 14,500 Malaysians and 1,500 foreigners and most of them were tested positive after the event. Since then, Malaysia imposed tight safety measures to raise their defense by restricting movements, curfews, lockdowns, travel bans, and closure of borders (OECD 2020b). The Malaysian Authorities announced to introduce a stimulus package of RM400 billion and in addition to tax breaks and provision of financial assistance to the affected communities and businesses (KPMG 2020d).

Myanmar had a relatively low spread of Covid-19 infection however, there were looming fears of an increase in spread rate due to lack of testing capacity. Initially, Singapore and South Korea donated 8,000 testing kits which were insufficient compare with the overall population. Later on, the United Nations intervened and donated 50,000 testing kits to enhance the testing capacity. The country is vulnerable to the spread of disease due to poor health system and financial inequality in the system. Instead of fully locking down the country, the government imposed partial curfew hours in seven major townships, banned mass gathering, and canceled all the sports events. To cater to the needs of affected businesses and people, the government announced a stimulus package of US$70 million. The general public was given other financial benefits such as a reduction in interest rate, borrowing relives for businesses and individuals, and tax waivers on goods (KPMG 2020e).

Philippines had the highest infection rate in ASEAN despite its enhanced testing capacity and comparatively better health facilities. The authorities in the Philippines placed the entire Luzon Island community under quarantine in April 2020 and extended until May 2020 (OECD 2020b). The policymakers suggested to impose lockdowns, restriction of movements, and curfews to curtail the spread of the virus. The country stopped issuing visas to foreigners and canceled all its domestic flights and prohibited the mass public gathering, closure of schools, and encouraged the public to practice social distancing. The government announced to provide financial assistance to the workers lost their jobs due to lockdowns, declared a subsidy for 18 million citizens having a low household income, and banks deferred payments of loans for one month (KPMG 2020f).

WHO regarded Singapore's response to the pandemic as satisfactory and aggressive as it used technology to verify home quarantine, contact tracing through a mobile-based software. Despite fears of a rise in Covid-19 cases, the mortality rate is relatively low as Singapore has an infrastructure, prior experience with SARS pandemic, and facilities to control the spread of infection (OECD 2020b). The government introduced stimulus packages of S$90.5 billion to cushion public, businesses, and workers affected by the Covid-19 outbreak. These packages were announced in four phases and each phase catered to the needs of different demographics and industry sectors in the country (KPMG 2020g).

Thailand's government responded typically according to the WHO global framework of health and safety during Covid-19. All major events in the country were canceled, the mass gathering was prohibited, closure of schools, sports complex, museums, libraries, and the restriction of movements to minimize the spread of infection. All domestic and international flights were canceled and banned tourists from gaining entry to Thailand. The financial assistance to fewer privileged communities, workers, businesses, and certain industry sectors was provided through a stimulus package of 400 billion baht. Other financial relives were an extension of timelines to repay the loans, tax rebates, and reduction and delay in utility bills (KPMG 2020h).

Vietnam responded exceptionally to limit the spread of Covid-19 as there was a fear of a massive outbreak in the country due to its large population and border with China. The authorities' readiness and enhanced safety measures successfully capped the spread of the pandemic. The first immediate action was the cancellation of all the flights to and from Wuhan and closure of the border with China. Vietnam imposed strict quarantines, contact tracing of infected patients, and the government consistently remained transparent in releasing the actual situation of Covid-19 in the country (OECD 2020b). The local government declared a financial stimulus package of US$12 billion focus on the welfare and assistance to the public, businesses, and the industries most affected due to the current pandemic (KPMG 2020i). Additionally, the government provided tax breaks, allowed to delay loan payments, and reduced land leasing fees.

The nature of the response and implemented domestic safety measures by ASEAN countries are represented in Table 2.

3 Research Methods

This is a qualitative study based on the secondary sources of data collected after reviewing and systematic evaluation of various documents (Bretschneider et al. 2017). The evaluation of documents helps in collecting background information and tracking changes and new development in the

Table 2 Summary of AMS' domestic response & safety measures

Safety measures	Countries									
	BRN	KHM	IDN	LAO	MYS	MMR	PHL	SGP	THA	VNM
Cancellation of major events	✓	✓	✓	✓	✓	✓	✓	✓	✓	✓
Lockdowns & curfews	–		✓	✓	✓	✓	✓	✓	✓	✓
Closure of schools & public places	✓		✓	✓	✓	✓	✓	✓	✓	✓
Restriction of movements	–	–	✓	–	✓	–	✓	✓	✓	✓
Contact tracing	✓	–	–	–	✓	–	✓	✓	✓	✓
International travel control	✓	–	✓	✓	✓	–	✓	✓	✓	✓
Public info campaign	✓	–	✓	✓	✓	–	✓	✓	✓	✓
Stimulus package	✓	✓	✓	✓	✓	✓	✓	✓	✓	✓
Wage support	✓	✓	✓	✓	✓	✓	✓	✓	✓	✓

Source Authors' own creation

case under investigation (Bowen 2009). Particularly, documents related to Covid-19 and its economic and financial impacts in AMS and existing literature is reviewed to provide solutions to combat the pandemic. Firstly, this study considered reports from the World Bank, IMF and OECD to outline the economic impacts of Covid-19 in AMS to develop the background information for the case under investigation. Secondly, policy documents of the World Health Organization (WHO), United Nations Economic and Social Commission for Asia and the Pacific (UNESCAP) and ASEAN were considered to propose the relevant policies to minimize the economic and financial shocks in AMS.

4 Findings and Discussion

4.1 Economic Risks of Covid-19 in ASEAN

The great challenges posed by the Covid-19 outbreak have brought the global economies to nearly a standstill which creates a high uncertainty in the economic integration across all ASEAN economies. Center for Strategic and International Studies' report projected a sharp economic downturn of ASEAN economies on a par with or even greater than the Asian Financial Crises in 1997–98. (CSIS 2020) IMF economic outlook released in April 2020 forecasted the growth of 5 ASEAN economies by -0.6% in 2020 (International Monetary Fund (IMF) 2020) whereas, the World Bank projected a negative GDP growth between −0.5 to −5.0% of 3 member states (except Singapore) in 2020 (The World Bank 2020). The optimistic scenarios (discovery of medical interventions) projected strong economic growth in ASEAN in 2021 yet, the future is highly uncertain as the case scenario studies found that economic outputs may fall more than 15% year on year in 2020 Q4 (OECD 2020a). The structural characteristics of the ASEAN region render it more vulnerable to exposure to the shocks of Covid-19 (OECD 2020a). Some of the economic fallouts of Covid-19 pandemic in ASEAN are as follows.

4.2 GDP Growth Downturn

IMF economic outlook projected that Asia and the Pacific to experience zero growth in 2020 which is a worse growth performance in over 60 years (Crisis Like No Other and Recovery 2020). These estimations are based on the fact that AMS are yet to develop immunity against the Covid-19 pandemic, by the the imposition of stringent domestic containment measures by the governments. The safety measures such as cancellation of large-scale events, suspension of flights, closure of schools, restaurants, and restriction of movements have negatively affected almost every sector of the economy. A few ASEAN countries have already started to ease lockdowns and curfews in phases however, the uncertainties associated with this pandemic are an obstacle to fully initiate the economic activities and recovery process. A projection of GDP growth before the start of the Covid-19 outbreak and during the pandemic presented in Table 3 compares and explains the pandemic effects on the GDP growth in ASEAN.

The table shows that before the start of the pandemic outbreak GDP growth in ASEAN was projected to increase by 4.9% on average between 2020 and24. However, the emergence of Covid-19 resulted in revised forecasts indicating that the growth prospects have severely deteriorated (Policy and Brief 2020). Even though a few ASEAN states have curtailed the spread of infection, yet, the GDP growth projections are negative which is perhaps due to the

Table 3 A comparison of AMS GDP growth before and during Covid-19

Country	Before Covid-19 outbreak		During Covid-19 outbreak		Source
BRN	1.5%	Sep 2019	2.0%	3 Apr 2020	ADB
KHM	6.8%	Sep 2019	2.3%	3 Apr 2020	ADB
IDN	5.3%	Official target, Aug 2019	−0.4% to 2.3%	1 Apr 2020	MOF
LAO	6.2%	Sep 2019	3.5%	3 Apr 2020	ADB
MYS	4.8%	Official target	3.2 to 4.2%, −2.0 to 0.5%	Feb 2020-April 3, 2020	MOF, BNM
MMR	6.8%	Sep 2019	4.2%	3 Apr 2020	ADB
PHL	6.5 to 7.5%	Official target	−0.6 to 4.3%	19 Mar 2020	NEDA
SGP	0.5 to 2.5%	Nov 2019	−4 to −1%	26 Mar 2020	MOTI
THA	2.8%	Dec 2019	−5.3%	8 Apr 2020	BOT
VNM	6.8%	–	6.09–6.27%	9 March 2020	MOPI

Source ASEAN policy brief, 2020

combination of factors such as plunge in oil prices resulting in pressure on asset prices of both equity and fixed income markets, countries' interdependence on trade and investments, informal economic nature of the most of ASEAN states, lack of a social protection system and most of the revenue-generating sectors in ASEAN are heavily affected due to Covid-19.

4.3 Trade, Tourism and Production Disruption

The socio-economic impacts of Covid-19 shocks have heavily affected the performance of the trade, tourism, and production sector. The restriction of movements imposed resulted in disrupted supply chains, a decline in demand for goods, and limited flow of trade and investment. China is the biggest trade partner and investor in AMS as it holds 17.1% share in cumulative trade and contributes 6.5% foreign direct investments. Similarly, other Covid-19 hard-hit countries such as the US and EU are also key strategic and investors in the region. According to World Trade Organization, global trade will plummet by 13% to 32% in 2020 which means a significantly low trade and flow of investments in ASEAN (World Trade Organization (WTO) 2020). Moreover, there is a fear that the trade is likely to fall in the countries dependent on complex value chains. An overview of AMS' trade volume with its global partners is presented in Table 4.

The spread of Covid-19 infection in ASEAN lead to the suspension of flights to and from China which negatively influenced the economies of all member states as the Chinese tourists account for 20% of inbound tourists in 8 AMS (OECD 2020a). Travel and tourism are significant contributors to the ASEAN economy which is about 12.6% in 2018. Among all AMS, Cambodia, Philippines, and Thailand are the most vulnerable states as these sectors largely contribute to the GDP, employment, and export revenue. The temporary closure of businesses, schools, and cancellation of all major events to necessitate social distancing declined the demand for goods and many firms hesitated to increase their production capacity.

4.4 Covid-19 Impact on MSMEs Business

Most of the government stimulus packages provide support for the businesses during Covid-19 however, the pandemic shocks have exerted a steep pressure on their balance sheets as many businesses are already loaded with debt due to slow economic progress (BIS 2019). Businesses are doubtful about their survival due to the current duration of the Covid-19 crises for instance, in the UK five out of six businesses reported that the current crises have created high uncertainty about their existence (European Commission 2020). This will result in businesses scrambling for bankruptcy which will start a chain motion of new bankruptcies due to a decline in demand and supply of goods and services from the suppliers. Especially, ASEAN economies have a large number of micro, small and medium enterprises (MSMEs) that are in need of economic support to cushion their survival during the current economic downturn. MSMEs in ASEAN are more vulnerable to economic shocks as they have lower access to resources and information which is mandatory for their survival. While, there are many sectors affected due to pandemic outbreak, increasing risks of bankruptcy, SME worker's furlough and large-scale business and household loans will result in losses that will undermine confidence in the financial system.

Table 4 ASEAN share with global trade partners

Trade partners	Trade (US$ billion)			Share to ASEAN total, in %		
	Total trade	Export	Import	Total trade	Export	Import
ASEAN total	2,825.3	1,436.4	1,388.8	100.00	100.00	100.00
Intra-ASEAN	650.7	346.5	304.3	23.03	24.12	21.91
China	483.8	199.0	284.8	17.12	13.85	20.51
EU	160.9	127.3	9.17	10.20	11.20	288.2
US	263.0	160.3	102.7	9.31	11.16	7.40
Japan	231.7	114.8	116.9	8.20	7.99	8.42
Korea	161.5	60.5	101.0	5.72	4.21	7.27
Hong Kong, China	118.3	100.2	18.1	4.19	6.98	1.30
Chinese Taipei	117.4	39.7	77.6	4.15	2.77	5.59
India	81.1	50.7	30.3	2.87	3.53	2.18
Australia	66.2	39.2	27.0	2.34	2.73	1.94

Source ASEAN policy brief, 2020

4.5 Financial Markets Disruption

The imposed safety measures of lockdowns, curfews, restriction of movements, and closure of schools, restaurants, and other public hotspots amidst Covid-19 have enhanced the risk of businesses temporary or permanent closure. Financial markets across the world have become more volatile due to hesitation among investors which has resulted in intensive crises worse than the global financial crises. The pandemic effect on the financial sector can be mapped by the spread of infection around the globe, economies, fiscal and monetary response, and measures developed for the protection of the fragile banking system.

Foreign investments were already moderating in ASEAN even before the start of the pandemic which was a result of trade tension between the US and China. Foreign equity portfolio stock in ASEAN plunged by 25.1 in 2018 as the key investors such as the US and EU withdrew. The most affected Covid-19 countries such as the US and EU are the largest (38.4, 27.1%) equity holders in ASEAN. Similarly, these major investors also control the cumulative debt investment stock: US 22.2% and EU 30.6%. The growth of the debt portfolio was sluggish in 2018 as it merely showed 0.3% growth in 2018. The FDI stock grew from 4.9 to 15.2% in the year 2018 and again the major investment was done by US (14.1%) and EU (18.7%). The current pandemic continues to spread and affect the countries around the world which will result in tight global financing conditions. In January 2020 the global stock markets experienced a brief upbeat trend however, the stock markets were unable to stabilize due to pandemic outbreak.

The news of the pandemic across the globe plummeted global stock markets. US Dow Jones Industrial Average shed 2,999 points on 16 March even it left behind the 'Black Monday' stock market crash in 1987. The unprecedented uncertainties associated with the pandemic has resulted in rapid capital outflow which has depreciated foreign exchange markets. The spread of infection in ASEAN has wiped out the stock market values in Indonesia, the Philippines, Thailand, and Vietnam. In ASEAN, Vietnam experienced the largest drop of 29.3% as the stock shed 274.1 points, however, the downtrend was relatively controlled in Malaysia as the stock market declined by 11.8% from the initial outbreak to the spike of Covid-19 cases. In terms of exchange markets Thailand, Indonesia, and Singapore experienced the largest depreciation while Indonesia shows the worse depreciation of 19.8% among all AMS.

A review of macroeconomic fundamentals indicates that many AMS have significant (more than 30%) debt in proportion to GDPs which relies on reserves of foreign exchange. If the exchange rate continuously depreciates it will lead to an increase in debt payment and will increase the risk of debt sustainability. Indebtedness can also result due to hesitation and fear among foreign investors as these investors tend to invest in safe assets. The borrowing cost will increase if the credit rating continues to decrease however, for factors such as broad liquidity, the significant current account balance can safeguard the economies of the countries.

The government capacities to introduce the stimulus packages may be limited in AMS due to the disproportional fiscal deficit. AMS have set aside their fiscal deficit targets and have substantially increased their debt by borrowings to curtail Covid-19 spread, to allocate budget for the health sector and to cushion the economy amidst pandemic crises. This again will increase the issues of debt sustainability and risks of foreign exchange depreciation particularly, when these governments continuously tap foreign credit and capital markets. Finally, oil-exporting AMS economies are capped due to pandemic which alternatively has yielded a lack of demand and influx of oil supply in the global market resulting in a sharp decline in prices.

5 Conclusion

This study analyses the economic and financial impacts of the Covid-19 outbreak in ASEAN and provides regulatory and policy implications for the governments thriving to rebuild the domestic and regional economies. Our study indicates that the characteristics of ASEAN economies and the current situation of the Covid-19 pandemic poses significant impacts on the GDP growth, trade, tourism, supply chains, MSMEs, and financial markets. These risks can be mitigated provided ASEAN governments and regional banks to develop a comprehensive and holistic approach by bolstering regional response, effective mobilization of policy tools, maximiszng production capacities, preventing leaning supply chains, and switching to digital trade.

5.1 Policy Implications

Globally, millions of people are infected by the Covid-19 pandemic and it continues to claim lives and impose a direct impact on everyday life. Besides mortality affects the morbidity effects are significant, large, and perhaps irreversible. Some of the common impacts of Covid-19 are economic and productivity loss, breakage of the supply chain, workers' furlough, financial pressure on businesses, and household. Generally, it is narrated that the world has already entered into a recession hence, government interventions precisely need to cater to the most significant components of the economy at the regional and domestic level to ensure public safety, restore people's confidence, preserve financial stability and initiate the recovery process.

5.1.1 Bolster Regional Response

There is a high risk of pandemics like Covid-19 in the future but it is obscure and the intensity of future pandemics is unspecified. The experience from the current pandemic signifies the urgency of developing a comprehensive and holistic regional response mechanism. This response mechanism should extend beyond the implication of health and contemporarily resolve and mitigate the economic, business, and people risks. These response mechanisms need to cater to cross-sectoral, cross-pillar, and multidimensional solutions to minimize the impacts of the pandemic within the socio-economic structure and capacity of AMS. From an economic perspective, the developed response mechanism immediately needs to provide a pragmatic solution related to financial stability, macroeconomy, supply chain connections, production, and readiness to restore the economy once the pandemic subsides. In the face of current and future pandemics, ASEAN countries need to strengthen national and regional cooperation with the global community so that health authorities take every possible intervention to protect and upgrade and save the lives of people.

5.1.2 Effective Mobilization of Policy Tools

AMS need to ensure that it effectively mobilizs all of its macro-financial and structure tools as the economic risk of Covid-19 is being posed with unprecedented speed and magnitude. It is difficult at this stage to gauge the supply effects triggered due to lockdowns, curfews, and restriction of movements however, for economic sentiment it is mandatory to estimate the impacts and develop a strategy to resolve the demand issues through financial fiscal, structural and social tools. Therefore, a holistic approach is required to address the supply and demand issues through targeted support which will cushion economic impacts and social damage caused by Covid-19. Policymakers need to ensure that their policy tools are mobilized in an implicit manner which strengthens the social safety nets and helps in poverty alleviation. ASEAN countries have a significant population employed on daily wages which is most affected by lockdowns and restriction of movement measures. Hence, governments must ensure that all vulnerable communities are protected and supported through the mobilization of their policy tools.

5.1.3 Maximizing Production Capacities

As most of the AMS embark on the fourth phase of lockdowns and prepare to resume economic activities, policymakers are required to ensure that the firms start with a maximum production capacity so that economic and financial losses during the outbreak can be covered. The policymakers need to ensure that firms and businesses have sufficient support to resume their operations and their debts are postponed which will lessen their burden that will maximize their production capacity. Additionally, preservation of production capacities will allow AMS to diversify production for export purposes which will develop resilience and it will also preserve an open competitive market environment. The preservation of production capacities will also allow firms to maintain their existence in the market and do not furlough its workers especially MSMEs.

5.1.4 Functional Supply Chains

The prolonged state of the current pandemic has strained the supply chains which will poise challenges to the food supplies for the agricultural businesses, processing plants, shipping industries and retailers involved in the import and export of essential medical equipment. ASEAN countries need to ensure that supply chains are free from bureaucratic and taxation hurdles so that supply chains remain functional and firms continue to yield the maximum output. AMS need to review their trade and taxation protocols to create a conducive environment for the flow of essential supplies and to warrant a proportional balance between demand and supply.

5.1.5 Switch to Digital Trade

While the future remains highly uncertain about pandemic subsiding, ASEAN countries need to leverage digital trade to resume the economic frontiers. Switching to digital platforms will help these countries in mitigating existing and future production losses and will provide an opportunity to learn to work in a remote environment. Social networks are a potential beneficiary of digital trade as the escalating fear among the public to get affected by virus had shunned consumers away from physical stores and crowded places. AMS need to address digital trade divide at the regional and domestic level on an urgent basis and enhance cybersecurity to grab the low hanging fruits of digital trade.

5.1.6 Financial Implications

The world is facing the worst health crises after a century that signifies that government and regulators support to uphold the economies. Additionally, financial agencies such as IMF, The World Bank, and Asian Development Bank (ADB) are the driving forces to sustain the ASEAN economy. Especially, banks need to have sufficient capital and buffers to absorb the economic shocks and provide contemporary support for the various stimulus initiatives focused on the welfare of the community. It is impossible at this stage of the pandemic to generalize the actual impacts on the community however, banks need to play their role in the smooth transmission of stimulus measures to the economy. Almost all ASEAN governments have addressed the immediate need of marginalized communities and vulnerable sectors and declared the financial assistance yet, the banks hold responsibility in ensuring access to these facilities.

Firstly, banks need to design a response strategy based on immediate, reboot and react, and adoption to the new world to cater to the needs of governments, investors, and its customers. Secondly, banks should leverage pandemic as an opportunity to fast forward their strategy focused on crisis management, operational efficiency, customer protection, and review of the business model. This will help to dvelop resilience in the financial sector and potentially contribute to the management of current crises. Lastly, financial sector players such as banks can play their role in the efficient transmission of money across banks and real economies which will help ASEAN governments to widen their fiscal monetary policies and provide support for businesses.

References

Anderson RM, Heesterbeek H, Klinkenberg D, Hollingsworth TD (2020) How will country-based mitigation measures influence the course of the COVID-19 epidemic? Lancet 395(10228):931–934

ASEAN Policy Brief (2020) Economic impact of COVID-19 outbreak on ASEAN. https://asean.org/storage/2020/04/ASEAN-Policy-Brief-April-2020_FINAL.pdf

ASEC (2020) ASEAN policy brief: economic impact of COVID-19 outbreak on ASEAN. ASEAN Secretariat, Jakarta. https://asean.org/storage/2020/04/ASEAN-Policy-BriefApril-2020_FINAL.pdf

Asian Development Bank (2020) Asian development outlook (ADO) 2020: what drives innovation in Asia? https://www.adb.org/publications/asian-development-outlook-2020-innovation-asia

Association of Southeast Asian Nations (ASEAN) (2020) About ASEAN. https://asean.org/asean/aboutasean/overview/

BIS (2019) Annual economic report: June 2019. Bank for International Settlements, Basel. https://www.bis.org/publ/arpdf/ar2019e.pdf

Bloomberg (2020) S&P 500 erases June losses after record home sales: market wrap. https://www.bloomberg.com/news/articles/2020-06-28/asian-stocks-to-decline-yen-edges-higher-markets-wrap. Accessed 10 July 2020

Bowen GA (2009) Document analysis as a qualitative research method. Qual Res J 9(2):27–40

Bretschneider P, Cirilli S, Jones T, Lynch S, Wilson N (2017) Document review as a qualitative research data collection method for teacher research. Sage Res Metho Cases

Center for Strategic and International Studies, (CSIS) (2020) The economic toll of Covid-19 on Southeast Asia: recession looms as growth prospects dim. https://www.csis.org/analysis/economic-toll-covid-19-southeast-asiarecession-looms-growth-prospects-dim

Ernst & Young (2020) How banks respond to the pandemic will define tomorrow's winners. https://assets.ey.com/content/dam/ey-sites/ey-com/en_sg/topics/covid-19-financial-services/how-banks-can-prepare-for-the-post-covid-19-reboot/ey-steps-banks-need-to-consider-now-to-prepare-themselves-for-the-post-covid-19-reboot-and-adapt.pdf?download. Accessed 31 July 2020.

European Commission (2020) Business and consumer surveys. https://ec.europa.eu/info/business-economy-euro/indicators-statistics/economicdatabases/business-and-consumer-surveys_en

Ferguson NM, Laydon D, Nedjati-Gelani G, Imai N, Ghani AC (2020) Impact of non-pharmaceutical interventions (NPIs) to reduce COVID-19 mortality and healthcare demand. https://www.imperial.ac.uk/media/imperial-college/medicine/sph/ide/gida-fellowships/Imperial-College-COVID19-NPI-modelling-16-03-2020.pdf

Financial Times (2020) Pandemic is causing the biggest disruption in decades to economies across the world. https://www.ft.com/content/e5879009-f451-4a54-9374-03472f2c4085

International Monetary Fund (IMF) (2020) World economic outlook, April 2020: The great lockdown. https://www.imf.org/en/Publications/WEO/Issues/2020/04/14/weo-april-2020

International Monetary Fund (IMF) (2020) IMF data mapper: Real GDP growth. https://www.imf.org/external/datamapper/NGDP_RPCH@WEO/OEMDC/ADVEC/WEOWOD

International Monetary Fund (IMF) (2020) World economic outlook update, June 2020-a crisis like no other, an uncertain recovery. https://www.imf.org/en/Publications/WEO/Issues/2020/06/24/WEOUpdateJune2020

Jorda O, Singh SR, Taylor AM (2020) Long run economic consequences of pandemics. Federal Reserve Bank of San Francisco. Working Paper 2020–09. https://www.frbsf.org/economic-research/files/wp2020-09.pdf

KPMG (2020a) Brunei Darussalam government and institution measures in response to COVID-19. https://home.kpmg/xx/en/home/insights/2020/04/brunei-darussalam-government-and-institution-measures-in-response-to-covid.html

KPMG (2020b) Government and institution measures in response to COVID-19-Cambodia. https://home.kpmg/xx/en/home/insights/2020/04/cambodia-government-and-institution-measures-in-response-to-covid.html

KPMG (2020c) Government and institution measures in response to COVID-19-Lao PDR. https://home.kpmg/xx/en/home/insights/2020/04/lao-pdr-government-and-institution-measures-in-response-to-covid.html

KPMG (2020d) Government and institution measures in response to COVID-19-Malaysia. https://home.kpmg/xx/en/home/insights/2020/04/Malaysia-government-and-institution-measures-in-response-to-covid.html

KPMG (2020e) Government and institution measures in response to COVID-19-Myanmar. https://home.kpmg/xx/en/home/insights/2020/04/Mynmar-government-and-institution-measures-in-response-to-covid.html

KPMG (2020f) Government and institution measures in response to COVID-19-Philippines. https://home.kpmg/xx/en/home/insights/2020/04/Philippines-government-and-institution-measures-in-response-to-covid.html

KPMG (2020g) Government and institution measures in response to COVID-19-Singapore. https://home.kpmg/xx/en/home/insights/2020/04/Singapore-government-and-institution-measures-in-response-to-covid.html

KPMG (2020h) Government and institution measures in response to COVID-19-Thailand. https://home.kpmg/xx/en/home/insights/2020/04/Thailand-government-and-institution-measures-in-response-to-covid.html

KPMG (2020i) Government and institution measures in response to COVID-19-Vietnam. https://home.kpmg/xx/en/home/insights/2020/04/Vietnam-government-and-institution-measures-in-response-to-covid.html

Martin, I (2020) Here's why the WHO thinks 'The Worst Is Yet to Come' from coronavirus. Forbes-30. https://www.forbes.com/sites/iainmartin/2020/06/30/heres-why-the-who-thinks-the-worst-is-yet-to-come-from-coronavirus/#45b381937c49

Mikic M, Puutio A, Gallagher J (2020) Healthcare products trade and external shocks: the US-China trade war and COVID-19 pandemic. ARTNeT Working Paper Series No 190. https://ssrn.com/abstract=3650972

Ministry of Finance and Economy (MOFE) (2020) Initiatives in combating the impact of COVID-19 to Brunei Darussalam's socio-economy. https://www.mofe.gov.bn/Lists/News/NewDispForm.aspx?ID=118

OECD (2020a) Enterprise policy responses to COVID-19 in ASEAN. https://asean.org/storage/2012/05/Policy-Insight-Enterprise-Policy-Responses-to-COVID-19-in-ASEAN-June-2020.pdf

OECD (2020b) COVID-19 crisis response in ASEAN member states. http://www.oecd.org/coronavirus/policy-responses/covid-19-crisis-response-in-asean-member-states-02f828a2/

The Economist (2020) The 90% economy that lockdowns will leave behind. https://www.economist.com/briefing/2020/04/30/the-90-economy-that-lockdowns-will-leave-behind

The World Bank (2020) The global economic outlook during the COVID-19 pandemic: a changed world. https://www.worldbank.org/en/news/feature/2020/06/08/the-global-economic-outlook-during-the-covid-19-pandemic-a-changed-world.

The World Bank (2020) World bank East Asia and pacific economic update, April 2020: East Asia and pacific in the time of COVID-19. World Bank, Washington D.C. https://openknowledge.worldbank.org/handle/10986/33477

World Health Organization (WHO) (2020) WHO coronavirus disease (COVID-19) dashboard-situation by WHO region. Retrieved from https://covid19.who.int/

World Health Organization (WHO) (2020) WHO calls for urgent, aggressive actions to combat COVID-19, as cases soar in South-East Asia region, Press release-17 March 2020. https://www.who.int/southeastasia/news/detail/17-03-2020-who-calls-for-urgent-aggressive-actions-to-combat-covid-19-as-cases-soar-in-south-east-asia-region

World Health Organization (WHO) (2020) Rolling updates on coronavirus disease (COVID-19). https://www.who.int/emergencies/diseases/novel-coronavirus-2019/events-as-they-happen

World Trade Organization (WTO) (2020) Trade set to plunge as COVID-19 pandemic upends global economy. https://www.wto.org/english/news_e/pres20_e/pr855_e.pdf

Behaviour of Islamic and Socially Responsible Indices in Crisis Period (COVID19): Case of Emerging Markets

Oussama Ennajar and Soufiane Lagsir

Abstract

The COVID-19 was an unexpected health crisis that propagated into several countries as a result of globalization, where it was quickly transmitted to the stock markets by decreasing value, and the same thing was observed since the 2007–2008 subprime crisis. These crises are without doubt part of the undesirable effects of the stock markets since they negatively impact their behaviour, although the developed markets are less affected than emerging markets by the effects of crises reflecting on their growth, and in our case study (COVID19) health crise. It's in this context that during this period several indices that attempt to replicate the performance of a market move downwards as well as upwards, hence the need to understand this behaviour in particular during this period. As traditional indices, ethical indices appeared in the 1980s and developed until the 1990s, where they are defined as a subset of their traditional benchmarks after going through a filtering process and constitute a separate investment area offering investors investment opportunities in line with their personal convictions and strategic orientations; These indices have been the subject of a few studies on their behaviour in the period of crisis, particularly in a developed country context. This article, therefore proposes to analyse the behaviour of ethical indices both socially responsible and Islamic in times of health crisis (COVID19) in a context of emerging countries from two different regions, Africa and Asia by reviewing their context, via their filtering criteria and an in-depth graphical analysis. Our results show that there is a highl correlation between these indices and the absence of a difference in performance in times of crisis.

Keywords

Socially responsible index · Islamic index · Screening · Financial market · Sustainable finance · Covid-19

1 Introduction

The reference to ethics is becoming more popular than ever because of the succession of financial crises. Indeed, finance itself is at least due to the multiplicity of unethical financial practices, it is in this context that ethical finance responds to the ethical character of finance through the regulation of the allocation of savings based on social, economic, moral and governance guidelines etc.

Ethical finance does not have a universal definition, the majority of definitions are complementary (El khamlichi 2012). According to (Spiteri 1993) ethics is of a general nature and morality is more individual. Ethical finance can be socially responsible, manifested by socially responsible investment as the most dominant form or morally responsible (Ghoul and Karam 2007), and in the case of Islamic finance, the latter has similarities with socially responsible investment (Novethic 2009) in terms of filtering and selection criteria.

In view of ensuring the sustainable and efficient functioning of stock markets, good ethical behaviour on the part of market players is essential in this respect, indeed financial engineering has enabled several stock exchanges to make available a range of products and services that meet the demand of ethically minded investors. The case of

O. Ennajar (✉)
University of Chouaib Doukkali, El Jadida, Morocco
e-mail: oussama.ennajar@gmail.com

S. Lagsir
University of Hassan II, Casablanca, Morocco

A. Salman and A. Tharwat (eds.), *Smart Designs for Business Innovation*,
Advances in Science, Technology & Innovation, https://doi.org/10.1007/978-3-031-49313-3_7

socially responsible and Islamic stock market indices is the subject of this paper.

Since their launch in the 1980s, these indices have been the subject of several studies, the first work focuses on the feasibility and functioning of these indices and then extended to their financial and extra-financial performance. This remains a debate that has not yet been resolved. Few studies have focused on the behaviour of ethical indices in a context of crisis where the majority of them have been in developed countries and these are all the interest of this study that comes manifested by the ethical commitment of emerging scholarships by studying the behaviour of ethical indices in a context of emerging countries since they are the most affected by the crisis.

South Africa and Malaysia are one of the emerging markets that have socially responsible and Islamic indices with different approaches of selection and filtering. We try in the following to study the behaviour of these indices in times of health crisis such as COVID19 as the research question, with the hypothesis if there is a significant impact on the behaviour of these indices or not during this period?

The remainder of this paper will be structured as follows. The first section presents literature review and the previous studies related to SRI research and Islamic indices, then the second section will analyse the behaviour of these indices in health crises context and the data. The next section elaborates on the methodology used followed by the result and the discussion. Finally, conclusion and recommendation for future research are discussed.

2 Socially Responsible Indices

The successive crises have provided an opportunity to review investment practices, which is obvious given the performance of the stock markets. This can be seen in the case of socially responsible practices developed in recent years and are considered as an important factor for the development of the financial market. As well as this plan is made explicit in the corporate social responsibility, allowing a strategic choice for the company to raise capital within a framework of responsible practices, or for the socially responsible investor's aims to generate social impact through an investment selection process based on compliance with ESG standards. Therefore, the commitment is reflecting the willingness of these actors to change the world view towards sustainability. This concept began to take off since the publication of the Brundtland report (1987) who used the definition of "sustainable development", as "development which meets the needs of the present without compromising the capacity of future generations to meet their own needs". It was reinforced by the holding of other events such as the Conferences of the Parties (COP), climate summits (the most recent were held in Paris 2015, Marrakech 2016, Bonn 2017, Katowice 2018, Chile 2019), the RIO summit etc., and all these events contribute to the reinforcement of respectful practices.

Looking for the interest in ethical practices growing, financial markets are no exception in order to satisfy all stakeholders, where the main goal is to create an environment of trust that allows for good behaviour by market players. In recent years several stock exchanges have set up their socially responsible indices in order to meet the demand of ethical investors, the use of these indexes allows calculating the performance of market or the performance of a share that meet ESG (environment, social, governance) criteria.

In this regard stock market index can be defined as an indicator that makes it possible to measure the evolution over time of the performance of a stock market, a sector of activity, or a sampled portfolio (Topsacalian 2000, p. 54). In the literature review there are two principal types of index:

- A broad index is an index that represents all economic sectors in a market. This sign allows managers to make sector forecasts in order to judge performance,
- A narrow index is calculated from the floating capitalization; it includes the most active stocks in the market selected on the basis of several criteria such as liquidity, etc. This indicator is perfectly suited to portfolio management.

Stock market indices help investors to judge the performance of the stock market, where they are calculated by four technical of weighting:

- Price weighting: its method of calculating the arithmetic average of prices, which means that securities have a low value and a low impact on the index and vice versa.
- Equal weighting: its method of calculating the average percentage change in listed financial securities. The example of the S&P 500 can be given, which is an equally weighted index in the United States.
- Market capitalization: most indices are capitalization-weighted; the capitalization of security its market value defined by the company's weighting in the market
- Float weighting: used by the main international stock exchanges, the calculation of the floating market capitalization takes only the securities available in a market. For example, the CAC 40 in France.

These methods are also a way to compare each index with the others, and it could sometimes give opposite results due to several parameters, like the calculation method chosen, the representativeness of the sample, the specificity of each market, etc. There are other methods that allow evaluating the performance like Sharpe ratios, Treynor and Jensen's alpha, which also have certain limitations, such as distributions of returns that can deviate from the normal law or the variability of betas (Grinblatt and Titman 1989).

However, in their conception the classic index differs from an ethical index, which is obtained after filtering a conventional index on the basis of criteria defined by rating agencies that meet ethical principles. These criteria are generally defined on the basis of extra-financial selection that differs from one rating agency to another. This is due to the lack of standardization of ethical stock market indices Pérez-Calderón et al. (2012) or the fact of the legitimacy of these agencies.

In the history ethical indexes appeared in parallel with social rating agencies, where the first index was the Domini 400 social index (DSI) proposed by the KLD agency, then other indexes appeared during the 1980s such as the FTSE4Good, ASPI proposed by the Viego agency, or the Dow Jones Sustainability Group Index (DJSGI). The literature of ethical indexes remains mixed given the recent nature of these indices, but the subject is beginning to gain momentum in the face of ethically conscious investors, who question the model of Western financial capitalism, which assumes that the creation of shareholder value is the only performance criteria. Indeed, these investors are interested in financial performance but more specifically in ethics.

2.1 The Performance of SR Stock Market Indices in the Literature

A few studies have focused on the performance of ethical indices (Fowler and Hope 2007), however, most of the studies analyse the financial performance of an SR index by comparing it with a traditional index which is a case of the studies below:

In the United States, Sauer (1997) compared the DSI400 index with two benchmarks, the S&P 500 and the CRSP, and concluded that there is no difference in performance between the two indices, which can be explained by the absence of the impact of ethical screening on performance. Then El Khmlichi (2019) conducted a study comparing the S&P 500 Environmental and Socially Responsible Index with its conventional index (S&P 500) using the daily quotations of the two indices for the period from September 2010 to March 2016, where the comparison showed that there is no significant difference in performance between the two indices.

In an attempt at an international study, the study by Hamid and Sandford (2002) focused on the analysis of European and American ethical indices. The study revealed constraints to the comparison, in particular the selection criteria that differ between these indices. The same comparison study was adopted by Saout (2005) when comparing the ethical indices of the Dow Jones family and those of FTSE4Good. He pointed out that the indices raise some differences in size, weighting, calculation method, and index construction, which makes comparison difficult. In addition, the authors Maux and Le Saout (2004) analyzed the performance of four ethical indices in the FTSE4good range and the DJSGI index over this period from 1 January 1997 to 1 December 2002 and concluded that their performances are equivalent to traditional indices and may in some cases outperform if the market is bullish and underperform if the market is bearish. They even noted that in the UK market the ethical index outperforms the FTSE 100 index.

A more exhaustive study was carried out by Vermeir and Friedrich (2006). They studied six socially responsible indices with their traditional counterparts during the period from 31/12/97 to 31/12/04: it's about the indices ASPI versus Stoxx Euro Index, ESIE versus MSCI Europe, ESIG versus MSCI Word, Dow Jones Sustainability Group Index versus Dow Jones Global Index, Domini Social Index versus S&P 500 and finally the FTSE4Good Europe versus FTSE Europe. The results indicate that four out of six indices outperform their benchmarks, and the return of socially responsible indices is statically not different from traditional indices but the risk is high. The authors state that the comparison of returns does not allow to define which part is allocated to profitability and which part is allocated to the financial style that is why they used the model of (French and Fama 2003); The authors conclude a positive sustainable effect on five out of the six sustainability indices and explain the difference in returns that they are not attributable to the CSR filter but to other elements of risk and style (small caps/large caps).

Besides the studies that have analyzed the performance and volatility are very rare testified by the study of Sudha (2015) who analyzes simultaneously the performance and volatility of the S&P ESG India index with two major market indices, namely the Nifty and the S&P CNX 500 using daily index data. The study indicates that while the daily compound returns of the ESG India Index are not statistically different from those of the Nifty or the CNX 500, the annualized returns of the ESG India Index were better than the returns of the other two indices.

In the context of the crisis El Khamlichi (2013) analyzed the behavior of stock market indices during the financial crisis, the choice of comparison was made on three SR stock market indices representing Europe, Canada and the United States by comparing them with their traditional counterparts during the period December 2007 to January 2010. The study concludes that the SR indices follow the same trend as the traditional indices in times of crisis, where the author's idea is similar to Saout 2005 which confirms that there is no difference in returns between these indices.

Ethical indexes can provide superior performance as they allow for the selection of companies according to inclusion criteria or even eliminate certain risks such as ESG risks.

All in all, more than thirty years later, the debate does not seem to be over yet on the under or over performance of socially responsible indices and seems very limited in a crisis context.

2.2 Presentation of Stock Market Indices Around the World

The growing share of the socially responsible investment has given rise to the concept of socially responsible indices, which is not recent but dates from the 1980s. This paragraph proposes to study the emergence and a sample of these ethical indices around the world.

United States

Ethical practices have increased significantly since the Second World War and the following events such as racial discrimination, the fight against child labor and lobbying against the arms and nuclear industries. It is in this context and in the early 1980s that the first ethical index (South Africa Safe Equity) appeared at the initiative of the Boston Bank in the United States due to the government's request that calls companies to stop the trade activities with South Africa on the way to purify their ethical investment portfolio a country known at the time of racial segregation against blacks. The appearance of rating agencies allowed the launch of the DOMINI 400, based on the classic S & P 500 index launched in May 1990 by the KLD agency, it is a capitalization-weighted index comprising 400 U.S. stocks of the top-performing companies in terms of sustainability and was in several years the only ethical index (Maux and Le Saout 2003), it is a benchmark for socially responsible investors. Sectors that are excluded are Tobacco, Alcohol, Weapons, Gambling and Nuclear… A new index appeared in June 2020 which is the Calvert US Responsible Core Responsible Index created by the management company Calvert Investments, based on positive and negative filtering. This index is a reference for measuring the performance of large socially responsible companies.

Europe

Socially responsible stock market indexes in Europe appeared at the end of the 1990s, and companies were selected on the basis of their positive results in sustainable development practices, the rating criteria of which differ from one rating agency to another. The review of the inclusion or exclusion of companies in these indexes is carried out either quarterly, annually or half-yearly, depending on the criteria of each rating agency.

The famous index in Europe is ASPI: (Advanced Sustainable Performance Indices) created in 2001 by the French agency viego, whose stock selection does not exclude any sector and uses a scoring system. ASPI is a benchmark index in Europe made up of 120 of the best performing stocks in the DOW Jones Euro Stoxx index according to sustainable development criteria.

Other Indices in a Context of Emerging Countries

As for emerging markets, the Casablanca Stock Exchange was the first stock exchange in the Maghreb region to reward the social commitment of the listed companies, by launching in 2018 a CSR index named ESG10 launched by the Viego rating agency. The index is composed of ten listed securities which represent more than 68% of the total capitalization of its benchmark index, MASI, and whose inclusion principles are set on the basis of ESG criteria. Next Turkish Stock Exchange also launched its BIST Sustainability Index in 2014 in cooperation with Ethical Investment Research Services Limited (EIRIS), which evaluates the companies listed on Borsa İstanbul on the basis of international sustainability criteria. In the same context of emerging markets, the Brazilian stock exchange has had its own ethical index since 2005 in collaboration with the Brazilian ethics agency FGV-EAESP, where the index is considered the first in Latin America. Adding also the South African stock exchange which also has its own ethical index in 2004, the Johannesburg stock exchange is the first emerging market in association with FTSE Russel to have formed in 2004 a series of socially responsible index FTSE/JSE SRI Index.

2.3 Screening Process

Socially responsible indices are subsets of investment universes (Le Saout 2005, p. 24) of their benchmark indices. Several selection methods exist in the constituents of these indices, where we present in the following a set of main methods going from the selection process to the filtering criteria used by the rating agencies.

The selection process or component of an ethical index starts with the universe by choosing a benchmark index, then the agency applies extra-financial criteria by excluding certain securities (if the filtering is negative). Agencies may also integrate market capitalisation criteria such as the DJSI Word or free float criteria such as the FTSE4GOOD.

The methods of screening are passive; they can be either positive, including thematic funds that focus on environmentally friendly sectors, or best-in-class approaches to select companies with the best ESG scores. They can also be negative; this technique is widely used by many funds in the United States and excludes sectors such as tobacco, alcohol, armament, etc., or combined between the two criteria positive and negative, giving the example of the American agency KLD or the British agency EIRIS. This approach makes it possible to obtain an overall financial and extra-financial performance.

Concerning the filtering processes are also subjective because of the lack of standardization between the rating agencies, one can find security that excludes in one market and present in another market and this comes back to the ethical vision of each agency and country.

In general, three principal approaches are identified:

- **Best in class**: consists in retaining the most convincing values of sector activities in terms of ethical behaviour that allow giving rise to a good degree of diversification as this approach does not exclude any sector that differs from sectoral or ESG approaches;
- **Best Effort**: This approach leads to focus on companies that demonstrate the best ESG efforts, it allows an objective development perspective to more efficient practices;
- **Best in universe**: This is a method of selecting the companies with the best ESG ratings, regardless of their sector of activity;

It is also noticeable that investors in their socially responsible investment processes use additional techniques known as normative exclusion based on international standards defined by international bodies such as the United Nations or combined with ESG factors.

The presence of security in an ethical index increases its visibility among investors, and its weight in a financial market becomes more important since it has gone through a filtering process that allows it to include an ethical index that is generally more concentrated than its benchmark index.

Talking about ethical indices refers to screening processes, the SR indexes focus on ESG criteria, but Islamic indices have more detailed rules in accordance with sharia principles. The following part will be devoted to literature of Islamic indices (Table 1).

Table 1 Methodologies employed by the major sustainability indices

Indices	Index tracked	Methodology
Calvert Group: The Calvert Social Index	Benchmark Index: None	Negative Screening Criteria: Excludes companies with bad environmental records and those operating in nuclear power, weapon, tobacco, alcohol or gambling
Dow Jones/SAM: Dow Jones Sustainability Index	Benchmark: Dow Jones Global Index	Positive Screening Criteria: Includes companies that score highest on a comprehensive list of sustainability criteria
Ethibel/S&P: Ethibel Sustainability Index	Benchmark Index: S&P Global 1200	Positive Screening Criteria: Evaluates companies according to four main criteria: internal social policy, environmental policy, external social policy, and ethical economic policy
FTSE FTSE4Good	Benchmark Index: Fortune 500	Mixed Screening Criteria: Excludes companies operating in: tobacco, nuclear systems, weapons systems and uranium. Includes companies based on qualitative judgments about: environmental sustainability, relations with stakeholders, and human rights
KLD Analytics: Domini 400 Social Index	Benchmark Index: Fortune 500	Negative Screening Criteria: Excludes companies operating in: weapons, alcohol, tobacco, nuclear power and gaming. Also excludes companies based on qualitative judgments about the environment, diversity, employee relations, and product
Viego: Advanced Sustainability Performance Indices	Benchmark Index: DJ EURO STOXXSM	Positive Screening Criteria: Rewards companies for introducing sustainability criteria

Source Fowler and Hope (2007)

3 Islamic Indices

Islamic finance is based on the laws of Islam, known as the principles of Sharia, which are considered the economic course of action for Muslims. The sources of Shariah can be found in the Qur'an, the Sunnah (the words and actions of the Prophet), the Ijmaa (consensus of Islamic scholars), the Qiyas (authenticated analogy), and the Ijtihad (rational intellectual efforts).

As was pointed out in the introduction of this part, five principles fundamental of Islamic finance are defined:

1. The prohibition of interest (riba) and usury: Allah said in the Coran "Allah has permitted trade and forbidden riba" (Surah Al Baqarah, verses 275–81)
2. The rule of profit and loss sharing: This principle finds its source in Hadith of our Prophet (ﷺ) in the Messenger of Allah said: "Profit follows responsibility".
3. The prohibition of Gharar and Maysir: futures, options and speculation, etc. …
4. Financial assets must be backed by a tangible asset (Asset Banking).
5. The prohibition of investing in illicit sectors (Haram).

As known Islam is one of the big important religion in the word with about 1.8 billion Muslims, Islam is focused on ethical practices with respect of sharia. The Islamic financial system is one of those and is composed of the Zakat, Waqf, Islamic banks, Islamic microfinance and Islamic capital market, represented by Islamic indices that constitute the universe of investment etc. These will be one of our paper subjects.

Establishing the context background, the emergence of Islamic banks around the world are the first system that initiates financial Islamic system, however the Islamic capital market was in an embryonic stage, but nowadays, the development of Islamic capital market becomes indispensable in order to meet the demand of investors who want to grow their capital without compromising their religious beliefs.

In this context the first Islamic fund was established in 1986s, however until 1990s Islamic jurisprudence allowed Muslims to invest their capital in "Shariah-compatible" funds (Peillex and Ureche-Rangau 2012). Though, Islamic stock market indices were launched for the first time in April 1998 considered as important factors that allow the development of Islamic capital markets. That's was extended to other Islamic indices like the creation of (Dar al Mal al-islami) DMI index, then, the American Bank Klein and Shrinea (Social Aware Muslim Index) SAMI, measure the financial performance of 500 Shariah compliant companies, as well as the Dow Jones Islamic index DJIMI created in 1999. Moreover the Global Islamic Index Series (GIIS) was launched by The FTSE, and Standard and Poor's which create the shariah Global Benchmark indices in 2006 as well. For the Eurozone and Europe, Stoxx Limited has launched a package of indices that are shariah compatible. Although the previous indices that had an international geographical coverage, some financial markets have introduced their own Islamic indices with a local focus (Amina Haoudi, Ayoub Rabhi).

3.1 The Performance of Islamic Stock Market Indices: A Literature Review

The literature review has shown that, a lot of researchers studied two major topics: the financial performance of Islamic funds and the performance of Islamic indices. These convergence items have contributed to enriching the literature on Islamic finance in general.

Also despite the difference in context and the methodologies used, several studies are interested in financial performance between Islamic and conventional indices, and most of them conclude that there is no significant financial performance between them. It seems to an prove that the Islamic screening process doesn't have any negative impact on the financial returns. The case of this study was first with Atta (2000), who tried to study the performance of the Dow Jones Islamic Market Index versus his conventional index using statistical and econometric methods between 1996 and 1999 as a result of his research he found that Islamic index outperformed the benchmark index, and outperformed the risk-free rate as well.

After that, more extensive research has been carried out by Hassan (2011) where he developed Atta's research by studying six Islamic indices of the Dow Jones family from 1996 to 2000. He analyzed empirically the issue of efficiency, as the evolution of risk/return ratio. In effect, he confirmed Atta's results, by using an econometric model (GARCH) then he concluded that DJIM is more efficient than the conventional index. Regarding the study of cointegration and efficiency of Islamic indices, it was found after analyzing nine indices "shariah-compatible" that there is an absence of cointegration, and argues that Islamic index is efficient as the conventional one, as well. It can provide a diversification opportunity for investors.

In the same research context, from the analysis of financial performance (DJIMI), the performance and volatility between Dow Jones Islamic Market Index (DJIMI), with DJ United States, DJ World, S&P 500 and MSCI World from 1996 to 1998 was compared. The Islamic index (DJIMI) is more rentable then the others indices, in contrast, it has the same level's volatility. This comparison shows that the Islamic index performance is highly correlated with the other indices, with statistically insignificant level of volatility.

Then the study of Hussein and Omran's (2005) was considered as original research is the fact of analyzing the performance of the DJIMI by introducing the effect of sector and size. The results suggest that Islamic indices outperform their conventional counterparts. The authors explain this outperformance by the composition of Islamic index, which is composed of a small-cap and low-indebtedness stock's companies.

As for emerging markets Abdullah et al. (2007) analyze the returns of Islamic and conventional Malaysian funds between 1995 and 2001. As well, they found that Islamic funds are less profitable than conventional ones. Indeed, they confirm the hypothesis that shariatic screening negatively impacts the level of diversification. The same opinion was confirmed by, Hayat (2006) who found in his study that the Malaysian Islamic funds were underperformers than the conventional ones, even statistically not being significant.

Recently, a few researchers have shown a neutral aspect, Hassan (2011) analyzed seven Islamic indices from Dow Jones[1] series between 1996 and 2005 and they conclude that there is no difference in returns of Islamic indices and their conventional benchmark. Also, in his article "performance of Islamic indices: a meta analyze", El khamlichi argue with other authors that Islamic indices are not of less performance than the conventional ones. The same idea was supported by El Bousty and Oubdi (2017), where they reported also that Islamic and conventional indices have the same level of volatility.

A more exhaustive study was carried out by Elfakhani et al. (2005) where they investigated the data from 46 funds (shariah compatible), between 1997 and 2002. Those funds were classified by sectors into eight categories. They measured and compared their performance with Islamic and conventional indices. They found constantly that there is no significant difference between the performance of Islamic funds and their benchmarks.

In crises context, Merdad et al. (2010) examined the performance of Islamic and conventional funds, using a various of risk-adjusted return's methods such as: Sharp ratio, Treynor and alpha of Jensen. Their results show that Islamic funds underperformed conventional funds during the "Full" period, in contrast they outperformed in the crisis period. Hussein's (2004) found the same results by examining the performance of the FTSE Global Islamic Index and FTSE All World Index. The return adjusted to risk of both indices seems equivalent, in addition, he analyzed the comportment of those indices in two different periods "Full" and "Bull", and concluded that the Islamic index underperforms the classic index in the crisis period, and conversely in the bullish.

By drawing on the following results, the conclusion that can be given is that Islamic funds provide hedging opportunities for investors in the crisis period, through restrictions that the shariah board imposes on the portfolio selection process (Firano et al. 2017).

3.2 Creation and Composition of the Islamic Index

Islamic indices are a subset of conventional indices after going through a screening process, and two kinds of screening are available: extra financial (qualitative or sectoral) and financial (quantitative) screening. For notice it's up only to Shariah scholars to carry out the screening of values in accordance with the Muslim law principles defined by the Shariah Board who are the Ulemas (scholars) with very specific theological, legal and financial knowledge, recognized internationally.

Qualitative Screening

First, companies which composed the origin index (conventional) must past through a sectoral screening or extra financial screening. The objective is to eliminate companies which are considered illicit by the Shariah board,[2] such as:

- Pig industry
- Defence and armament
- Tobacco
- Cinema and entertainment
- casinos/gambling
- Pornography
- Alcohol
- non-Islamic banking and financial services
- Insurance

According to this sectoral screening, three following cases are possible:

Firstly, companies with a main and secondary activity are completely legal. Second, companies whose activities are totally illegal and third, companies that operate in several sectors, some of which are legal and some of which are illegal. However, the integration or exclusion from the Islamic index for the last kind of companies don't make the

[1] Dow Jones Islamic Market World Developed Index, the Dow Jones Islamic Market World Emerging Markets Index, the Dow Jones Islamic Market U.S. Index, the Dow Jones Islamic Market Europe Index, the Dow Jones Islamic Market Asia/Pacific Index, the Dow Jones Islamic Market Canada Index, and the Dow Jones Islamic Market U.K. Index.

[2] Shariah board published a list of illicit sectors.

Table 2 Level of debts ratio: calculation method for the most popular Islamic Index

Index	Calculation method
DOW JONES ISLAMIQUE	$\frac{\text{Total Debts}}{\text{Average Market Capitalization(Trailing 24 month)}} < 33\%$
S&P SHARIAH	$\frac{\text{Total Debts}}{\text{Average Market Capitalization(Trailing 36 month)}} < 33\%$
MSCI ISLAMIC	$\frac{\text{Total Debts}}{\text{Total Assets}} < 33\%$
FTSE SHARIAH	$\frac{\text{Total Debts}}{\text{Total Assets}} < 33\%$
STOXX ISLAMIC	$\frac{\text{Total Debts}}{\text{Total Assets or Global Market Capitalization}} < 33\%$

Source Amar et al. (2017)

Table 3 Interest bearing debts ratio: calculation method for the most popular Islamic Index

Index	Calculation method
DOW JONES ISLAMIQUE	$\frac{\text{Total cash and interest-bearing securities}}{\text{Average Market Capitalization(Trailing 24 month)}} < 33\%$
S&P SHARIAH	$\frac{\text{Total cash and interest-bearing securities}}{\text{Average Market Capitalization(Trailing 36 month)}} < 33\%$
MSCI ISLAMIC	$\frac{\text{Total cash and interest-bearing securities}}{\text{Total Assets}} < 70\%$
FTSE SHARIAH	$\frac{\text{Total cash and interest-bearing securities}}{\text{Total Assets}} < 50\%$
STOXX ISLAMIC	$\frac{\text{Total cash and interest-bearing securities}}{\text{Total Assets or Global Market Capitalization}} < 33\%$

Source Amar et al. (2017)

Shariah Board unanimity (Khatkhatay and Nisar 2007). But some scholars prohibit investing in these companies, while others allow it on the condition that the return's weight of the illicit activity must not exceed 5% of the company's overall income.

Quantitative Screening

After passing from the sectoral screening, companies composed the Islamic index must pass at the second step of screening, and it's about a financial screening process. It includes those companies in the index according to their financial structures.

The financial screening uses a series of ratios and with respect to criteria helps integrate the Shariah compatible index.[3] The quantitative screens differ from one Islamic index to another and don't make the Shariah Board unanimity; they are only doors of tolerance. The screens are the level of debts, receivables and interest-bearing securities. Violation of one of these levels results in the company exclusion from the index.

- Level of debts Ratio:

It's the first financial screening that measures the company's level of indebtedness to ensure that it is moderately indebted with respect to the principle of interest's prohibition. This filter is expressed as a ratio of the following:

$$\text{Level of debts} = \frac{\text{Total Debts}}{\text{Average Market Capitalization}} < 33\%$$

This highlights that the holders of shares must purify their dividend by removing the interest-bearing. However, the part of these dividend must be donated to charity, but they are independent of Zakat's payment (Table 2).[4]

- Interest bearing debt Ratio:

This ratio makes investors ensure that a company's main assets are not predominantly cash or cash-related. If a company's main assets are cash based, trading of its shares is equivalent to trading of cash for cash. This will trigger the issue of riba' (interest) because, in trading currencies or cash, the Shariah rules of currency exchange (bay'al-sarf) should be observed. This filter is expressed as a ratio as follows (Table 3):

$$\text{Interest bearing debt} = \frac{\text{Total cash and interest-bearing securities}}{\text{Average Market Capitalization}} < 33\% \text{ at } 70\%$$

- Receivables Ratio:

To ensure that a company is not involved directly or indirectly in riba'-related activities that exceed the tolerable benchmark specified within the criterion. The riba'-related activities of a company can be in two forms: Investment and/or placement of cash in conventional or interest-based instruments; and acquiring funds from the capital market or banking sector through interest-based facilities. This filter is expressed as a ratio of the following (Table 4 and Fig. 1):

$$\text{Receivable Ratio} = \frac{\text{Total receivables}}{\text{Average Market Capitalization}} < 33\% \text{ at } 70\%$$

4 Analysis of the Behavior of Islamic and Socially Responsible Indices in Crisis Period COVID-19: Case of South Africa and Malaysia

We consider two ethical indices, both socially responsible and Islamic, from two emerging countries, South Africa and Malaysia. The study covers the period from the first

[3] Cited by Mohamed Lamine Mbengue, 2017.

[4] The Messenger of Allah said, "O people! Allah is Pure and, therefore, accepts only that which is pure" **Abu Hurairah.**

Table 4 Receivable ratio: calculation method for the most popular Islamic Index

Index	Calculation method
DOW JONES ISLAMIQUE	$\frac{\text{Total receivables}}{\text{Average Market Capitalization(Trailing 24 month)}} < 33\%$
S&P SHARIAH	$\frac{\text{Total receivables}}{\text{Average Market Capitalization(Trailing 36 month)}} < 49\%$
MSCI ISLAMIC	$\frac{\text{Total receivables}}{\text{Total Assets}} < 70\%$
FTSE SHARIAH	$\frac{\text{Total receivables}}{\text{Total Assets}} < 50\%$
STOXX ISLAMIC	Shariah board of STOXX ISLAMIC don't use this Ratio

Source Amar et al. (2017)

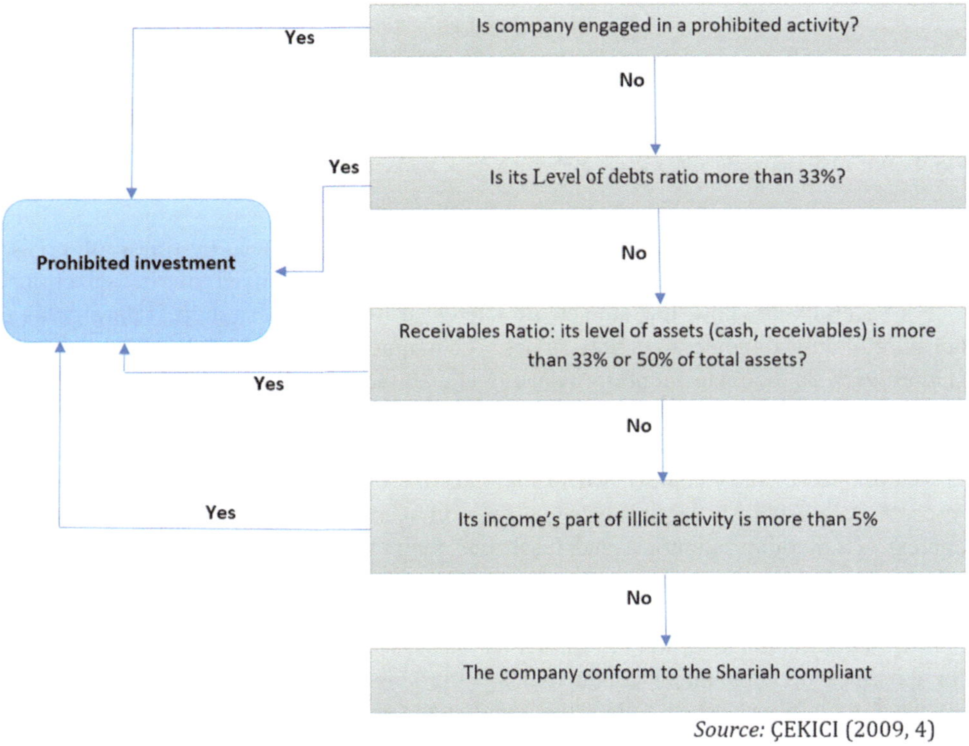

Fig. 1 Islamic index screening process

declaration of the COVID 19 pandemic discovered in Wuhan for the first time on December 31, 2019 (according to World Health Organization) until June 2020. The data come from the database of the two stock exchanges.

Then the choice was made to focus on two emerging countries that have two ethical indices on their stock exchanges at the same time in order to avoid any sector bias, which is the case of the indices below:

- Malaysia
  - FBM EMAS Shariah index regulated by the Shariah Advisory Board of the Securities and exchange Commission, where all securities must go through a screening process in accordance with Shariah principles. tTis index includes the components of the FTSE Small Cap Index and FTSE Bursa Malaysia TOP100 Index;
  - FTSE4GOOD BM Index measures the performance of companies that meet ESG standards
- South Africa:
  - The FTSE/JSE responsible investment Top 30 Index (J110) is an equally weighted index calculated on a real Time basis. It is tradable and comprises the Top 30 companies ranked by FTSE Russell ESG Rating;
  - The Shariah Top 40 (J140) Index is an index that includes the top 40 Shariah-compliant companies selected by Yasaar, its starting universe is the Top 40 Index (J200) and its weighting methodology is based on free float market capitalization weighted.

Fowler and Hope (2007) in their article "A Critical Review of Sustainable Business Indices and Their Impact" highlighted the methodological bias of comparison which reflects certain limitations such as differences in size, country and weighting in index comparisons, where the case for their study was the comparison of SR indices with their traditional counterpart, that is, tour study will follow the same approach for this reason. The focus of our study will be on

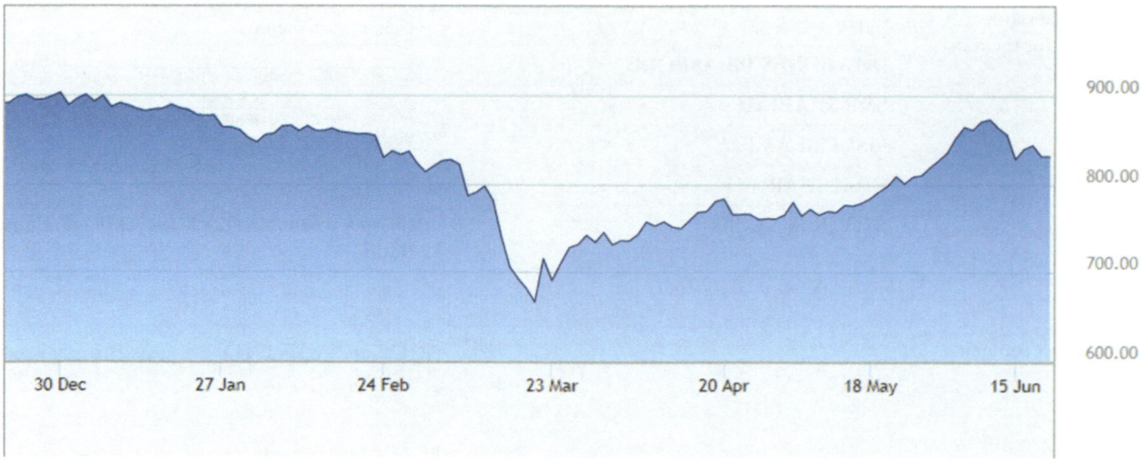

Fig. 2 Socially responsible index in the Malaysian stock market: FTSE 4GOOD

advanced graphical analysis to derive results on the behaviour of ethical indices in times of health crisis (COVID 19).

For several years now, few studies are interested on the behavior of ethical indices in context crises. The majority of studies work on the financial performance of ethical indices by comparing them with their benchmark, in particular the socially responsible index with its traditional counterparts in a developed country context, where the objective of our research is to establish the link between these indices in a context of emerging countries, and reach the comprehension of their behavior on crises context.

First of all, as we notice that the similarity between the ethical indices is the selection criteria based on the respect for the rules of good moral conduct, it is surprising that all the four indices chosen follow the same stock market behavior. as shown in the graphs below. All four graphs are in "v" format, with a sharp decline in the first quarter of 2020 to a point of bearish reflection. in the month of MARCH followed by an increase in the second quarter.

South Africa J140 index and J110 index are highly correlated, and achieve the same performances; we can therefore deduce neither under performance or overperformance. As for the indices listed on the stock exchange of the Malaysia FBM EMAS Shariah and FTSE4GOOD BM indices in the same way the behaviour of these indices is not different than the South African indices.

We can deduce that the impact of the selection criteria has not an impact on the financial performance of these indices, also the results show that the behavior of ethical indices is the same as their counterpart traditional, as well as they are following the same market trends. This indicates that ethical indices don't ensure protection against market downturns in times of crisis.

To conclude, our results have contributed to enriching the literature based on the subject of the behavior of ethical indices, especially socially responsible and Islamic ones, in times of crisis. We have also highlighted the impact of the selection criteria and the performance of these indices during this period. The academic approach or methodology used is supposed to be a more rigorous investigation (Figs. 2, 3, 4, 5, 6 and 7).

5 Conclusion

Ethical indices both socially responsible and Islamic indices, are a subset of conventional ones after going through a screening process, two kinds of screening are available: extra financial (qualitative or sectoral) and financial (quantitative) screening, defined by a sharia board in accordance with the Muslim law principles for Islamic index, also for the socially responsible index the screening process is defined by the rating agency in accordance with ethical principles known as ESG standards, this criteria differs from one agency to one other depending on the specificity of each country, religion…. Therefore, the convergence point of these indices is the screening process where it reduces the investment universe, and according to modern portfolio theory (Markowitz 1952), the lack of diversification may also penalize their performance.

In a context of health crisis COVID 19 announced by International Health Organization in December 2020 as a global pandemic, a financial crisis has been triggered in both developed and emerging countries. This crisis appears two months later in the financial markets of emerging countries and is characterized by a massive deterioration of market indices. Our study was about analyzing the behavior of ethical stock market indices during this period of crisis.

The objective of this paper is to analyse the behaviour of socially responsible and Islamic indices in two emerging country contexts during the crisis period of COVID-19. We perform a selection of stock market indices that meet

Fig. 3 Islamic index in the Malaysian Stock Market: FBM EMAS Shariah

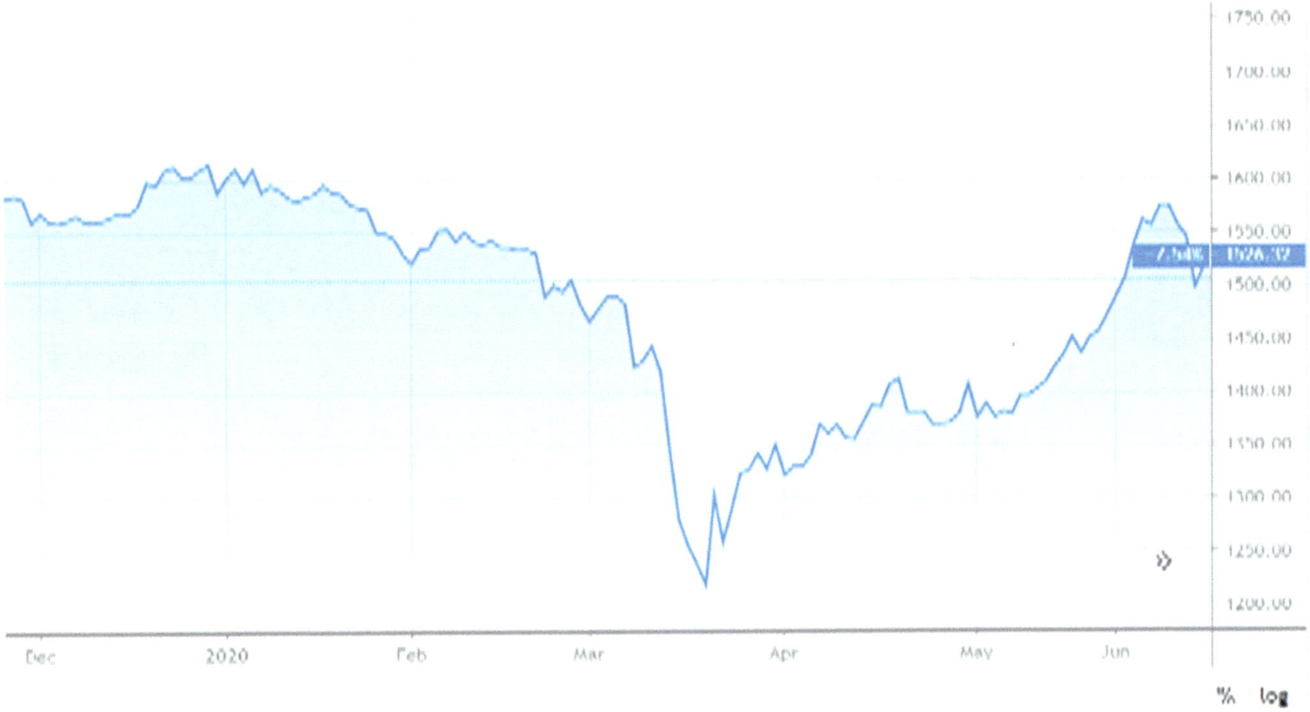

Fig. 4 Malaysian stock market index: KLSE

Islamic principles and SRI criteria known as ESG, the choice was reported to FTSE 4GOOD and FBM EMAS SHARIAH in the Malaysian market as J1140 and J110 in the South African stock market, the main goal is to compare these indices each other as well as with their benchmark. From the graph of the indices we use technical analysis as the method, where it can be concluded as follows: Islamic and socially responsible indices are highly correlated and they're following the same trend of their market as "V" form with a sharp decline in the first quarter of 2020 to a point of bearish reflection. in the month of MARCH followed by an increase in the second quarter of 2020.

The results of this research support the idea that there is no significant difference in the performance of ethical indices as well as compared with the conventional one, Therefore the investors will not scarify about a part of returns on their portfolio investment due to the screening process as a fact. Whilst this study did not confirm the idea

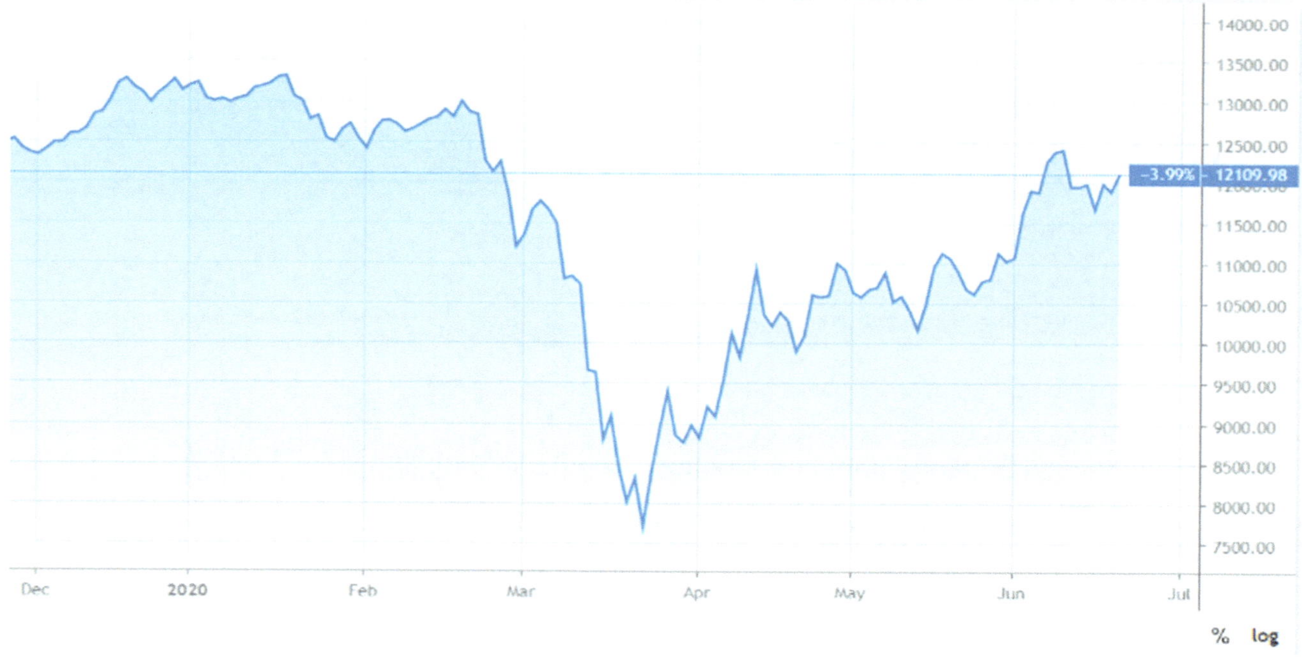

Fig. 5 Socially responsible index in the South African stock market: J110

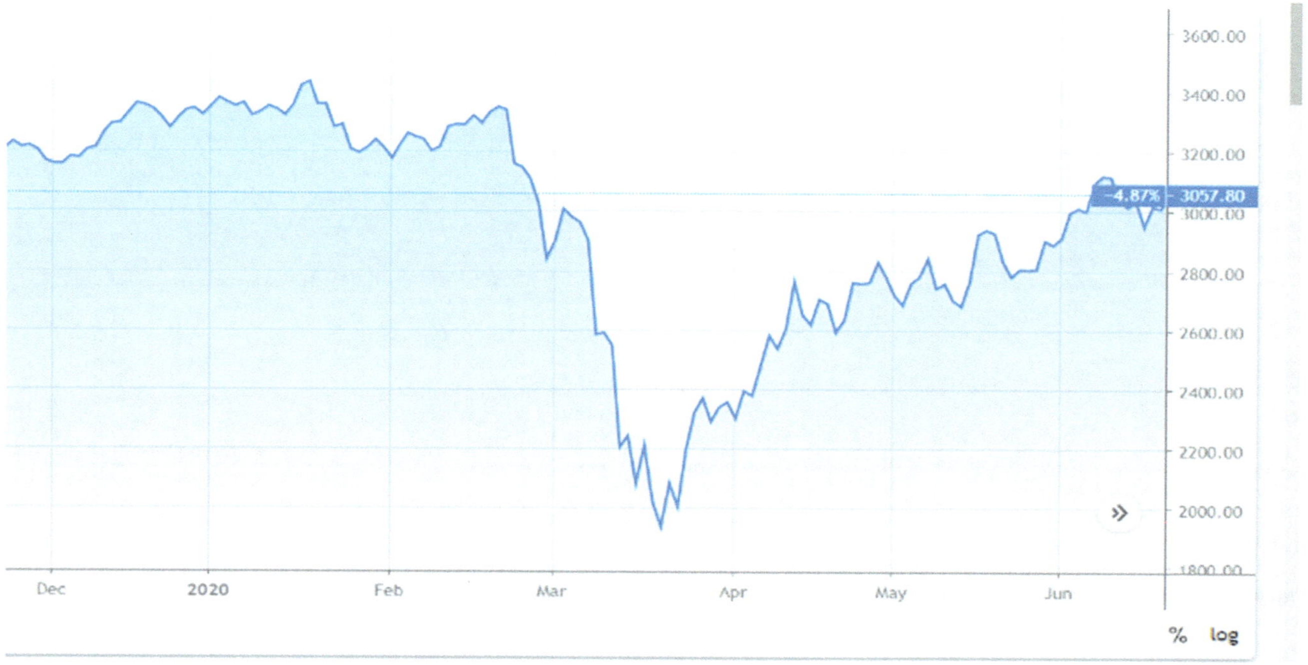

Fig. 6 Islamic index in the South African stock market: J140

about ethical indices underperform or outperform in the crisis period, but it has shown, however, that investors can invest in ethical products rather than conventional products even in times of crisis in order to meet their own personal convictions. For further research, we recommend that this study will be extended to other emerging markets with a use of others approach.

References

Abderrezak F (2008) The performance of Islamic equity funds: a comparison to conventional, Islamic and ethical benchmarks. Thèse, université de Maastricht

Abdullah F, Hassan T, Mohamad S (2007) Investigation of performance of Malaysian Islamic unit trust funds: comparison with conventional unit trust funds. Managerial Finance

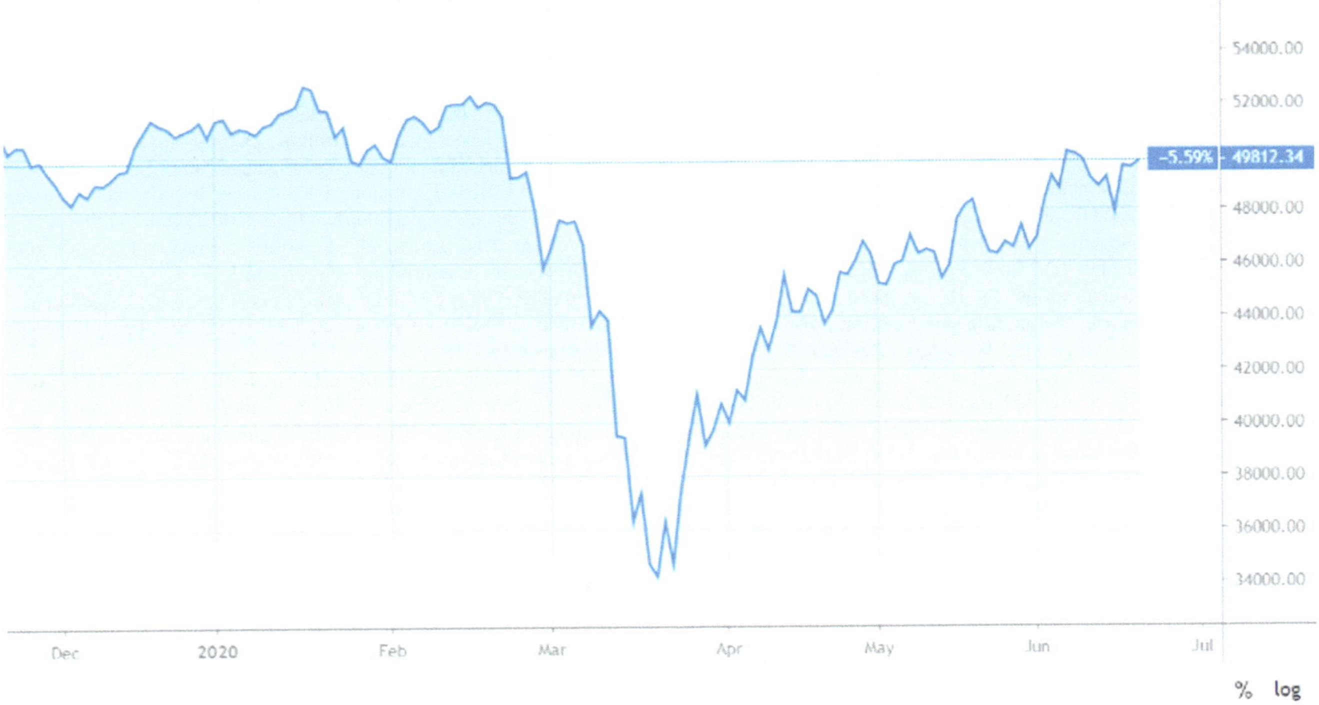

Fig. 7 South African stock market index: SA40

Alam N, Arshad S, Rizvi SAR (2016) Do Islamic stock indices perform better than conventional counterparts? An empirical investigation of sectoral efficiency. Rev Financ Econ 31:108–114. https://doi.org/10.1016/j.rfe.2016.06.003

Amar AB, Jerfel L, Bellalah M (2017) Du TUNIDEX au TUNINDEX-i: Structure et Performance. https://doi.org/10.13140/RG.2.2.23576.80645

Atta H (2000) Ethical rewards, an examination of the effect of Islamic ethical screens on financial performance and of conditioning information on performance measures. Working paper, University of Durham, Etats-Unis

El bousty MD, Oubdi L (2017) Les indices boursiers islamiques sont-ils plus performants que leurs homologues conventionnels ? Étude comparative entre pays émergents et pays développés. Recherches et Applications en Finance Islamique 1(2):100–120

El Khamlichi A (2010) L'éthique en bourse: le cas des indices boursiers socialement responsables. Université Réalité et Prospectives du développement durable – Clermont

El Khamlichi A (2012) Éthique et performance: le cas des indices boursiers et des fonds d'investissement en finance islamique

El khamlichi A (2019) Les indices boursiers socialement responsables: Quelle contribution pour la durabilité? Paradigmes, modèles, scénarios et pratiques en matière de durabilité forte, MSH Clermont Fd, Dec 2019, Clermont Ferrand, France. ⟨hal-02541291⟩

El khamlichi A (2013) Le comportement des indices boursiers socialement responsables en période de crise. Revue Manage Avenir 61:30–49

Firano Z, El Marzouki A, Laaguid A (2017) Analyse Comparative des Performances des Indices Islamiques et Éthiques. بحوث وتطبيقات في المالية الإسلامية 60 1:132–21. https://doi.org/10.12816/0037413

Fowler SJ, Hope C (2007) A critical review of sustainable business indices and their impact. J Bus Ethics 76:243–252

Girard E, Hassan MK (2005) Faith-based ethical investing: the case of Dow jones Islamic indexes. FMA Annual Meeting, Chicago

Grinblatt M, Titman S (1989) Mutual fund performance: an analysis of quarterly portfolio holdings. J Bus 62(3)

El Hajjaji H, Moutahaddib A (2019) Création d'un indice boursier islamique sur la place de Casablanca. Recherches et Applications en Finance Islamique (RAFI) 3(1):88–110

Hamid N, Sandford Y (2002) Are SRI indices responsible? Deutsche Bank Equity Research

Hassan K (2011) Risk, return and volatility of faith-based investing the case of the Dow Jones Islamic index. Center for Middle Eastern Studies, Harvard University, pp 43–67

Hussein KA (2005) Islamic investment: evidence from Dow Jones and FTSE Indices. In: 6th international conference on Islamic banking and finance, Jakarta, Indonesia

Hussein K, Omran M (2005) Ethical investment revisited: evidence from Dow Jones Islamic indexes. J Invest 14(3):105–124

El Khamlichi A, Viallefont A (2015) La Performance des Indices Boursiers en Finance Islamique: une Meta-Analyse. Revue de Gestion et d'Économie 3(1):1–15

Khatkhatay MH, Nisar S (2007) Investment in stocks: a critical review of Dow Jones Shariah screening norms. In: International conference on Islamic capital markets, Jakarta, Indonesia

Lelart M (2014) De la finance éthique à l'éthique en finance. Document de Recherche

Markowitz H (1952) Portfolio selection. J Finance 7(1):77–91

Maux J, Le Saout E (2003) La performance des fonds socialement responsables: mirage ou réalité? Working Paper, Université Paris 1 Panthéon Sorbonne

Maux JL, Le Saout E (2004) The performance of sustainability indexes. Finance India 18:737–750

Mbengue ML (2017) Creation of an Islamic stock index in West Africa. Res Int Bus Finance 41:105–108. https://doi.org/10.1016/j.ribaf.2017.04.017

Merdad H, Hassan MK, Alhenawi Y (2010) Islamic versus conventional mutual funds performance in Saudi Arabia: a case study. J King Abdulaziz Univ: Islamic Econ 23(2):163–200

Peillex J, Ureche-Rangau L (2012) Création d'un Indice Boursier Islamique Sur La Place Financière de Paris : Méthodologie et Performance on JSTOR. Revue d'économie financière : revue trimestrielle de l'Association d'Economie Financière. - Paris : Assoc., ISSN 0987–3368, ZDB-ID 23878–8. - Vol. 107.2012, pp 289–313

Pérez-Calderón E, Milanés-Montero P, Ortega-Rossell FJ (20125) Environmental performance and firm value: evidence from Dow jones sustainability index Europe. https://doi.org/10.22059/IJER.2012.571

Rabhi A, Haoudi A (2017) Islamic finance in frontier financial markets: an alternative or a complement to conventional finance? In: Finance: Vers Un Renouvellement Des Approches et Des Pratiques, pp 173–198. https://hal.archives-ouvertes.fr/hal-02432619

Saout E (2005) Indice, mon bel indice : dis-moi qui est le plus performant-Le cas des indices éthiques. Banque & Marchés 74:24–31

Sauer DA (1997) The impact of social-responsibility screens on investment performance: evidence from the domini 400 social index and domini equity mutual fund. https://doi.org/10.1016/S1058-3300(97)90002-1

Sauer DA (1997) The impact of social-responsibility screens on investment performance: evidence from the Domini 400 Social Index and Domini Equity Mutual Fund. Rev Financ Econ 6(2):137–149

Sourang MD (2013) La finance islamique et les marchés boursiers. https://corpus.ulaval.ca/jspui/handle/20.500.11794/24739

Sudha (2015) Risk-return and Volatility analysis of sustainability index in India. Environ Develop Sustain J

Topsacalian P (1996) Les indices boursiers sur actions. Economica

Topsacalian P (2000) Le point sur...les indices boursiers. Banque & Marchés 47:54–58

Vermeir W, Friedrich C (2006) La performance de l'ISR. Revue D'économie Financière, Programme National Persée 85(4):107–120

von Wallis M, Klein C (2015) Ethical requirement and financial interest: a literature review on socially responsible investing. Bus Res 8:61–98

Carbon Accounting: A Social and Corporate Perspective

Muhammad Safdar Sial, Muthanna G. Abdul Razzaq, Asma Salman, Lara Al-Haddad and Muhammad Tahir

Abstract

Global greenhouse gas emissions and the escalating implications of climate change need the development of new, more comprehensive approaches in preventing and reducing the harmful effects of climate change. As a result, governments, enterprises, academic institutions, and non-profit organizations will require improved methods of anticipating and fulfilling new information responsibilities and guidance on using evolving accounting systems to promote transparency. Scientific, political, economic, and corporate carbon accounting are only a few of the several developed types of accounts. They are related in policy or strategy, but they are not sufficiently interwoven in execution. Corporations may benefit from carbon accounting in two ways: using carbon accounting to identify and eliminate unsustainable behavior and improving sustainability. Manufacturing, distribution, procurement, supply chain management (SCM), innovation, communication, and marketing are just a few corporate services becoming more reliant on both methodologies. It makes little difference if a department's principal purpose is to ensure compliance with regulations, better organize energy and material flows to minimize large reduction impacts, increase eco-efficiency, product innovation, or legitimacy, or any combination of these objectives. Carbon management accounting has the potential to benefit decision-makers at all levels. It is hoped that the findings of this study would assist academics and policymakers in understanding how businesses respond to the requirements imposed by governments and non-governmental organizations (NGOs) to report their carbon emissions.

Keywords

Carbon accounting · Carbon disclosure · Social · Corporate perspective

1 Introduction

1.1 Contextualizing Carbon Accounting for Sustainable Development and Climate Change

As one of the six primary sustainability challenges (together with deforestation and biodiversity loss, population growth, poverty, water scarcity, and climate change), climate change is probably the most pressing issue facing the world right now (Yohe and Tol 2008). Many of climate change's most severe consequences may be traced back to a variety of economic and societal activities. The following figure indicates the top Carbon-di-Oxide producers, expressed in gigatons of carbon produced. One has to keep in mind that the overall production of 465 Giga tons of Carbon will end up raising the global temperature by 2 °C, resulting in massive amounts of changes in global weather patterns. Therefore, it is paramount that this importance as with passage of time the CO_2 accumulation in the

M. S. Sial · M. Tahir
Department of Management Sciences, COMSATS University Islamabad, Islamabad, Pakistan
e-mail: safdar.sial786@gmail.com

M. Tahir
e-mail: m_tahir@comsats.edu.pk

M. G. A. Razzaq · A. Salman (✉)
College of Business Administration, American University in the Emirates, 503000, Dubai, United Arab Emirates
e-mail: asma.salman@aue.ae

L. Al-Haddad
Department of Finance and Banking Sciences, Yarmouk University, Irbid, Jordan
e-mail: Lara.haddad@yu.edu.jo

A. Salman and A. Tharwat (eds.), *Smart Designs for Business Innovation*,
Advances in Science, Technology & Innovation, https://doi.org/10.1007/978-3-031-49313-3_8

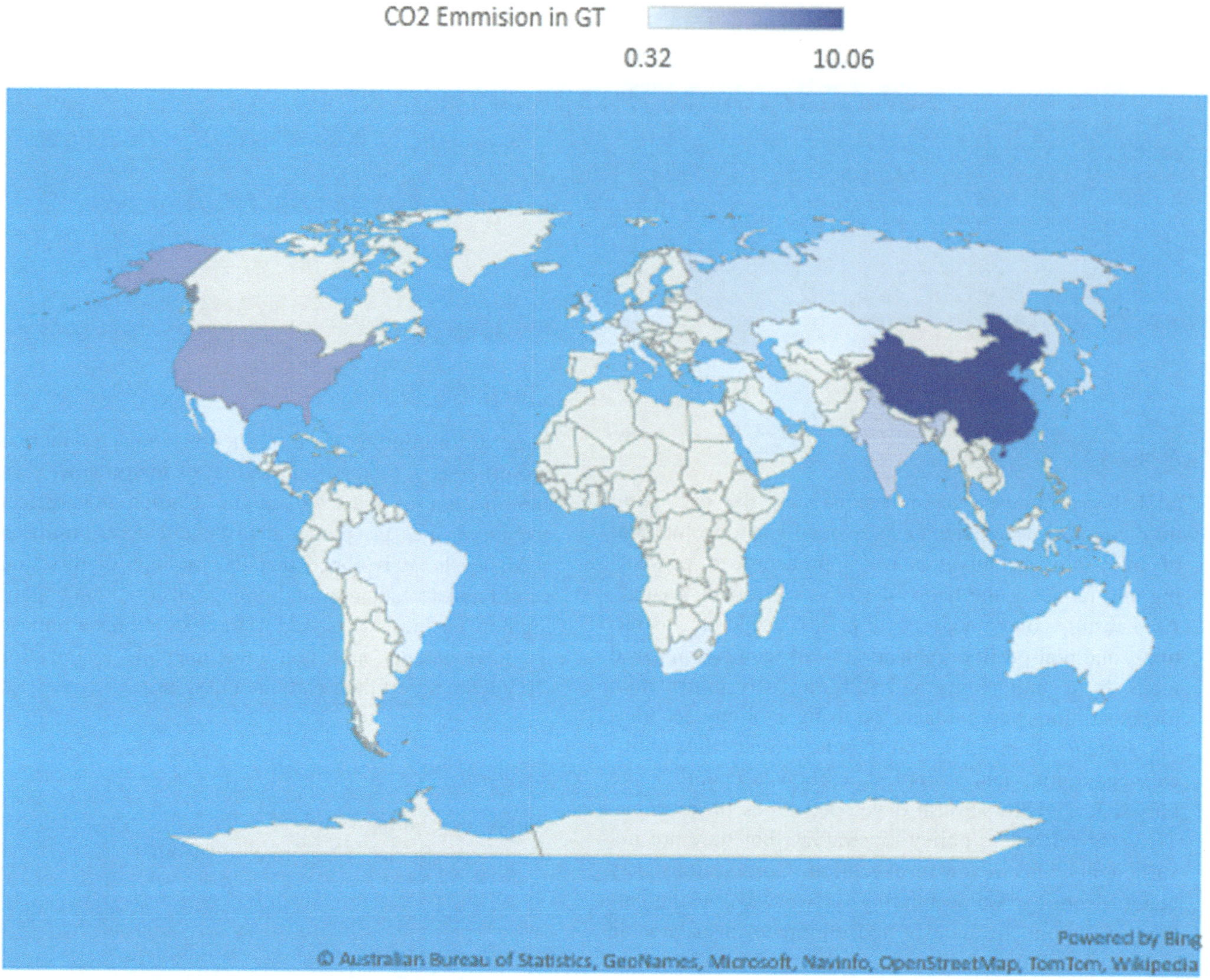

Fig. 1 Map indicating the top 20 countries w.r.t CO_2 omissions.

atmosphere is rising by the day, as indicated by the Figs. 1 and 2.

When it comes to the issues related to accumulation of Greenhouse gasses and their adverse impact on global climate and overall ecology, most of the time carbon di oxide is taken as standard, the simple reason being that it makes up almost 75% of the global "Green House Gas" emission as depicted in Fig. 3.

When it comes to global emissions the main cause is the fuel combustion, mainly the combustion of fossil fuel and in this respect China leads the global trend. Figure 4 depicts the total contribution of top economies in terms of their part in global CO_2 emissions.

The problem of global emission does not stop here as with passage of time not only the global emissions are increasing but at the same time one has to keep in mind that many economies have scaled up their CO_2 emissions. One of the parameters for measuring this is the per capita emissions. The top twenty countries in this respect are presented in Figs. 5 and 6.

The above stats also provides information regarding the extant of the problem as many new countries such as Saudi Arabia, Kazakhstan and Iran have joined this club. This also indicates how much damage is caused in terms of CO_2 emission as a consequence of their economic growth. Apart from this in-depth analysis of the greenhouse gas emission it is indicated that that almost two third of these gasses including CO_2 are produced as result of production of electricity used for industrial processes and heating for domestic and industrial purposes, along with the use of carbon-based fuels for manufacturing processes, the snapshot of which is provided in Fig. 7.

Uncontrolled use fossil fuel for economic development and progress already is having severe consequences on the global weather pattern and in countries where population density is high, there is rising sea level and constant

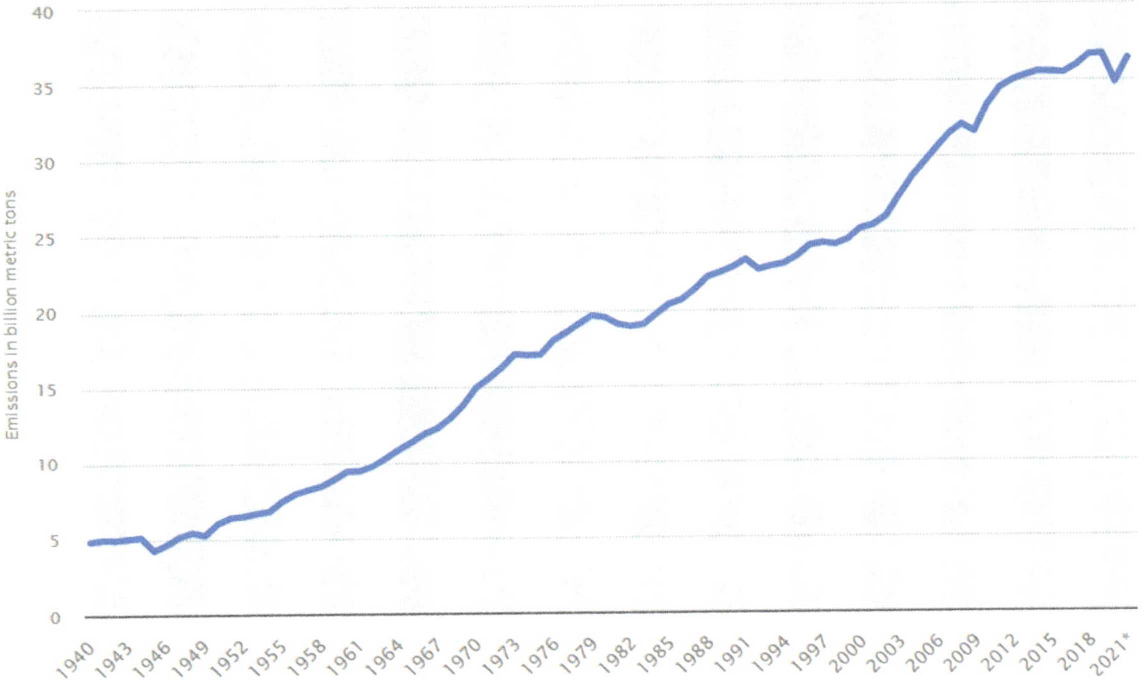

Fig. 2 Global CO_2 emissions from 1940 upto 2020

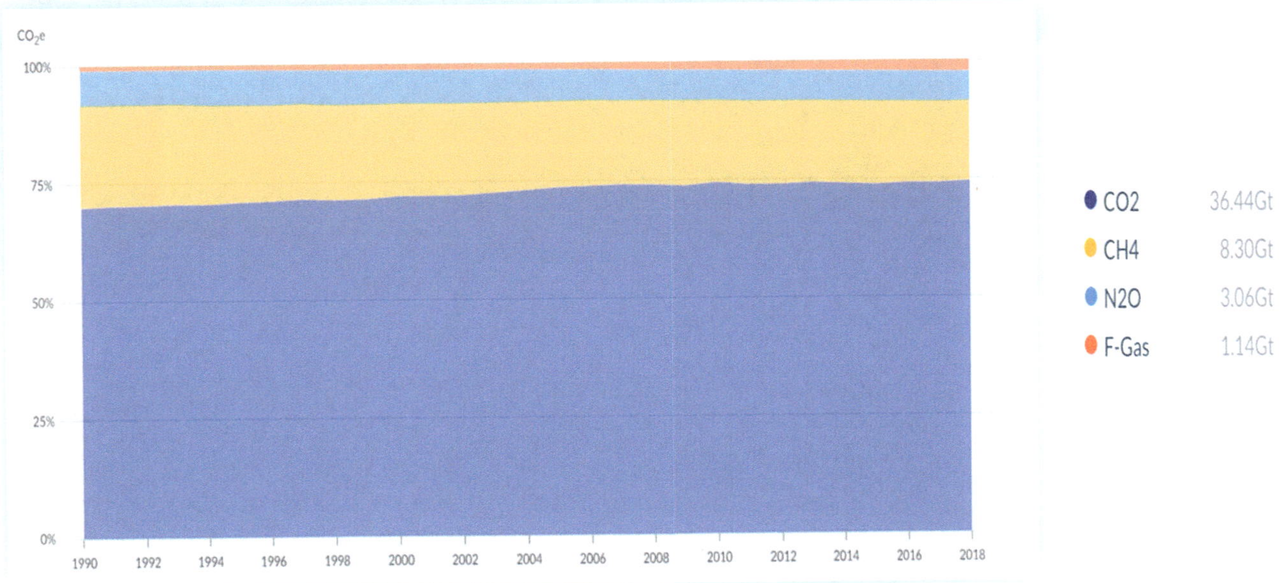

Fig. 3 Composition of global green house gas emission from 1990 upto 2018

changes in weather patterns that have resulted in droughts, typhons, and other natural disasters. The implication of such changes has a devastating impact on the population both in terms of social and economic issues. The battle against climate change is a critical problem for the long-term development of the world economy (Banuri and Opschoor 2009). Scholars have discovered that the global 'carbon bottom line' is continuously growing, putting ecosystems and present economies at risk of collapse on a scale never seen before in human history. Climate-changing greenhouse gas emissions have increased significantly over the past decade, mostly attributable to ever increasing emission of greenhouse gasses such CO_2, whose underlying cause is rapid urbanization and population growth in emerging economies such as India and China. while the developed economies such as USA, have paid little to no

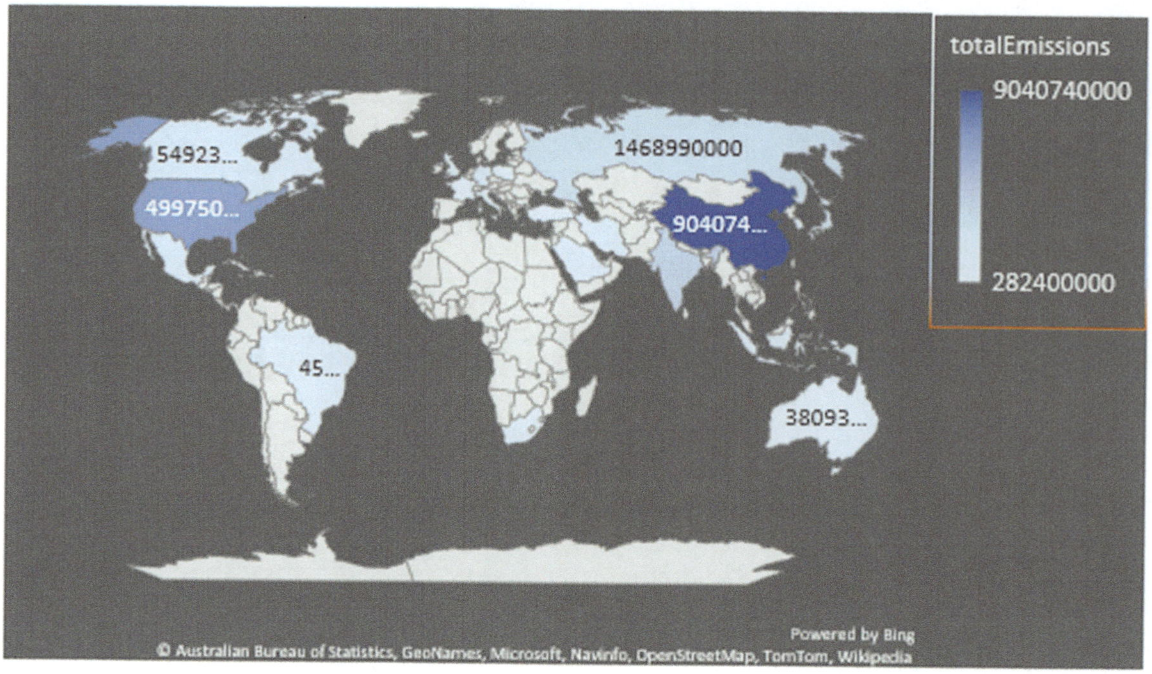

Fig. 4 Data is for carbon dioxide emissions from fuel combustion in tons in 2015

Fig. 5 Top 20 countries ranked according to Per-capita CO_2 Emissions

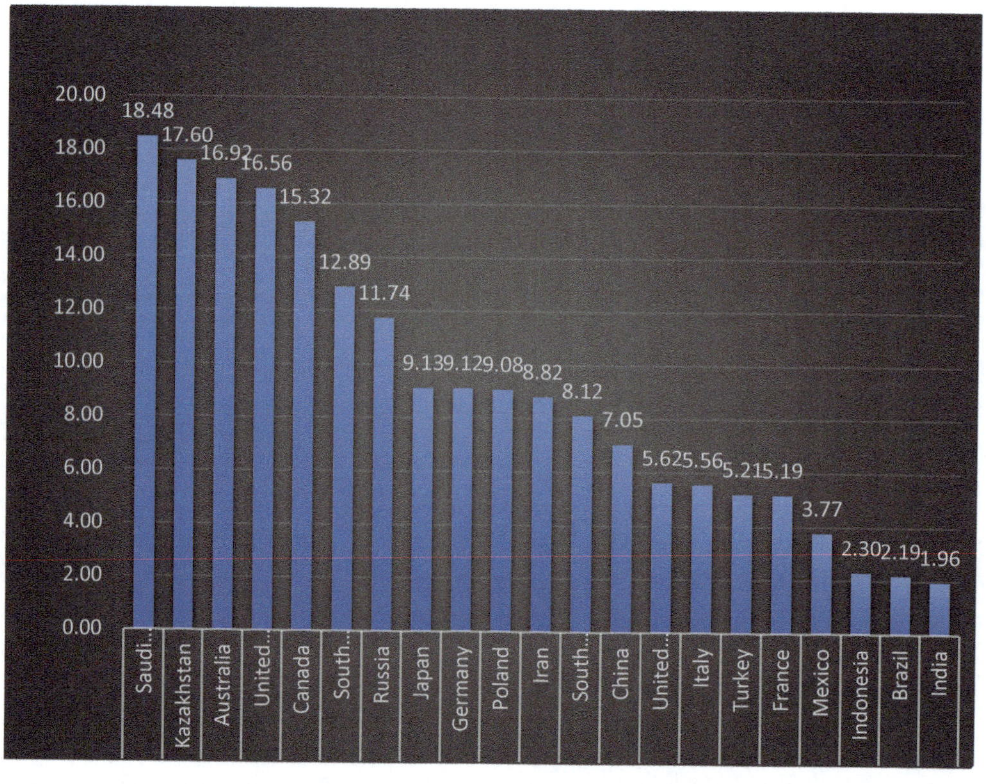

attention to decreasing their carbon emissions. The following Figs. 8 and 9 provide an overview of these emissions by world's major economies and economic zones. These figures also indicate the targets set by these countries, and their actual performance in terms of controlling and reducing their emissions' targets from 1995 to 2005.

As it the above graphics clearly indicate that, in the absence of any policy the emissions will have devastating

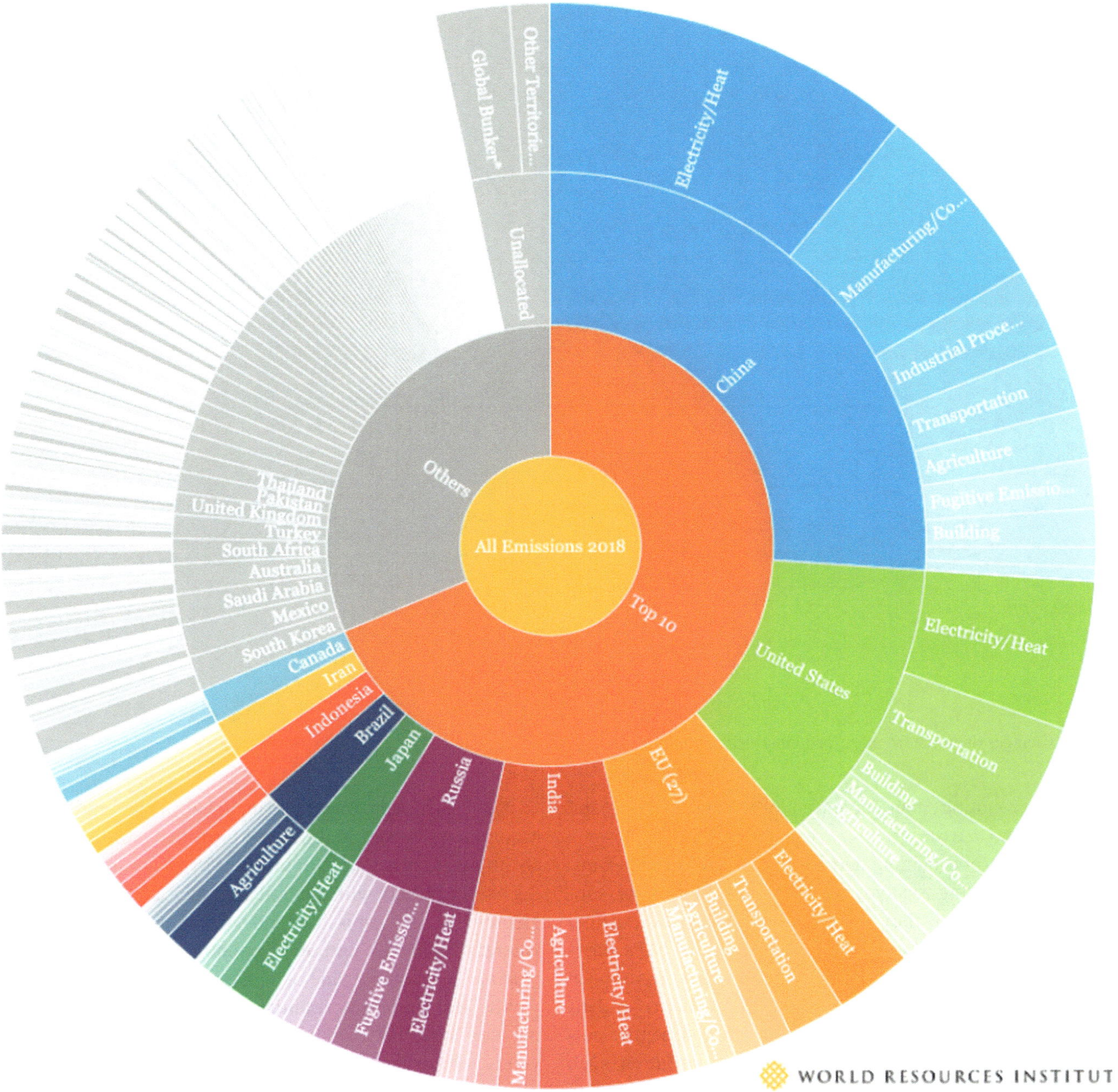

Fig. 6 The top 10 GHG emitters contribute over two-thirds of global emissions

consequences for the entire planet while in the case of adopting and flowing the Paris agreement the global emissions cannot only be controlled but can also be curtailed. In the fight against climate change, Germany and the Netherlands are at the forefront of reducing greenhouse gas emissions. At the same time, vulnerable countries such as those in the 'Coalition of Pacific Island States' encourage the international community to become more involved in climate change prevention and adaptation activities. In their efforts to reduce per capita carbon emissions, other countries, such as Australia and China, are following their predecessors' footsteps. Through technological advancements, Europe has partially isolated GHG emissions from GDP growth over the previous two decades.

Improvements in process efficiency and more energy-efficient consumer products are presently being utilized as indicators of greenhouse gas reduction. However, despite this being an important subject of study, the world's population and economic growth, particularly in big emerging economies, currently overwhelm the efficiency improvements. As a result, substantial reductions in the overall carbon emissions are more difficult to achieve through

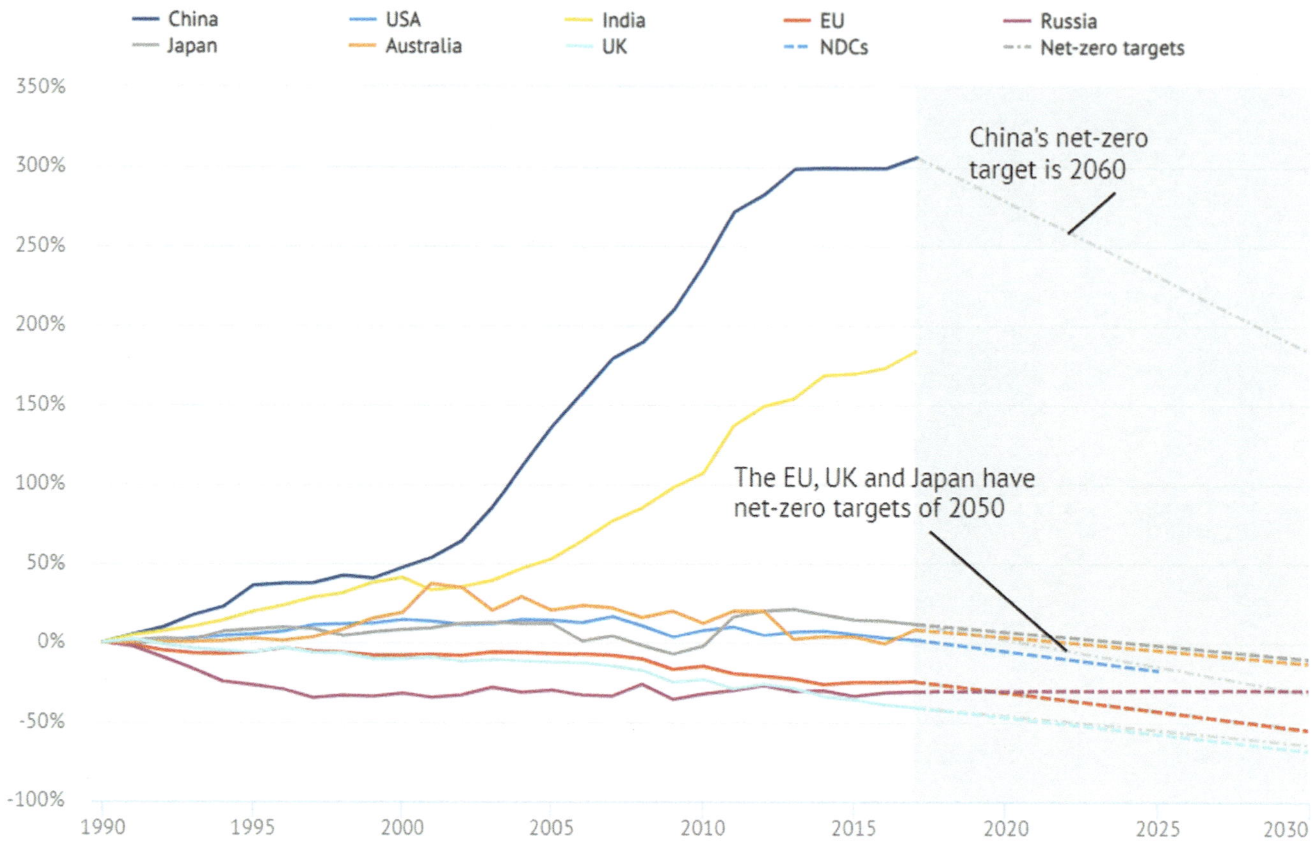

Fig. 7 Changes in emissions major economies since 1995

carbon accounting than increased efficiency (Busch and Lewandowski 2016).

Product carbon tagging and life cycle pricing are examples of accounting systems that consider the whole supply chain. However, they are not yet relevant in the actual world due to technological limitations. In the EU's environmental policy, product-oriented indicators have been added to industrial process control rules to improve their effectiveness. So far, product-related environmental policy has focused on large-scale sources of pollution such as industrial emissions and waste management rather than on smaller-scale causes of contamination. There are, however, raising concerns about the need for rules that cover the whole product life cycle, including the use phase, which are becoming more prevalent. Environmental effects across the life-cycle should be dealt with in an integrated way, rather than just changing from one phase of the life-cycle to another," this should ensure that the environment is protected throughout the life-cycle (Wilting and Vringer 2009).

Because it reveals where emissions originate and where they are absorbed, carbon accounting is critical in the battle against global warming. Earth's sinks and sources have changed throughout time, therefore those who make choices on how to reduce global emissions utilize the most accurate data available.

Many different things are included in the word "carbon accounting," which is a general term that can imply different things to various individuals. Physical carbon accounting is concerned with quantifying the actual quantities of greenhouse gas emissions released into the atmosphere, whereas financial carbon accounting is concerned with placing a monetary value on carbon.

Physical carbon accounting is one method of calculating emissions of carbon dioxide into the atmosphere. If you're a business person, you can use this to figure out how much carbon you're releasing into the atmosphere. Goals for reducing carbon emissions may be set after it is understood how much carbon is being emitted. Furthermore, this approach is critical in that it enables us to determine who is accountable for each individual's contribution to global warming emissions (Fig. 10).

2 Importance of Carbon Accounting

When it comes to dealing with climate change, carbon accounting is becoming more important. People who are interested in businesses want them to do what they can to help. You need to know where you are now and how it will change in the future to be able to make good decisions.

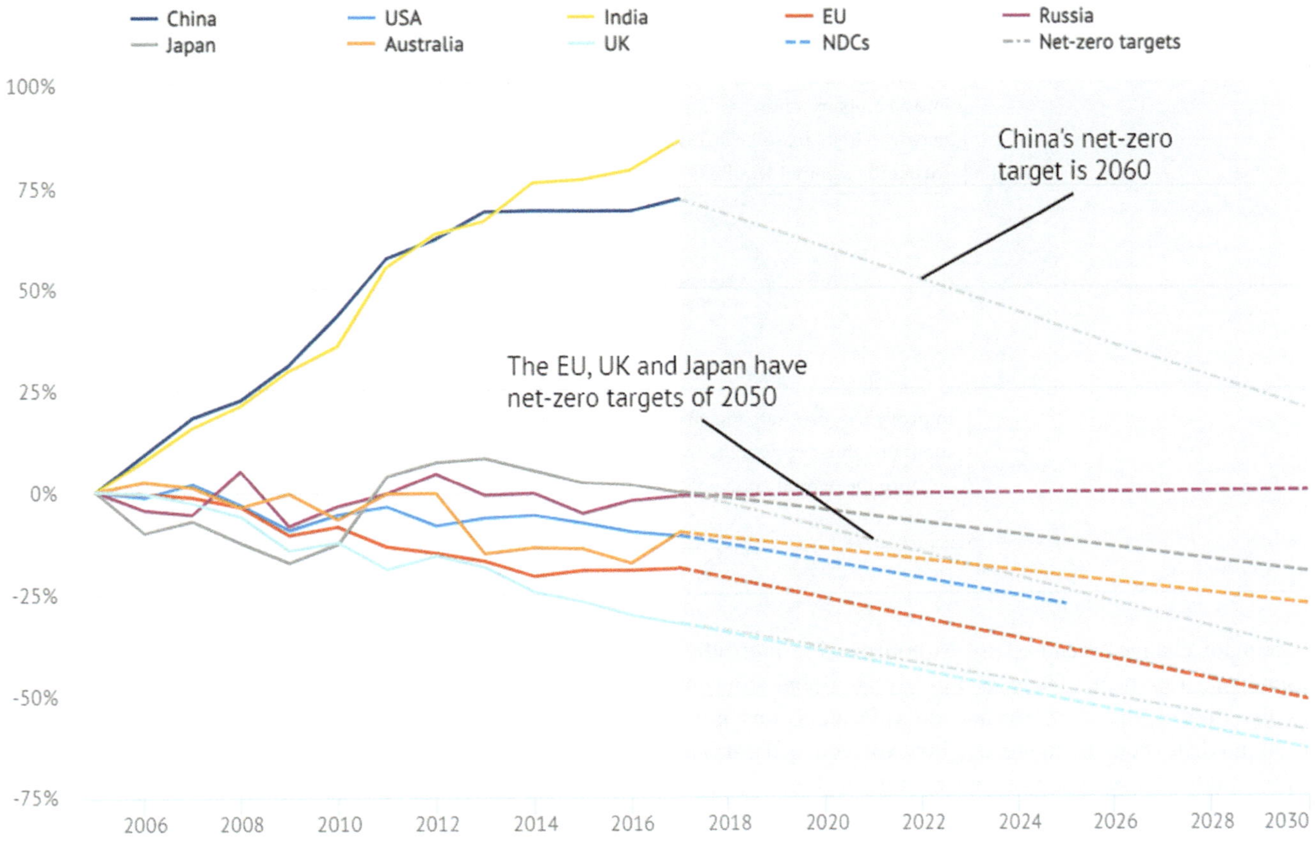

Fig. 8 Changes in emissions major economies since 2005

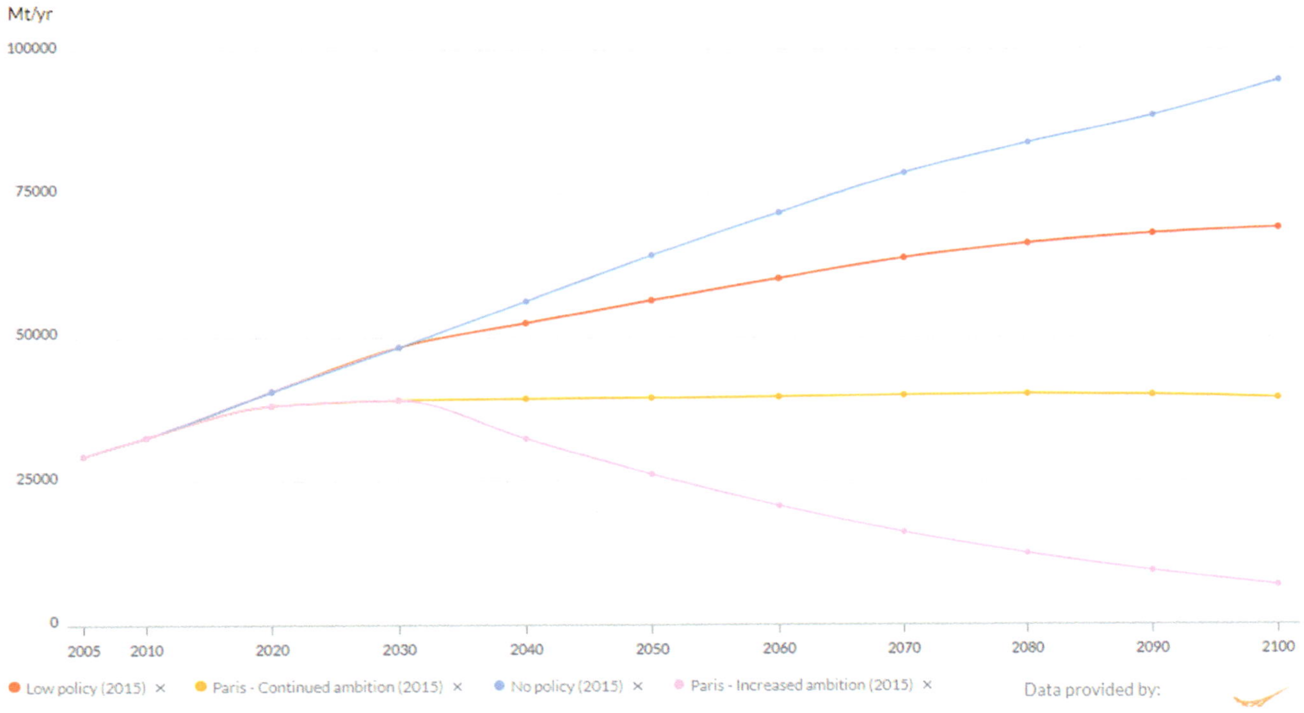

Fig. 9 Projections of CO_2 emissions in different scenarios

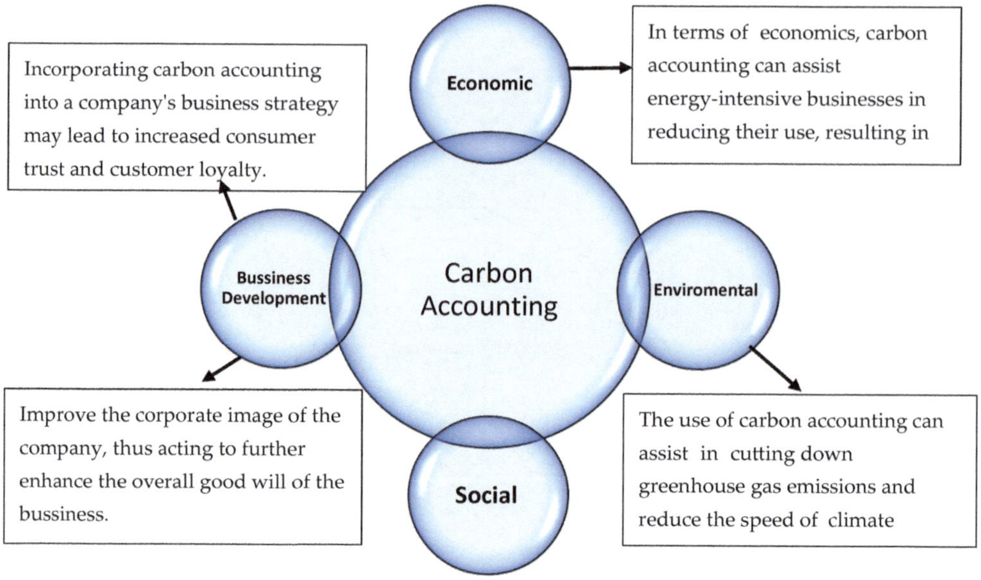

Fig. 10 Different aspects of carbon accounting

Climate change is caused by carbon dioxide and other gases that trap heat. There is already a global consensus that this is the case. Carbon dioxide emissions must be counted in order to figure out how to reduce them and improve the air and water on our planet. In this case, carbon accounting can be used to help. In the fight against climate change, one of the most important things governments and businesses can do if a disaster is near is to use carbon accounting to figure out how much carbon they use (Delay et al. 2009).

Carbon accounting might imply different things to different people. According to experts, it is the "process of obtaining scientifically rigorous and trustworthy measurements of GHG [greenhouse gas] emissions" (Green et al. 2017). With the United Nations Clean Development Mechanism (CDM) market, emissions reductions are measured against a hypothetical baseline. Additional processes are carried out to form a new trading commodity: carbon credits (Ministry of Environment 2009). When it comes to emissions trading systems, the International Accounting Standards Board (IASB) is particularly interested in accounting for tradable emission rights and liabilities (Lovell and MacKenzie 2011). Because of the increasing number of businesses that are reporting to the Carbon Disclosure Project (CDP), The Climate Registry, or other similar schemes, it is necessary to monitor and disclose greenhouse gas emissions, for which the businesses take varying degrees of accountability (Bebbington and Larrinaga-Gonzalez 2008). In various methods, carbon accounting is used in many of society's most significant climate change solutions, including governmental emission limits, corporate climate change goals, and carbon markets. Despite this, it is usually overlooked in its significance and influence. Even more significantly, the interconnections between various carbon accounting firms have not received nearly enough rigorous consideration (Kauffmann and Tébar Less 2010). There are distinct institutional structures, normative practices, and academic literature for carbon accounting distinct from those for other types of carbon accounting. This research provides a complete picture of what carbon accounting includes across industries and organizations to make sense of the inconsistencies between different types of carbon accounting (Allan Cook 2009).

Today's carbon accounting field is characterized by the convergence of at least five primary "framing" processes, where the "hot" new world of political commitments and carbon markets meets the somewhat "cooler" foundations of physical carbon accounting, financial accounting, and social/environmental accounting. Understanding different aspects of carbon accounting and their interconnectedness more effectively solve the accounting-related challenges that hamper attempts to mitigate climate change (Hahn et al. 2015).

When discussing the "political" aspect of accounting of carbon in terms of national inventories. In that case, physical carbon measurement predates and influences the more technical literature on "market-enabling" carbon accounting, as well as the literature on "market-enabling" climate change. The financial accounting of rights and duties in carbon markets has only lately been brought to the attention of financial accountants, even though such markets have begun to have significant ramifications for corporate balance sheets (Lovell and MacKenzie 2011). A significant amount of research on social and environmental accounting has been conducted concerning examining corporate carbon disclosure and reporting practices. There has been little research on the politics and practices of carbon accounting (Allan Cook 2009); thus, this is a welcome addition to the field. Discussions about carbon accounting have tended to occur in isolated settings with only a few ties between them (Alrazi et al. 2015).

3 Literature on Carbon Accounting

The Kyoto Protocol, approved by 195 countries, provides a market-based framework for countries to limit or control their greenhouse gas emissions. In the wake of establishing the carbon emissions trading market, new accounting issues have arisen, which must be addressed. The new method has ignited a debate in the accounting literature about various climate change mitigation and adaptation measures (Milne and Grubnic 2011). Collective experiments to reinvent "the forms of organization of economic, political, and scientific activity" are now underway in the carbon market, and they are referred to as "ongoing collective experiments." It's also worth mentioning that there is some skepticism about the success of various climate change programs in terms of cutting greenhouse gas emission.

(Andrew and Cortese 2013; Boston and Lempp 2011), as well as (Çalışkan and Callon 2009) state that while the policy debate focuses on the general impact of climate change on business, some academics are more interested in the particular accounting implications of the shift and the problems involved with carbon accounting, both in terms of study and in terms of practical application. There is a thorough discussion of the issues associated with carbon trading and accounting and numerous ways that accounting may be utilized to communicate the various climate risks and uncertainties (Hahn et al. 2015). From the perspective of management accounting, carbon accounting is discussed to stimulate more research into carbon management and control. The early conceptual inquiries into carbon accounting will greatly assist future research in the field (Hartmann et al. 2013).

3.1 Financial Accounting for Carbon Assets and Liabilities

With the advent of a new emission related restrictions and taxes, the question of how to report carbon emissions in financial statements arises. The argument places a strong focus on the value of free allowances and the volatility caused by varied asset values, and the recognition of obligations in the financial statements and other documents. The difficulty in calculating carbon allowances is a significant factor in the problem. It is both a financial instrument that may be traded on the market and a carbon emission permits, with the latter functioning as a legislated upper limit on carbon emissions (Bebbington and Thomson 2013) Standard-setting agencies have found it challenging to develop a universal accounting standard that is compatible with both carbon-related assets and liabilities as well as other general assets and liabilities because of this distinguishing characteristic.

According to the IFRS,[1] Due to a dispute over the accounting of carbon allowances, Emission Rights were abolished in June 2005 as reported by (Kollmuss et al. 2008). Because the actual standards for accounting for emissions allowances have not yet been determined in practice, and there are three widely used methods.

Allowances can be accounted for in various ways, including net liability, gross liability, and inventory techniques. There are two approaches to accounting for free allocations: a gross liability technique that accounts for free allocations at fair value and an inventory method that accounts for free allocations at zero value. Because corporations can choose whether carbon allowances should be classed as assets, liabilities, or even expenses, accounting discrepancies might make, issues with standards related to disclose the nature of business, the comparison of financial statements for different types of business becomes difficult (Warwick and Ng 2012). Because of this, academics have called for accounting standard-setters to adopt a standardized approach to accounting (Trifts and Asare 2015).

Since 2014, there has been no mention of carbon allowance accounting in accounting literature or textbooks. However, there is still an issue, and it may worsen if additional countries worldwide choose to employ ETSs to control their greenhouse gas emissions. More research into the issue of carbon financial accounting may be beneficial to the field of carbon financial accounting. One of the many climates change-related difficulties in financial accounting is the management of carbon allowances, which is only one example. (He et al. 2020) develop a model that considers a wide range of carbon-related characteristics, including emissions allowances, carbon sequestration, and emissions control capabilities. Assets that are stranded and assets that regulate emissions are also worthy of consideration (Dr Lovell et al. 2010). It can be that accounting's increased inclusion of carbon concerns will be a rewarding study subject to examine further as the effects of climate change on the value of business assets become more substantial (Pitrakkos and Maroun 2020).

[1] In November 2021 the Trustees published a revised *Constitution* and a Feedback Statement that responds to the feedback from Exposure Draft *Proposed Targeted Amendments to the IFRS Foundation Constitution to Accommodate an International Sustainability Standards Board to Set IFRS Sustainability Standards*.

4 Carbon Disclosure

Net-zero carbon emissions are becoming more and more difficult to achieve, and their success depends on a worldwide effort by governments, businesses, financial institutions, and people to remove or capture carbon emissions. It all begins with simple activities like calculating and reporting carbon emissions each year. A considerable improvement in measuring and reporting corporate carbon emissions has occurred, although the vast majority of publicly traded corporations and even fewer privately owned businesses continue to avoid disclosing the amount of carbon they emit. Another issue with present voluntary disclosures is that they lack a consistent methodology for measuring and reporting information: "Firms publish reams of meaningless puffery, while often failing to reveal the few items that matter. An ideal situation would be for an asset manager to be able to calculate their portfolio's carbon footprint and track changes over time. As a result, many companies have failed to disclose their emissions in a comprehensive manner, and the metrics made public by different companies sometimes overlap, resulting in double counting" (The Economist 2021).

Capital markets are built on the foundation of mandatory disclosures of important financial information. As the climate situation worsens, it's critical that we learn more about how much carbon dioxide we're producing. Individual firms' progress toward the net zero target may be gauged by requiring both publicly listed and private enterprises to publish their carbon emissions. Our suggested reporting obligation has already been enacted in certain jurisdictions, notably the United Kingdom (Bolton et al. 2021).

Businesses publish their emissions disclosures in a number of ways. It is a legal requirement for certain firms to disclose their GHG emissions to government agencies, while other companies choose to do so voluntarily through the Carbon Disclosure Project (CDP) or other sustainability or social responsibility reporting. Carbon accounting has given a considerable deal of attention to the subject of carbon disclosure. One of the most common types of carbon disclosure studies is qualitative or quantitative. As of now, there are three distinct study areas focused on the factors that impact organizations' decisions about whether or not to disclose their carbon footprints, including the quality and appropriateness of such disclosures, among other things (Hahn et al. 2015).

4.1 Determinants and Motivations of Carbon Disclosure

The legitimacy theory, stakeholder theory, signaling theory, and institutional theory are a few of the most prevalent theories on voluntary carbon disclosure. These are typically cited as supporting ideas in inquiries into the causes and motivations for carbon disclosure. A firm's readiness to reveal its genuine stance on carbon emissions and management is linked to social, commercial, economic, regulatory and institutional constraints when they are translated into disclosure incentives, according to the theories (Louche et al. 2021). Based upon the previous literature the following model has been formulated to reflect the relationship between different factors that impact the decision regarding the disclosure related to carbon accounting or in simple terms the disclosure of carbon emissions at the firm level (Fig. 11).

4.2 External Pressures

The impact of governmental and institutional mandates on company carbon disclosure is also a topic of debate in

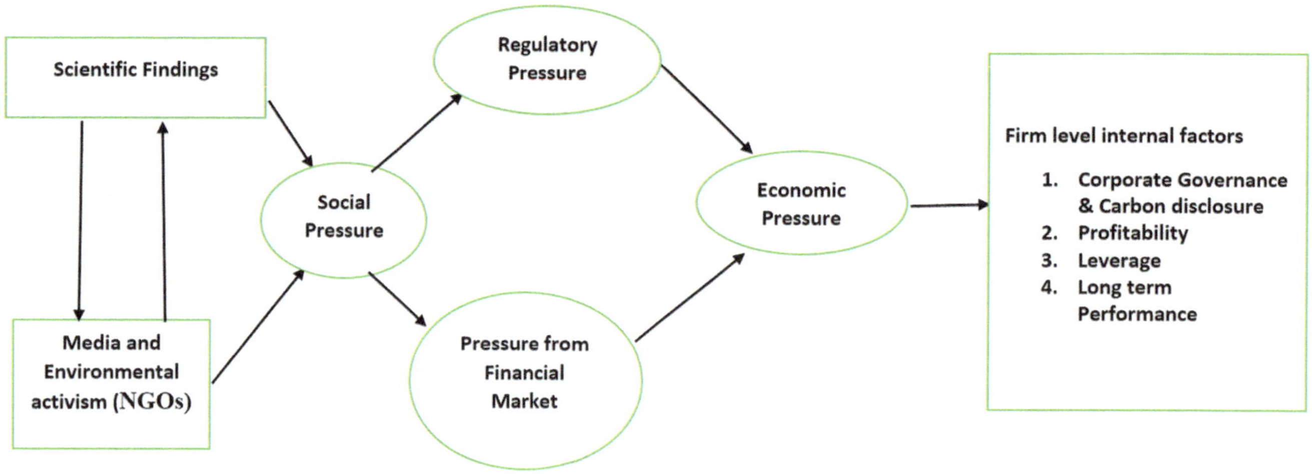

Fig. 11 Disclosure of carbon emissions at the firm level

academic circles. According to a new research, voluntary carbon disclosure is more likely to occur in nations where investors are well-protected and have stringent environmental regulations (Nor et al. 2016). Due to the stricter laws that apply to these businesses, Companies in carbon-intensive businesses are more likely than their peers in other industries to disclose their carbon footprint (He et al. 2020, 2021a). According to research conducted in Australia, the United Kingdom, the United States, and China, the reporting requirements of emission imposed by governments and financial markets disclosure have a beneficial influence on the willingness of corporations to voluntarily disclose information about their carbon emissions (Yang and Farley 2016). Furthermore, non-governmental organizations corporate carbon disclosures can benefit from non-governmental organizations like the Global Reporting Initiative (GRI) and the Carbon Disclosure Project (CDP) (Green et al. 2017).

Certain studies have also considered the impact of economic pressure on carbon disclosure as a potential driver of carbon disclosure. As a result of the implementation of climate legislation, internalized carbon pricing has emerged as one kind of economic pressure (Bebbington and Larrinaga-Gonzalez 2008; Bebbington and Thomson 2013; de Aguiar and Bebbington 2014) Researchers at the World Resources Institute found that companies with headquarters in countries that have signed the Kyoto Protocol are more likely to disclose their efforts and outcomes when they are compelled to do so by the Protocol's regulations. Economic pressure can also be exerted on a company through the operational environment it operates in. According to (Ott et al. 2017) businesses' decision to voluntarily publish their carbon emissions may be impacted by competitive pressures. Researchers at the World Resources Institute found that companies with headquarters in countries that have signed the Kyoto Protocol are more likely to disclose their efforts and outcomes when they are compelled to do so by the Protocol's regulations. Economic pressure can also be exerted on a company through the operational environment.

In addition to social and financial market dynamics, the literature has addressed the role of government in the economy. Because the media and authorities are more interested in and examining larger organisations, academics frequently use their data on company size as a proxy for social pressures. According to a growing body of studies, people's willingness and ability to report their carbon emissions is strongly influenced by societal pressure (Freedman and Park 2014; Freedman and Park 2017). A major factor in growing financial market pressure on management to reveal more information about greenhouse gas emissions is the involvement of investors, who are expected to play an important role. However, empirical research also shows that capital raising or ownership concentration and public carbon disclosure have no connection and, in some situations, a negative correlation (He et al. 2021b).

4.3 Firm Characteristics

The firm's board of directors' structure has been investigated as a potential element in carbon disclosure requirements. Research done in Australia by (Green et al. 2017) indicates a positive relationship between a company's overall governance quality and the probability and extent to which it discloses carbon emissions. It has been demonstrated that having a higher proportion of carbon disclosure preparedness is correlated with the presence of female directors on the board of a corporation (Pitrakkos and Maroun 2019). Several studies, including that of (Alrazi et al. 2015) and (Green et al. 2017), talk of their various experiences and lack of financial investment in the company, where independent directors advocate greater comprehensive carbon disclosure (Cooper et al. 2018). Those who have a higher interest in the firm may be hesitant to engage in carbon abatement initiatives, such as transparency, due to the uncertainty of a financial return on such a significant environmental investment. Contrary to the popular belief, those who have found a link between corporate ownership and carbon disclosure believe the exact opposite (Pitrakkos and Maroun 2019). They argue that management ownership would enable managers to better align their own interests with those of their shareholders, increasing their willingness to engage in climate change discussions with their shareholders.

Financial characteristics like profitability, leverage, and long-term development possibilities are explored in the academic literature. In accordance with (Freedman and Park 2014), because higher profitability improves the company's available financial resources, researchers often assume a positive link between corporate profits and carbon disclosure. According to a past study, a company's profitability has no significant influence on the likelihood or extent to which it discloses its carbon footprint. To put it another way, a large corporation with a great deal of power may be expected to disclose information about its carbon impact if asked (He et al. 2020, 2021b). Nonetheless, a heavily leveraged corporation may choose to keep sensitive information like carbon risk under wraps for fear that full disclosure of such information could damage its bargaining power in the future (Luo 2019). Some studies have found a negative correlation between the carbon disclosure and profitability of the firms (Luo and Tang 2014), with the majority finding no correlation at all (He et al. 2020, 2021a, 2021b; Luo 2019); firms with significant development potential, particularly in less developed countries, are less likely to declare carbon emissions than other enterprises.

Firms emphasize financial objectives over environmental concerns, resulting in a reduction in the amount of time and money spent on lowering carbon emissions and publicizing the results of their research. Additionally, management's opinions and attitudes toward environmental preservation may impact a company's decision to disclose carbon data. Because cultural influences might significantly impact responses to major changes in climate (He et al. 2020). Observe the relationship between national culture and the replies of firms to the CDP survey. They come to the conclusion that cultural traits like masculinity, power distance, fear of the unknown, individualism, and a long-term outlook have a significant impact on whether or not people are willing to share their carbon statistics. Management systems for the environment are more likely to succeed than those that are not, managed firms to inform investors and the general public about their efforts to combat climate change (Bowen and Wittneben 2011; Haigh and Shapiro 2011) either because they have significantly lower disclosure propensity and credit risks associated with climate change (Ott et al. 2017) or because they have significantly lower disclosure propensity and credit risks associated with climate change.

4.4 Carbon Disclosure, Quality and Adequacy

Some experts are concerned about the quality of corporate carbon disclosure because it is still optional in the majority of countries (Cowan and Deegan 2011). Several studies have shown that corporate climate change disclosures are skewed in favor of what they consider to be the best outcomes (Haque 2017). Five of the seven pillars of (Comyns and Figge 2015) self-created disclosure quality index include accuracy; Completion, consistency, credibility, relevance, timeliness, and transparency round out the checklist. During their investigation, they find that disclosure quality has not much improved, and they believe that regulation is important to keep the practice under check (Haslam et al. 2014) have expressed dissatisfaction with present methodologies that provide irreconcilable numbers and narratives that contradict one another. According to (Haigh and Shapiro 2011), investors can benefit from more information about a company's carbon emissions. Still, carbon performance information may have minimal influence on investors' portfolio selections. Researchers discovered that investors were taking advantage of recognized inadequacies in public reporting on climate change by employing the accounting and reporting procedures that can be termed as deceptive (Andrew and Cortese 2013).

The inadequacy of corporate carbon disclosure information can be attributed to a misalignment amongst different stakeholders' and managers' expectations on the disclosure of carbon emissions. Climate change is a topic that management doesn't seem to care much about, even though green communities and environmental authorities are worried. Directors are more concerned with the costs and dangers of complying with rules and financial success for shareholders than they are with the impact of operations on carbon emissions. It is consistent with previous research (Haque 2017). The fact that carbon dioxide emissions declarations are purely voluntary enhances the prospect of inconsistency in statistics due to methodological heterogeneity, which may be addressed if mandatory regulation were implemented (Andrew and Forgie 2008).

Sustainability accounting and disclosure had its early detractors who were concerned about the reliability and quality of voluntary carbon disclosures in the literature which were shared by other early critics of sustainability disclosure and accounting (Hopwood 2009). According to (He et al. 2020, 2021b), the CDP system has improved, and carbon disclosure assists investors in making decisions about the market value of a firm (Matsumura et al. 2014). Because voluntary carbon disclosure is only advantageous if it correctly represents a company's true carbon performance, individuals worried about its quality are justified in questioning whether it does so. A common explanation for the relationship between carbon performance and disclosure is found in two conflicting theories: the signaling and legitimacy hypotheses. According to signaling theory, top performers are motivated to offer more trustworthy, objective, and quantitative disclosures to distinguish themselves from low performers and avoid being removed from the competition (Hughes 1986). Unfortunately, the empirical data in this particular study subject is unclear. The findings of (He et al. 2020, 2021b) provide validity to the signaling concept by revealing a relationship between a company's effectiveness in carbon moderation and the extent to which it discloses its carbon emissions and greenhouse gas emissions (Ott et al. 2017) have comparable evidence; however, it is of poor quality. As described by (He et al. 2020; Luo 2019), if carbon institutions are tight, firms' incentives to use carbon disclosure for legitimation attempts might be restrained. On the other side, using Chinese data, (Momin et al. 2017)discovered evidence that supports the legitimacy hypothesis.

According to (Pitrakkos and Maroun 2019), businesses in carbon-intensive sectors rely more on releasing behavioural information to demonstrate their genuine efforts to prevent global warming than their counterparts in low-carbon industries. Disclosures made by participating firms in the UK ETS and Energy Efficiency Scheme were used to make the organizations look more credible and shift the responsibility for fighting climate change to the government or suppliers, which slowed down progress. Businesses can influence their disclosure behavior in two ways: by reporting their carbon emissions and by failing to declare their carbon emissions. Regardless of whether the goal of carbon disclosure is to achieve legitimacy or to send a signal, (Schaltegger and Csutora 2012) argue that the disclosure encourages subsequent organizational reform from the outside-in, rather than the other way around. According to the findings of the researchers, changes in carbon disclosure levels are linked to changes in carbon emissions performance in the future.

5 Conclusion and Outlook for the Future

It is doubtful that the carbon reporting obligation will solve the climate situation. Nevertheless, research shows that simply requiring corporations to record their past emissions will motivate them to reduce their emissions faster because of the attention that will be generated by future emissions reporting. In addition, a slew of multinational firms has lately established voluntary objectives (milestones) on their projected routes to net-zero energy usage. Companies may enhance their required yearly direct emissions reporting with extra optional disclosures. Mandatory and voluntary disclosures will eventually give additional information about a company's actual success of prior reduction goals. One such example was the agreement of global community on Montreal Protocol to adopt mandatory emission reporting in 1987, in regards to the emissions of Green House Gasses in order to save the rapid depletion of the Ozone layer. This led to recovery of the Ozone layer in following decades. Emission caps and the wider range of international mechanisms made available as a result of their adoption by more countries could help address some of these issues. A small number of countries will continue this effort, and it still raises questions about internationalizing policy and incentives in the most problematic areas, such as transportation and some land uses. Carbon accounting can serve as a bridge, which can be used to achieve the climate related targets in both long and short terms.

5.1 The Future of Carbon Accounting Will Be Based on Reasonable Targets Based on Science and Reduced Emissions.

Regarding the future of carbon accounting, the notions of quality versus quantity of disclosure present a significant challenge. The carbon footprints of both large and small businesses are investigated and the disclosure medium that businesses employ (integrated vs sustainability report). Carbon disclosures tend to be driven mostly by a desire to be perceived as legitimate, and corporations appear to be hesitant to commit to high-quality carbon reporting practices. Because of the "plethora of third-party ESG verifier companies" (Nasralla and Bousso 2019), as well as the "numerous voluntary initiatives and frameworks to unify carbon accounting and target setting; some overlap, but none have been universally adopted," investors are left to fend for themselves in a confusing maze of carbon accounting rules and regulations.

Management research has proposed that "science-based targets" for climate change implementation be established. Their comparison of four different science-based techniques (Faria and Labutong 2019) contributes to the literature on carbon accounting. When it comes to set target values, it is demonstrated in this study that mitigating possibilities are equally as important as the allocation principle, which is a noteworthy finding, assists businesses in their GHG emission reduction efforts, and policymakers must encourage them to pick models that are far less polluting than the 2degree C limitations. As part of their value propositions, several firms are altering their offerings to help clients minimize emissions from existing business models. For example, (Revellino 2020) in his research, discusses how this concept may be employed in an organization what it means for future attempts to reduce greenhouse gas emissions and adapt to climate change. While (Revellino 2020) examines how "climate change calculations become seductive forces for public engagement."

References

Cook A (2009) Emission rights: From costless activity to market operations. Acc Organ Soc 34(3–4):456–468

Alrazi B, de Villiers C, van Staden CJ (2015) A comprehensive literature review on, and the construction of a framework for, environmental legitimacy, accountability and proactivity. J Clean Prod 102:44–57. https://doi.org/10.1016/j.jclepro.2015.05.022

Andrew J, Cortese C (2013) Free market environmentalism and the neoliberal project: the case of the Climate Disclosure Standards Board. Crit Perspect Account 24:297–409

Andrew R, Forgie V (2008) A three-perspective view of greenhouse gas emission responsibilities in New Zealand. Ecol Econ 68(1–2):194–204. https://doi.org/10.1016/j.ecolecon.2008.02.016

Bebbington J, Larrinaga-Gonzalez C (2008) Carbon trading: accounting and reporting issues. Eur Account Rev 17:697–717

Bebbington J, Thomson I (2013) Sustainable development, management and accounting: boundary crossing. Manag Account Res 24:277–283

Bolton P, Kacperczyk M, Leuz C, Ormazabal G, Reichelstein S, Schoenmaker D (2021) Mandatory corporate carbon disclosures and the path to net zero. CEPR Cent Econ Policy Res 111:1–14. https://cepr.org/sites/default/files/policy_insights/PolicyInsight111.pdf

Boston J, Lempp F (2011) Climate change: explaining and solving the mismatch between scientific urgency and political inertia. Account, Audit Account J 24:1000–1021

Bowen F, Wittneben B (2011) Carbon accounting. Account, Audit Account J 24(8):1022–1036. https://doi.org/10.1108/09513571111184742
Busch T, Lewandowski S (2016) Corporate carbon and financial performance: a meta-analysis. Acad Manag Proc 2016(1):11657. https://doi.org/10.5465/ambpp.2016.11657abstract
Çalışkan K, Callon M (2009) Economization, part 1: shifting attention from the economy towards processes of economization. Econ Soc 38(3):369–398. https://doi.org/10.1080/03085140903020580
Kauffmann C, Tébar Less C (2010) 10th OECD roundtable on corporate responsibility
Comyns B, Figge F (2015) Greenhouse gas reporting quality in the oil and gas industry. Account, Audit Account J 28(3):403–433. https://doi.org/10.1108/AAAJ-10-2013-1498
Cooper SA, Raman KK, Yin J (2018) Halo effect or fallen angel effect? Firm value consequences of greenhouse gas emissions and reputation for corporate social responsibility. J Account Public Policy 37:226–240
Cowan S, Deegan C (2011) Corporate disclosure reactions to Australia's first national emission reporting scheme. Account Financ 51:409–436
de Aguiar TRS, Bebbington J (2014) Disclosure on climate change: analysing the UK ETS effects. Accounting Forum 38:227–240
Dr Lovell H, Dr Sales de Aguiar T, Bebbington J, Dr Larrinaga-Gonzalez C (2010) Accounting for Carbon. CertifAccountS Educ Trust, 3–32
Faria PCS, Labutong N (2019) A description of four science-based corporate GHG target-setting methods. Sustain Account, Manag Policy J 11(3):591–612. https://doi.org/10.1108/SAMPJ-03-2017-0031
Freedman M, Park JD (2014) Mandated climate change disclosures by firms participating in the regional greenhouse gas initiative. Soc Environ Account J 34:29–44
Freedman M, Park J (2017) SEC's 2010 release on climate change: shifting from voluntary to mandatory climate change disclosure. Soc Environ Account J 37:203–221
Green W, Taylor S, Wu J (2017) Determinants of greenhouse gas assurance provider choice. Meditari Account Res 25(1):114–135. https://doi.org/10.1108/MEDAR-08-2016-0072
Hahn R, Reimsbach D, Schiemann F (2015) Organizations, climate change, and transparency. Organ Environ 28(1):80–102. https://doi.org/10.1177/1086026615575542
Haigh M, Shapiro MA (2011) Carbon reporting: does it matter? Account, Audit Account J 25(1):105–125. https://doi.org/10.1108/09513571211191761
Haque F (2017) The effects of board characteristics and sustainable compensation policy on carbon performance of UK firms. Br Account Rev 49:347–364
Hartmann F, Perego P, Young A (2013) Carbon accounting: challenges for research in management control and performance measurement. Abacus 49:539–563
Haslam N, Loughnan S, Perry G (2014) Meta-Milgram: an empirical synthesis of the obedience experiments. PLoS ONE 9(4):e93927. https://doi.org/10.1371/journal.pone.0093927
He R, Luo L, Shamsuddin A, Tang Q (2021a) Corporate carbon accounting: a literature review of carbon accounting research from the Kyoto Protocol to the Paris Agreement. Account Financ, acfi.12789. https://doi.org/10.1111/acfi.12789
He R, Luo L, Shamsuddin A, Tang Q (2021b) Corporate carbon accounting: a literature review of carbon accounting research from the Kyoto Protocol to the Paris Agreement. Account Financ, 1–38. https://doi.org/10.1111/acfi.12789
He R, Luo L, Tang Q (2020) Usefulness of corporate carbon information for decision-making. In: Information for efficient decision making. World Scientific, pp 451–476. https://doi.org/10.1142/9789811220470_0015
Hopwood AG (2009) Accounting and the environment. Acc Organ Soc 34:433–439
Hughes PJ (1986) Signalling by direct disclosure under asymmetric information. J Account Econ 8(2):119–142. https://doi.org/10.1016/0165-4101(86)90014-5
Trifts JW, Asare KN (2015) A cash flow approach to analyzing long-term liabilities: a pedagogical exercise. J Financ Educ 41(2):129–156
Kollmuss A, Zink H, Polycarp C (2008) Making sense of the voluntary carbon market: a comparison of carbon offset standards
Louche C, Young S, Fougère M (2021) Cross-sector dialogue for sustainability: to partner or not to partner? Sustain Account, Manag Policy J 12(6):1161–1177. https://doi.org/10.1108/SAMPJ-02-2021-0045
Lovell H, MacKenzie D (2011) Accounting for carbon: the role of accounting professional organisations in governing climate change. Antipode 43(3):704–730. https://doi.org/10.1111/j.1467-8330.2011.00883.x
Luo L (2019) The influence of institutional contexts on the relationship between voluntary carbon disclosure and carbon emission performance. Account Financ 59(2):1235–1264. https://doi.org/10.1111/acfi.12267
Luo L, Tang Q (2014) Does voluntary carbon disclosure reflect underlying carbon performance? J Contemp Account Econ 10(3):191–205. https://doi.org/10.1016/j.jcae.2014.08.003
Matsumura EM, Prakash R, Vera-Mu-noz SC (2014) Firm-value effects of carbon emissions and carbon disclosures. Account Rev 89:695–724
Milne MJ, Grubnic S (2011) Climate change accounting research: keeping it interesting and different. Account, Audit Account J 24(8):948–977. https://doi.org/10.1108/09513571111184715
Ministry of Environment GJ (2009) Japan's national greenhouse gas emissions for fiscal year 2009.https://www.env.go.jp/en/headline/1580.html
Momin MA, Northcott D, Hossain M (2017) Greenhouse gas disclosures by Chinese power companies: trends, content and strategies. J Account Organ Chang 13(3):331–358. https://doi.org/10.1108/JAOC-07-2015-0054
Nasralla S, Bousso R (2019, October 19) Investors get lost in big oil's carbon accounting maze. Reuters.www.reuters.com/article/us-oil-carbon-climatechange-insight/investorsget-lost-in-big-oils-carbon-accounting-maze-idUSKBN1WO0F6
Nor NM, Bahari NAS, Adnan NA, Kamal SMQAS, Ali IM (2016) The effects of environmental disclosure on financial performance in Malaysia. Procedia Econ Financ 35:117–126. https://doi.org/10.1016/S2212-5671(16)00016-2
Ott C, Schiemann F, Günther T (2017) Disentangling the determinants of the response and the publication decisions: the case of the Carbon Disclosure Project. J Account Public Policy 36(1):14–33. https://doi.org/10.1016/j.jaccpubpol.2016.11.003
Pitrakkos P, Maroun W (2019) Evaluating the quality of carbon disclosures. Sustain Account Manag Policy J 11(3):553–589. https://doi.org/10.1108/SAMPJ-03-2018-0081
Pitrakkos P, Maroun W (2020) Evaluating the quality of carbon disclosures. Sustain Account Manag Policy J 11(3)
Revellino S (2020) Accounting for carbon emissions: simulating absence through experimental sites of material politics. Sustain Account, Manag Policy J 11(3):613–640
Schaltegger S, Csutora M (2012) Carbon accounting for sustainability and management. Status quo and challenges. J Clean Prod 36:1–16. https://doi.org/10.1016/j.jclepro.2012.06.024
Banuri T, Opschoor H (2009) Climate change and sustainable development. United Nations, Department of Economics and Social Affairs, Working Papers

The Economist (2021, May 22) Sustainable finance is rife with greenwash. Time for more disclosure. The Economist Newspaper Limited
Delay T, Grubb M, Willan C, Counsell T (2009) Global carbon mechanisms emerging lessons and implications
Warwick P, Ng C (2012) The 'cost' of climate change: how carbon emissions allowances are accounted for amongst European Union companies. Aust Account Rev 22:54–67
Wilting HC, Vringer K (2009) Carbon and land use accounting from a producer's and a consumer's perspective – an empirical examination covering the world. Econ Syst Res 21(3):291–310. https://doi.org/10.1080/09535310903541736
Yang HH, Farley A (2016) Convergence or divergence? Corporate climate change reporting in China. Int J Account Inf Manag 24:391–414
Yohe GW, Tol RSJ (2008) The Stern Review and the economics of climate change: an editorial essay. Clim Change 89(3–4):231–240. https://doi.org/10.1007/s10584-008-9431-z

GPSR Compliance

The European Union's (EU) General Product Safety Regulation (GPSR) is a set of rules that requires consumer products to be safe and our obligations to ensure this.

If you have any concerns about our products, you can contact us on ProductSafety@springernature.com

In case Publisher is established outside the EU, the EU authorized representative is:

Springer Nature Customer Service Center GmbH
Europaplatz 3
69115 Heidelberg, Germany

Batch number: 10755702

Printed by Printforce, the Netherlands